MEMORIES, REALITIES AND DREAMS
Aspects of the
South African Jewish Experience

*To Leonard Mendelsohn
a man who loved museums.*

MEMORIES, REALITIES AND DREAMS
Aspects of the
South African Jewish Experience

EDITED BY
MILTON SHAIN AND RICHARD MENDELSOHN

JONATHAN BALL PUBLISHERS
JOHANNESBURG & CAPE TOWN

All rights reserved.
No part of this publication may be reproduced or transmitted,
in any form or by any means, without prior permission from
the publisher or copyright holder.

© Selection by Milton Shain and Richard Mendelsohn
  (All contributions other than that of James Campbell arose
  out of a colloquium organised by the Isaac and Jessie Kaplan Centre
  at the University of Cape Town, 2000)
© The author of each essay retains the copyright of his own work.

Published by
JONATHAN BALL PUBLISHERS (PTY) LTD
PO Box 33977
Jeppestown
2043

ISBN Hard cover edition 1 86842 141 4
     Soft cover edition 1 86842 132 5

Design by Michael Barnett, Johannesburg
Cover photograph by courtesy of the South African Jewish Museum
  (Jewish immigrants arriving in Cape Town)
Typesetting and reproduction of covers by Collage Graphics, Johannesburg
Typesetting and reproduction of text by Alinea Studio, Cape Town
Printed and bound by CTP Book Printers, Caxton Street, Parow, Cape

Contents

Introduction MILTON SHAIN AND RICHARD MENDELSOHN	7
Growing Up Jewish DAN JACOBSON	15
Between Ideology and Indifference: *The Destruction of Yiddish in South Africa* JOSEPH SHERMAN	28
The Boer War, The Great War, and the Shaping of South African Jewish Loyalties RICHARD MENDELSOHN	50
Insiders on Outsiders: *Some South African Jewish Writers* MARCIA LEVESON	60
"If It Was So Good, Why Was It So Bad?" *The Memories and Realities of Antisemitism in South Africa, Past and Present* MILTON SHAIN	76
Beyond The Pale: *Jewish Immigration and the South African Left* JAMES T CAMPBELL	96
Accounting for Jewish Radicals in Apartheid South Africa GIDEON SHIMONI	163
The Road to Rivonia: *Jewish Radicals and the Cost of Conscience in White South Africa* GLENN FRANKEL	187
Jews and the Open Society DENNIS DAVIS	199
Endnotes	211

Introduction

MILTON SHAIN AND RICHARD MENDELSOHN

It is perhaps not surprising that a colloquium dealing with South African Jewry[1] only six years after the introduction of democracy in South Africa in 1994, and built around the concepts of 'Memories, Realities and Dreams', should result in participants grappling with, in one way or another, the immigration experience, adaptation to the new country and the construction of a new identity, the host society's response to the newcomers, and attitudes toward racism and apartheid. The latter topic in particular has become hotly contested, as South African Jews reflect on their individual and collective political behaviour under the old regime.[2]

Migration and the challenges posed in the new setting are clearly abiding and important features of the South African Jewish experience. Jews were only able to settle in South Africa in the early nineteenth century in the wake of the British occupation of the Cape. A trickle of English and Central European (mainly German) Jews took advantage of the new opportunities. The Cape Town Hebrew Congregation was established in 1841, preparing the way for congregations in the smaller centres. The discovery of diamonds in the 1860s and gold two decades later attracted an influx of fortune seekers. Their numbers increased with the influx of Eastern European (mainly Lithuanian) Jews escaping oppression and poverty in the Tsarist Pale of Settlement. By the early twentieth century communal institutions had evolved, including the South African Jewish Board of Deputies (the representative voice of the Jewish community), the South African Zionist Federation, and a range of educational, religious and welfare structures. By 1911 the Jewish population of the country numbered 46 919 or 3,7% of the total white population.³

As a community built essentially upon the great wave of Jewish migration from Lithuania in the four decades prior to the First World War, that experience, including the cultural baggage brought by the newcomers, cannot be ignored in the shaping of their new identity and their behaviour in the new country. It inevitably provides a leitmotif running though this volume. Equally inevitably, contributors differ markedly in the significance they attach to the processes of migration and adaptation. Whatever the differences, however, the connections between the 'old' and 'new' worlds demand exploration, as does the impact of changing cultural and political mores upon generations.

Dan Jacobson's quintessentially autobiographical account of growing up in the 1930s and 40s in Kimberley, a small South African mining town, as the child of immigrants, would be instantly recognisable to many South African Jews – notwithstanding Jacobson's assertion that with only 130 Jewish families it was atypical. Keenly observant and with a novelist's sensitivity, Jacobson portrays a new world far removed from the old country. The tensions, the ambience and the challenges are all considered through the eyes of a young boy. With his Lithuanian roots, Jacobson captures in many ways the essential South African Jewish experience of his generation: the formative impact of immigrant parents, the powerful influence of Zionism as an ideology in the home, the abiding sense of Jewish peoplehood, the overwhelmingly Christian character of the host society, the rupture of the Holocaust, and empathy for the underdog (which did not necessarily translate into political action). For Jacobson, the British Commonwealth served as a beacon of decency in an unfriendly world, at any time prey to antisemitism and bigotry. 'Self-division, self-doubt, self-rejection, anxiety, weariness, conflicting loyalties, envy, shame, the longing to be shot of the whole business' captures for Jacobson the angst of Jewishness in the new milieu.

The challenges Jacobson faced in a relatively homogenous small town differed from those encountered in the more variegated larger centres. In the latter there was more room for personal choice and ideological contestation, and for a greater range of debate and forms of identification. One such fierce debate was over the valence of Yiddish and Hebrew, or in Joseph Sherman's characterisation, the battle between the *mameloshn* and the *tateloshn*. This at times ferocious intramural debate within the community was integrally tied to a Yiddishist battle against Zionists who 'demanded the revival of Hebrew as a precondition for fulfilling Jewish national aspirations in a restored Jewish homeland'.

Clashes between Yiddishists and Hebraists become a window through which to examine an important part of the immigrant experience. The 'old world' is jettisoned in what Sherman describes as 'the destruction of Yiddish'. Upward social mobility had enormous implications for self-definition and identity, and Jewish educationists, most importantly Isaac Goss, cemented the hegemony of Hebrew (and with it Zionism) via the Jewish Day School system. Sherman draws our attention to the importance of the politics of language and the powerful influence of Israel. 'Yiddish is now dead, and cannot be recalled to life,' he laments. Nonetheless scholars, Sherman argues persuasively, ought to examine extant Yiddish writings for a fuller picture of South African Jewish history. Sherman's robust championing of the lost history of Yiddish creativity and culture in South Africa is an important corrective to established narratives.

Communal self-definition and identity are also the focus of Richard Mendelsohn, who explores the shaping of mainstream Jewish loyalties in South Africa in the formative years of the community in the first decades of the twentieth century. He compares the impact on the infant community of the two great upheavals of the period, the South African War and the First World War, arguing that both played a critical role 'in the shaping of the community's relationship with the wider society, in particular the locus of its members' broader political loyalties'. Whereas the former conflict allowed space for neutrality, the Great War 'threw into much sharper relief than had the South African War the issue of Jewish public loyalties'. While the South African War, Mendelsohn contends, 'settled the issue of where their public loyalty should lie, the First World War taught South African Jewry the necessity of embracing these loyalties enthusiastically and unconditionally, lest the Jewish community be singled out for unflattering and uncomfortable public attention'.

Marcia Leveson also explores the identity of Jews, focusing through South African Jewish writing on the problematics of insiders and outsiders, the impact of marginality, and responses to prejudice – the 'stigma of difference' as she puts it. Like Jacobson and Sherman, she reflects on Jewish attitudes towards the 'other', in this case the oppressed black majority. Unlike Jacobson, who characterises the Jews as marginally more sympathetic toward the plight of the underdog than their gentile peers, Leveson reminds us that, notwithstanding the frequent appearance of the image of the Jew as a 'Kaffirboetie' – a negrophile – as a powerful motif in South Afircan literature, most Jews 'were content to accept the norms and even the prejudices of the wider white society and to concentrate on communal and personal issues', a view with which Joseph Sherman concurs.

While Jews joined their white compatriots in 'othering' the black majority, they in turn were perceived as the classic 'other' by the white minority. Perceived differences are what informed host attitudes towards the newcomers as shown by Milton Shain. He clearly demonstrates how the Jew was constructed over time as the 'other', but also points out that the Jew was not always a target of hostility. 'My Joodje,' he tells us (quoting George Aschman, an historian of Oudtshoorn Jewry), 'was a term of endearment applied by Boers to those peddlars who had for years brought news of the "outside world" and "gossip from the town and the rest of the countryside"'. Shain traces the ebbs and flows of animosity, and the nature of anti-Jewish stereotypes, arguing that antisemitism was contingent on numerous factors unconnected to Jewish behaviour. Programmatic antisemitism, however, was only a short-lived consideration, rooted in the tensions and problems of political and socio-economic crises in the 1930s and 40s: '...the intensification of poor whiteism following the impact upon South Africa of the world depression, the emergence of Nazism in Europe and, most importantly, the rise of an illiberal, anti-modernist and exclusivist Afrikaner nationalism'.

In the apartheid era Jews were appropriated as whites into the apartheid project, and antisemitism receded rapidly. 'In 1953 Prime Minister DF Malan returned from a visit to Israel full of admiration for the "Jewish People". The National Party seemed to wish to put the tensions and excesses of the 1930s and 1940s behind it. In the apartheid system, Jews, as whites, were to have a rightful and welcome place.' This facilitated embourgeoisement and general material comfort. For the most part Jews accommodated themselves to the racial order, content to abide by the Board's apolitical and quiescent stance vis-à-vis apartheid and the tortuous moral conundrums of the day. Political choices were left to individual preference, and moral issues – at least formally – were deflected to the rabbinate. The latter, with the exception of an outspoken few, failed the challenge.[4]

Notwithstanding this communal timidity, perhaps understandable in the light of the intimidatory legacy of the ruling National Party's recent history of antisemitism, and a sense of Jewish vulnerability heightened by the Holocaust, a significant number of South African Jews did challenge the inequities of apartheid. Many fought for political rights for the disenfranchised majority, others for tolerance and liberty, and some for the rights of workers. Their efforts were manifest in mainstream and radical politics, legal aid, student activism, educational, cultural and health-care initiatives, philanthropic endeavours, trade unions, underground resistance and in the delegitimisation of the apartheid state from abroad. In short, Jews were conspicuously present – and overrepresented – in the struggle for democracy and human rights. More than half the 23 whites involved among the 156 activists in the Treason Trial of the 1950s were Jews, and all five whites apprehended at Rivonia (where leading ANC activists were arrested and subsequently charged with sabotage) were Jewish.

James Campbell is therefore surely correct in asserting that 'Jews were massively overrepresented in the ranks of opposition' to apartheid. Accounting for this, he discounts religious and cultural legacies and instead underlines the impact of migration, and the consequent disruption and alienation. 'The point, put simply, is that immigration was a profoundly disruptive experience, and that South Africa's celebrated Jewish radicalism may be less a product of community "tradition", handed down from generation to generation, than a function of historically specific processes of dislocation and conflict.' Drawing on a rich genre of recent South African Jewish autobiography, Campbell deals insightfully with the memoirs of Hyman Basner, Baruch Hirson, Pauline Podbrey and Joe Slovo, teasing out common features and experiences.

Marginality and dislocation are in Campbell's view of fundamental importance. Radical politics, he writes, 'and the Communist Party in particular, represented more than just a new political affiliation. It offered community, human contact, a warmth and solidarity otherwise absent from their daily lives.'

By contrast, Gideon Shimoni, addressing the same phenomenon, stresses 'cultural baggage' and the particular values within families as a possible key to explaining Jewish overrepresentation in activist politics. The immigrant home, 'especially with regard to communist sympathies or affiliations' was, he argues, a major factor. But Shimoni also reminds us that many radicals cut their political teeth in the Zionist movement which 'provided a stimulus for political awareness and sometimes a training ground for radical activism'. Huge dilemmas were generated for young Jews against the backdrop of a burgeoning European fascism, aped by the radical right in interwar South Africa. These dilemmas continued after the Second World War with the coming of apartheid and the birth of the state of Israel in 1948.

Glenn Frankel also treats 'Jewishness' as an important factor informing Jewish radicalism, although he also asserts that it certainly did not guarantee a radical choice. There were after all many conservative strands within the community. State Deputy Attorney General of the Transvaal (and prosecutor of Mandela) Percy Yutar was a case in point. Here was an Orthodox Jew, born in Cape Town, 'of parents who had come to South Africa, like so many of the radicals he pursued, from the ghettos of Lithuania'. Yutar's response, writes Frankel, 'came from a different tradition' – that of the medieval *shtadlan* or intercessor, the defender of 'Jewish interests in the court of the tyrant'. 'By prosecuting his fellow Jews, he offered protection for the larger community.'

Jewish radical politics in South Africa will clearly remain a field of ongoing enquiry. As the carefully nuanced arguments of Campbell, Shimoni and Frankel so richly illustrate, simple explanation cannot match empirical complexity. Shimoni is probably correct when he writes that ultimately we can only talk about 'common denominators' and 'no generalisation can cover every single case ... For every Denis Goldberg or Ruth First (Slovo) whose lives were totally divorced from Jewish or Zionist associations, there is an Arthur Goldreich or Baruch Hirson who passed through one or other phase of meaningful Jewish involvement, and so on. Imponderables such as idiosyncratic personality traits, chance exposures to inspiring role models, and the warm embrace of supportive social groups enter into the equation and are perhaps the ultimate differentiating factors.' Those wishing to explore the issue should heed Campbell's proposal that we ask questions about 'the sources and character of Jewish immigration to South Africa, changing Jewish settlement patterns, class formation, experiences of work and leisure, and, perhaps most importantly, about immigrant family life'.

While the road to radicalism remains contested, and a continuing challenge to scholars, the uncharted and corrugated road to the future is an immediate challenge to all South African Jews. The challenges for the immigrant generation might be over, but the 'New South Africa' – the 'Open Society' as Dennis Davis, employing Karl Popper's notion, calls it – provides a set of new challenges. Davis asks if Judaism is compatible with the critical spirit of modernity, built on 'an association of free individuals respecting one another's rights within a framework of mutual protection supplied by the state, and where policies are achieved through the making of responsible rational decisions'. Davis's highly personal contribution is clearly informed by concern for what he sees as a reactionary strain in contemporary South African Jewish Orthodoxy. Will closure to, or engagement with, the outside world prevail? Highlighting contradictions between accepting the principle of freedom and equality for all (as enshrined in the new South African constitution) but denying such tolerance to all Jews, Davis calls for respect for the 'other', including the 'deviant Jew'. There is no superior tradition, contends Davis, but there is a cost to denying contest and rational engagement.

The current challenge to South African Jewry identified by Davis is, as will be seen in this volume, only the latest of a series of historical challenges. Having been victims of discrimination and oppression, Jews arrived in South Africa to find themselves, simply by virtue of their skin colour, beneficiaries of a system built on racial exploitation. As this collection vividly demonstrates, this ironic reversal of fortune inevitably generated unfamiliar dilemmas for the newcomers. Some of these, and the associated responses, are explored here, although it should be noted that the contributions by no means encompass all the dilemmas and ambiguities of the South African Jewish experience. But the contributions to this volume do throw light on important dimensions of that experience, and hopefully further our understanding of a community in transition. The challenges remain.

Growing up Jewish

DAN JACOBSON

DAN JACOBSON was born in Johannesburg in 1929 and grew up in Kimberley. He settled in England in the mid-1950s. Since then he has produced ten novels, two collections of short stories, two critical works and a volume of autobiographical essays. His last two books, *The Electronic Elephant* and *Heshel's Kingdom* are eclectic in nature, bringing together public history, private memoir and accounts of the author's travels in southern Africa and eastern Europe. He recently retired from a chair in English Literature at University College, London.

There is an ironic contrast between our way of thinking about adulthood during childhood and how we look back on childhood once we have become adults. As children we long to become adults; we cannot wait to leave the state of subordination in which we are trapped, whether at school or in the home. Out there are grown-ups who do important work, go to bed when they like, spend money, have sex, drive cars ... and here we are, dependent on them, subject to their orders, knowing that we cannot cope without them – in short, living through what the poet WB Yeats, in one of his great phrases, and speaking in the masculine gender only, referred to as 'the ignominy of boyhood'.

And when we become adults? Even those not in thrall to the doctrines of psychoanalysis are likely to find themselves thinking that the experiences that ultimately shaped their consciousness took place during childhood. It was then that we perceived everything with an unparalleled sharpness and sensitivity; then that our emotional lives had an immediacy that has seldom been matched subsequently. In those respects, at least, much of what followed has been a falling-off.

Perhaps writers or writers-to-be are particularly prone to reaching forward in childhood to the unrealised future and then, in adulthood, looking back with longing or blame on the receding past. In any case, having volunteered to speak on the topic of 'Growing up Jewish', I promptly realised how much more appropriate to that task is the memoir or short story or poem. Imaginative writing is at home with confusion and multifariousness and an absence of clearly defined 'borders' on any side; discursive writing, on the other hand, seems to impel one towards a categorising, generalising mode of presenting experience, with strengths and weaknesses, good things and bad, credits and debits, placed side by side in neat bookkeeping columns. No aspect of our lives, however, is separable from any other, and almost any experience can be seen, especially in retrospect, as one of both gain and loss. All this is yet further complicated by the fact that 'growing up Jewish' is just one way of 'growing up anything', of going through the universal experience of being a child and then, at no definable moment, ceasing to be one.

Well, having proposed my topic I am not going to complain about it further. But before proceeding with it in the most direct, categorical fashion – by dividing the experience of growing up Jewish into good and bad things and listing them accordingly – I must insist that these categories are being set up only to be disrupted or even destroyed. Also that the references which follow to my own childhood are basically not intended to be particular and autobiographical in nature; rather I want to focus on events and complexes of feeling which had a general application to Jewish life in South Africa as a whole. I am acutely aware that my childhood took place a long time ago (in the late 30s and 40s of the last century) and in a setting (the small mining town of Kimberley, which then had a Jewish community of about 130 families) that was 'atypical' even by South African standards. But whether that strengthens or weakens the historical interest and the present relevance of what I shall say must be left for others to decide.

Now – what good things do I associate with having grown up Jewish in that place and at that time? The first must surely be the strength of feeling within the family about the family – as an institution, as a fixed framework for our lives – that was conveyed by my parents and I believe by most other Jewish parents in the town to their children. As it happens my own parents did not get on particularly well with each other, and both of them came from homes that had been disrupted in different ways – quite apart, that is, from the great upheaval of their migrations at an early age from Latvia and Lithuania. Yet none of their children ever doubted the strength of the commitment they had to us and the depth of responsibility they felt towards us. Moreover, this was made manifest not by way of explicit declarations and programmatic or sentimental appeals, but by what I would call their very opposite: through gestures, tones of voice, expressions of the face, assumptions unwittingly made, hopes and expectations left undeclared. By such means, too, I seem always to have been made aware – though from what age and in what terms I became conscious of this it is impossible for me to say – that in my parents' minds their feelings about their children were inextricably associated with the vulnerability and fragility of their position as Jews and immigrants; and that what was true of them applied in varying degrees to most other members of the community.

So there you are: I have already presented you with an example of my own inability, in talking of such matters, fully to separate good things from bad, weaknesses from strengths.

Obviously I am not suggesting that only immigrant Jewish parents gave a high priority to the welfare of their children and felt their responsibility towards them so keenly. What I have in mind, rather, is the style or manner of their caring and the powerful undercurrents that ran within it. Another aspect of my parents' lives into which and out of which their Jewishness flowed, in their own view as well as their children's, was their intellectual curiosity. My father was a businessman and my mother worked as an accountant in the firm, but they were both bookish by temperament. They read. They read different kinds of things, novels and biographies in the one case and books on current affairs in the other; but to both of them their reading was important, and they talked to us as well as to each other about what they were reading and the ideas it suggested to them. One consequence of growing up in such a household was that their children became readers too, from an early age, and we generally did well in school. So did a disproportionate number of other Jews in the school – a fact that one or two unpleasant teachers did not fail to point out to those Jewish boys, of whom there were of course several, who were not high achievers. To tell the truth, at such moments I could not tell to whom such teachers felt more hostile: the boys who fulfilled their stereotype of 'Jewish cleverness' or the ones who failed to do so.

The next gain or benefit I want to put on this list is the sense of kinship, or at least of a commonality of background, which the Jewish families in Kimberley shared with one another. Almost all of them were of Litvak or Latvian origin, as my parents were, and as was the case with the overwhelming majority of South African Jewry. Almost all of them, too, were relatively recent arrivals to the country, or the children of new arrivals. Since the community was so small, I imagine the members of it all knew one another by sight and name, even when they were not on closer terms. The organised nature of community life gave both adults and children regular opportunities of seeing one another and of pursuing the usual kinds of collective activities: synagogue services and the administrative business involved in running the synagogue, Hebrew lessons for the youngsters, Zionist meetings addressed by fund-raisers from abroad or from Johannesburg and Cape Town, women's gatherings, weddings, barmitzvahs, the burial society, a Young Israel Society and so on and so forth. As children, in short, we were provided with what could be called a ready-made milieu, which, though it did not cater for all our social needs and aspirations, nevertheless gave us many of our friends and much of our entertainment, and which helped us in a variety of ways to acquire a sense of what we might make of ourselves.

Related to all this was our consciousness that being Jewish involved us not just with the local community in Kimberley, and with other communities in South Africa, but with Jewry worldwide. During my boyhood the Jewish world was undergoing a catastrophe of proportions unlike any other even in its history. The full extent of it, perhaps fortunately, was not known to us; but we were aware that terrible, unspeakable events were taking place in Europe, and that these not only affected us morally and psychologically but threatened our physical existence too. Of all this I will say more shortly – on the debit side, clearly – but I hope it will not seem crass to add here, as a 'credit' of the most heavily qualified kind, that as children we learned that through our Jewishness we had a direct stake in world-shaking events; and what is more, that for us to have found ourselves in a small town in South Africa was not the random happening it might have appeared to be, but was part of a history of dispersion and suffering that had been going on for many centuries and might well go on for as many more. As Jews we may have been newly arrived at the foot of the African continent, but we were not newly arrived in the world; in fact we had arrived in the world long before almost any other group anywhere that could make a plausible show of possessing a continuous historical identity. The Zionist movement had something of the same effect on us: it incited us to believe that we were intimately involved in struggles that may have been physically distant but which could well have an important effect on our own futures. Not, by the way, that the Second World War was physically distant for the many young men of the town, my older brother among them, who served with the South African forces in North Africa and Italy.

In speaking of this 'international' dimension of growing up Jewish I also wish to draw into the discussion another worldwide phenomenon from which many South Africans (and not only those of British stock) derived a strengthened sense of their identity and self-importance. I mean the British Empire and Commonwealth. Those who lived 'under the British crown' in those days could think of themselves as attached to, a part of, a political system that exercised worldwide power and was held in worldwide esteem. However insignificant they may have been within that system, they had some kind of obscure claim for consideration not just wherever they happened to be but all over the place, in Canada and Australia, in Malaya and India, as well as in the so-called 'mother country' itself. The crown, the coinage, the buff envelopes marked 'On His Majesty's Service', the playing of 'God Save the King' at the end of cinema performances, some of the history we studied in school, some of the movies we watched, like the ardently imperialist *Rhodes of Africa* or *Lives of a Bengal Lancer* – all this, politically incorrect though it may be to say so today, was a source of an enlarged sense of selfhood, even for those who could at best claim to have been stepchildren of the empire.

As evidence for this I could point, for example, to the life of Chaim Weizmann, Zionist statesman and first president of Israel, who was a passionate admirer of the British imperial mission, or to the memoirs of major figures in the Indian struggle for independence like Gandhi or Nehru. More to the point here is to say that I can remember hearing echoes of such sentiments among those who, on the face of it, should have rejected them outright, like members of the large Cape Coloured community in Kimberley, and from blacks as well as resentful, republican-minded Afrikaners. Among the blacks I should mention my fellow-Kimberley-ite and fellow-writer, Sol Plaatje, translator of Shakespeare into the Tswana language and founder of the African National Congress, who repeatedly and unavailingly turned to London to intercede on behalf of his people against the 'colonial' whites'. Plaatje was also, incidentally, the first man to make a recording (in London, in 1920) of *Nkosi Sikelel' iAfrika* (Brian Willan, *Sol Plaatje: A Biography*, Johannesburg, 1984, p.290).

For Jews the imperial connection had a peculiar importance for two further reasons. First, South Africa's constitutional status as a self-governing British dominion within the Commonwealth made it seem 'natural' that the country should enter the Second World War against Germany on Britain's side (even if the vote in parliament to do so was a damned close-run thing, as the Duke of Wellington said about the battle of Waterloo). Secondly, Great Britain was the mandatory power in Palestine, where the struggle for the establishment of an independent Jewish state was gradually coming to its crisis.

Finally, on the credit side of growing up Jewish, I believe that it encouraged many of us to feel a quasi-instinctive sympathy with other despised and unjustly treated racial groups in South Africa, and a distaste, to put it no more strongly, with the way they were habitually spoken to, and spoken of, by most whites in those days. The Jewish boys at my school came in all sizes, shapes and dispositions, but I will say of them that I never heard them using the violent and abusive language against people of darker skin that was common coin among many of my schoolfellows. (Not all, needless to say.) Nor did I hear Jewish boys boasting of what they or their fathers or their uncles had done to this or that unfortunate black or brown servant or urchin or passer-by who had been (in the odious language of the time) 'cheeky'. This may not sound like much in today's climate, but it was something. I know too that the view my parents took of the voteless, rightless, poverty-stricken majority of people around us was explicitly derived by them from their own past and their feelings about that past. (The past of their individual lives, that is, and of their people.)

There is much discussion within the South African Jewish community today of how politically pusillanimous or otherwise the Jews were vis-à-vis the injustices perpetrated on other groups in the country, especially during the apartheid years; and some of what I will be saying shortly has a bearing on the pre-history of that debate. In other words, my remarks will raise the question of how secure politically, socially and even physically the Jews felt themselves to be at the time I am speaking of – which is roughly between the years leading up to the outbreak of the war in 1939 and the crucial electoral victory of the Afrikaner-dominated Nationalist Party nine years later.

I turn now to the debits, the bad things about growing up Jewish in those years. Many of them, as I warned you would be the case, have already been noted on the credit side of this exceptionally messy balance sheet. Before I do so, however, allow me another brief preamble.

I begin with a statement of the obvious. The overwhelming majority of the people of South Africa, black and white, espouse varying forms of Christianity. The languages they speak, the calendar they use, the customs they follow, most of the musical, literary, pictorial and cinematic modes of expression they are familiar with, to name just a few items, are all steeped in, or dependent on, Christian beliefs and assumptions. It would be pointless as well as improper for any non-Christian minority to feel aggrieved on that score. Next, as long as the people of South Africa (or anywhere else) are divided into ethnic, religious and linguistic groups – and I cannot imagine them not being so divided – there will always be group tensions and group animosities among them. It is always going to be difficult to get socially and racially diverse peoples to live harmoniously together within a single polity, and no talk of a Rainbow Nation will ever be enough to change that state of affairs. Finally, in speaking as bleakly as I am going to about the antisemitism I grew up with, I do not want to suggest that it was universal. Far from it.

Still, the fact remains that the heaviest item on the debit side of my experience of growing up Jewish, the bad thing which probably embraces all the others, was the antisemitism of a virulent and murderous variety, and of epidemic proportions, that was abroad during my boyhood. If the sentiment, the passion, the ideology of antisemitism – and it was all of these – never actually became murderous in South Africa itself, that was as much a matter of luck (and we knew it) as of any imperviousness within the society's own institutions. By 'luck' I mean, of course, that Britain did not surrender to the Germans at the time of Dunkirk and the Battle of Britain. If that had happened one can only speculate about the fate of the community, given the undisguised longing for a German victory expressed by the official Afrikaner Nationalist movement – not to speak of such now-forgotten but once actively and vociferously pro-Nazi outriders to it as the Ossewa Brandwag, the New Order and the Greyshirts.

By the early 1940s Nazism was at its peak. It seemed all-conquering. The Nazis had spread their poison worldwide, and we know from documents discovered after the war that they regarded South Africa as a territory particularly ripe for the harvesting. This was the climate in which we conducted our lives; and, just like the Jews who lived in countries much closer to the Nazi armies than we were, we did so by and large by carrying on just as if everything was normal and would go on being so. Fortunately for us, so did most of our non-Jewish neighbours.

But antisemitism did not affect only those who were openly or covertly pro-German. The Nazis did not invent antisemitism, and their version of it was so successful because in large part it merged with attitudes and beliefs that were ancient, insidious yet somehow casual too; taken for granted yet held with great tenacity and a kind of ebullient self-righteousness by all and sundry. Well, not all, obviously, but certainly sundry – businessmen, teachers, clergymen, directors of the De Beers Consolidated Mines (who would not employ Jews in the company), boys at school, their parents who discouraged their offspring from playing with Jewish boys, newspaper editors who wrote offensively about the Jews, indeed almost any category of person you wish to think of. They were not Nazis, but they were antisemites, whether they were wholly conscious of being so or not; and, emboldened by the climate of the time, they made their presence felt in all sorts of ways.

Let me give just a single instance of the kind of willingness to wound Jewish feelings I am thinking of here, and which helped to determine and to darken my feelings both about being Jewish and about the society at large. From Standard Four to the end of Standard Eight at school (between 1938 and 1942 I think – i.e. between my ninth and thirteenth years) not a school year passed without one of our prescribed literary texts containing a prominent Jewish figure whose unpleasantness was made central to his Jewishness by the novelists themselves. We had a child's version of Scott's *Ivanhoe*, with its crawling, money-crazed Isaac of York, followed by Baroness Orczy's *The Scarlet Pimpernel*, of all trashy items, which contained at least one chapter prominently featuring a miserly and treacherous Jew. Then there was an Afrikaans novel with a name I have forgotten which was similarly adorned, and finally Dickens's *Oliver Twist*, best known perhaps for its portrait of the unforgettably villainous Fagin, which we studied exhaustively over two years for our Junior Certificate examination. If, at that particular historical moment, such a succession of books was deliberately chosen by officials of the Cape Province Education Department, we know what we have to think of them. And if they chose the books accidentally? Do we have to think all that differently about them? Not in my view. *The Merchant of Venice* we managed to escape, incidentally, not because it was not on offer, but because our English teacher happened to choose *Hamlet*, which was the alternative Shakespeare text for the matriculation examination that year.

In the eyes of most South African whites the Jews were on the lowest rung of esteem and social acceptability among the whites. Not the lowest rung professionally or economically, by any means; that was reserved for the 'poor whites'. But the fact that I can bring the poor whites into comparison with a group whose menfolk were mostly shopkeepers and professional people, and which aspired earnestly to a middle-class way of life, illustrates just how anomalous and indeed oppressive was the situation in which the Jews found themselves. I know the word 'oppressive' will sound provocative in some ears, in view of the many other, more brutal forms of racial oppression and dispossession that were rife in the South Africa of 50 and more years ago, but I am going to stick with it. If the feminists have been able successfully to claim that throughout human history womankind as a whole, as a gender, has been slighted and marginalised by a masculine-dominated culture, regardless of whatever fame or influence might have been won by individual women, and that this amounted to a form of oppression, then a Jew can certainly say the same today in speaking of what it was like to be a ten-year-old boy in a small South African town 60 years ago.

Now add together the following: first, what I have just called the inevitable marginalisation of Jews in a largely Christian society (and notice that I have not gone into the question of the extent to which the Christian scriptures are themselves programmatically anti-Jewish in inspiration); second, the thoughtless readiness to speak and think ill of the Jews which was then so widespread in the society at large; third, the insanely paranoid, ideological anti-semitism that was being spread about by what was then the strongest military power in the world; and last but not least, the constant interaction and interchange between all these levels of attitude and belief. Take all this into account, think seriously about its effects on the minds and sensibilities of youngsters who are at the wrong end of it, and what will you find? I can tell you. Self-division, self-doubt, self-rejection, anxiety, weariness, conflicting loyalties, envy, shame, the longing to be shot of the whole business.

None of this, when the talk is of Jews and of growing up Jewish just before the middle of the twentieth century, should come as a shock or surprise to anyone. Jews have been saying for centuries that it's hard to be a Jew, and a vulnerability to the kind of moral and psychological pressures I have just described is one of the hardships that have faced them since they began to seek admission to the larger societies within which they lived – or towards which they were migrating. These pressures were and to some degree still are a source of great pain; they are also at the heart of much Jewish humour; they are at work behind and within Jewish ambition and creativity in a variety of fields of endeavour –

literature not least among them. (As a not-so-tiny example of the tortuosities of consciousness I am trying to describe, let me say that my early, humiliating acquaintance with *Oliver Twist* was the beginning of a lifelong addiction to the novels of Charles Dickens.) Of course not even the most self-hating Jew believes that all gentiles lead happy and unproblematical lives, and that they would do the same if only they could be released from servitude to their Jewishness. But anyone who has been the object of racial hatred knows that it is so wounding to its victims – more wounding than abuse directed against them as individuals – precisely because it denies them their individuality. It says to every member of the spurned race: to me you will never be a person with a life and interests of your own, but always a representative of a species. Whatever you do will reveal only your species-dom; and if you try to escape from it, that too will reveal the nature of the species you belong to.

I did say that the good things I spoke of were going to turn into bad things or be seen as the concomitants of bad things, and I have depressingly been as good as my word. No doubt some of you are wondering at this stage why I did not mention the consolations of religion among the good things about growing up Jewish. It is a serious question to which I have to give a serious answer. I have not mentioned the consolations of religion because I never felt them. Some of the rituals and observances of the Jewish festivals had a limited aesthetic appeal – those which took place in the home, like the table laid for the Seder, more than those in the synagogue; but as far back as I can remember they were vitiated for me by my inability to accept the specifically religious beliefs and teachings to which they owed their existence. The same readers might go on to suggest that the dismal states of mind itemised above would not be felt, or would be felt less keenly, by a believing Jew – which in all likelihood is the case. But that can hardly affect my own position. Belief adopted for instrumental or therapeutic reasons, rather than out of genuine conviction, is bound to strike someone like myself as a contradiction in terms; more of the problem, so to speak, rather than a solution of it.

To have grown up secular, as in effect I did – with the active encouragement of my mother and the compliance of my father, whose deep feelings about his people were manifested in his almost obsessive identification with the Zionist cause – was in fact quite a common way of growing up Jewish in my youth. And of subsequently staying Jewish too, in the sense of continuing to sustain an interest in the fate of the Jews both in Israel and in the Diaspora, as my own career and that of many of my contemporaries might suggest. Today it appears that just as more and more Jews are marrying 'out', so too more of them – a far smaller number, I am sure, than the first group – are returning to the religion of their forefathers. In my time the choice of the latter option was rare indeed. Of my contemporaries I can think of only one who later became truly observant; and even he had squared the circle by marrying a gentile woman who had then converted.

Much of what I have written here about growing up Jewish may sound excessively gloomy and negative, a going-back over old, unhappy things. I have not quite finished, however. History never ceases to surprise us, and not a few of the surprises that have come our way during the past 50 years – that is, from the time I crossed the invisible line between adolescence and adulthood – have been more encouraging than one then had any right to expect. My feeling about antisemitism, for instance, is that though the sentiment has not disappeared, and probably never will, as a political force it is now a busted flush. It may seem rash to say so, but I suspect that the antisemites themselves find it hard to convince themselves – even in Russia! – that antisemitism will again serve as the central inspiration for a mass movement that will carry them to the power they crave for. There are many reasons for this, among them social and demographic changes on a global scale that have nothing to do with the Jews as such. But among those reasons, too, is the existence of the state of Israel, which has done away with what in my view never failed to provoke the antisemites to their excesses: not the power of the Jews, as they always liked to claim, but its very opposite, the helplessness of the Jews, which fed the sadistic conviction of their enemies that this particular people could be driven and hunted from place to place, and killed outright when circumstances were propitious, because no country in the world would ever see it as its prime business to give them protection.

Those days are over. They are no more going to come back than a doctrine of white supremacy is going to return to power in South Africa. Or Marxism in the now non-existent Soviet Union. For all this, at the beginning of the new century, we should be grateful.

Between Ideology and Indifference:
The destruction of Yiddish in South Africa

JOSEPH SHERMAN

JOSEPH SHERMAN is a Corob Fellow in Yiddish Studies at the Oxford Centre for Hebrew and Jewish Studies, University of Oxford. His field of research is modern Yiddish literature, on which he has published widely in international journals. His translation into English of a hitherto untranslated novel by Isaac Bashevis Singer, entitled *Shadows on the Hudson*, was published in 1997. Dr Sherman has also been particularly concerned to make available in English translation much of the considerable body of Yiddish writing which has been produced in South Africa, and his volume of South African Yiddish stories in English translation, entitled *From a Land Far Off*, was published in 1987. In 1989 he edited and introduced an annotated English translation of Leibl Feldman's important Yiddish monograph, *Oudtshoorn: Jerusalem of Africa*, which was published in a limited edition in 1989. He has written several scripts for television, and has directed over 27 plays for various amateur and professional groups in Johannesburg.

Conflicting ideologies and communal indifference threw Yiddish writing in South Africa into almost total neglect. A vigorous body of work about the Jewish experience in South Africa has therefore effectively been erased, to the detriment of building a full picture of the growth, development and demise of the South African Jewish community.

Although the work published in Yiddish in South Africa has

been listed in three progressively enlarged bibliographies,[1] very little research has been undertaken to evaluate it. Most scholars of South African Jewish history have relied for their primary source material on minutes of Jewish communal organisations, and the work of earlier chroniclers, all written in English. While full sets of South African Yiddish books have been preserved in a few specialist libraries,[2] a number of other publications, chiefly journals and newspapers, have been lost. Among the most historically important of these are the short-lived early periodicals that, in exceptional circumstances, go back variously first to the time of the South African War, were then published in the years preceding the outbreak of the First World War, and subsequently appeared between the world wars. Although potential researchers regrettably have no access to this vanished material, much has survived from a later period that deserves assessment. It is worth sketching briefly the range of this available material, before identifying the forces that obliterated Yiddish in South Africa.

A century of Yiddish writing in South Africa

In 1890, in a remarkable burst of confidence about the viability of Yiddish as an international language, ND Hoffman immigrated to South Africa, carrying with him in his luggage a set of Hebrew typeface. The overseas correspondent for several Yiddish periodicals in Eastern Europe, Hoffman was determined, if he could, to develop Yiddish culture in South Africa. Thus for three months during the Anglo-Boer War, between October and December 1899, he produced a daily single-page news bulletin in Yiddish for what was evidently a sufficiently large number of interested readers. Hoffman continued to file reports about life in South Africa to overseas Yiddish newspapers, and in 1916 he used them to produce a volume of his *Zikhroynes*, the first Yiddish book to be published in South Africa.[3] From this early beginning, and in the teeth of setbacks, Yiddish writing in and about South Africa blossomed, reaching its full fruition between 1947 and 1975. During that time, South African Yiddish writers produced and published eight collections of essays and short stories, ten volumes of poetry, two novels, four historical or polemical pamphlets, one full-scale history, and a great deal of journalism. Active though small-scale, Yiddish writing continued in South Africa until the mid-1980s, appearing in both journals and limited-edition books. In 1983, to commemorate his 80th birthday, the uncollected poems of David Fram were published in a volume entitled *A shvalb oyfn dakh*. The most active of South African Yiddish writers continues to be the poet, critic and essayist David Wolpe, who in 1999, at the age of 91, published the second of two volumes of his memoirs.[4]

Notwithstanding the loss of the earliest South African Yiddish newspapers and journals, those published after the Second World War are readily available. Their pages offer a virtually untapped vein of insights into the moral complexities of life in apartheid South Africa. The monthly (later quarterly) journal *Dorem Afrike* (1947-1989) and the weekly newspaper *Der Afrikaner yidishe tsaytung* (1953-1983) are the two most significant of these serial publications of which complete sets exist. In addition, several volumes of historiography and socio-political commentary by Leibl Feldman offer idiosyncratic but informative perspectives on the South African Jewish community, not found elsewhere and well worth scholarly appraisal. The most important of these are *Yidn in dorem-afrike* (Vilna, 1937), *Yidn in yohannesburg* (Johannesburg, 1956), and the monograph *Oudtshoorn: Yerushalayim d'afrike* (Johannesburg 1940).[5]

Fiction and poetry predominate in the extant published material. Some of the poetry is undeniably work of world class. David Fram's two epic poems confronting the Holocaust, *Efsher* and *Dos letste kapitl*, were internationally acclaimed after their appearance in London in 1947. For his collected poems, published in Johannesburg in 1975 in one volume under the title *A volkn un a veg*, David Wolpe was honoured with the Itzik Manger Prize in Israel in 1983. In 1956 Jacob Mordecai Sherman published South Africa's first Yiddish novel, *Land fun gold un zunshayn*, a retrospect of the difficulties of an immigrant Jew's life in South Africa from the beginning of the twentieth century. Mendel Tabatznik provided a detailed picture of South African immigrant Jewish life between the world wars in a three-volume novel entitled *Kalman Bulan*, published between 1968 and 1971. Particularly prolific were the writers of short prose fiction, almost all of whom wrote from the rare perspective of working-class 'whites'. Many tales unsparingly portray the hardships and moral dilemmas faced by Jews in a country predicated on institutionalised racial discrimination. Perhaps the most striking in this regard are microscopic studies of the labouring lives of Yiddish-speaking immigrants employed in the abusive 'kaffir eating houses' established by concession on mine property along the Reef during the gold industry's boom period. The plight of these impoverished immigrants, exploited by rich fellow Jews, is bitingly contrasted with the smugness of unscrupulous get-rich-quick men who benefited handsomely from opportunities created by legislated racial discrimination.[6] Many stories highlight the contempt of large numbers of immigrants for traditional Jewish learning, and their attenuated respect for the tenets of Judaism. They probingly scrutinise the self-seeking materialism of the *nouveaux riches* who use the outward forms of religious and communal service as a convenient handle on social purchase. Overall, South African Yiddish fiction offers a startlingly enlarged view of the white immigrant experience in this country.

Such uncomfortable depictions undermine self-congratulatory assumptions about the nature of the Jewish enterprise in South Africa. Our Yiddish fiction makes clear that, by and large, Jews who immigrated here exploited to the full the ample scope for self-advancement opened up in a social formation that privileged whites at the expense of blacks. In doing so, of course, Jews were no different from any other groups of white immigrants. However, the disproportionately large number of men and women of Jewish parentage who shared in the struggle for black emancipation has fostered a popular belief that Jews in South Africa were ethically more sensitive than their gentile counterparts. The picture presented in our Yiddish fiction does much to dispel this myth. On the other hand, some of our Yiddish writing docs show itself profoundly disturbed by political injustice and racial inequality. Rakhmiel Feldman and Nehemiah Levinsky each produced a volume specifically entitled *rase-dersteylungen*, 'race-stories', which express shocked revulsion at South Africa's apartheid legislation, and which highlight the equivocal position of Jews forced to confront racial prejudice in themselves.[7]

Nowadays, though, the few interested researchers who might wish to examine this work have no entry into the available texts, because they know no Yiddish. Nor can it be expected that they should. Although the Jewish population of South Africa was virtually doubled by the influx of Yiddish-speaking immigrants from Eastern Europe between 1880 and 1930, their language and culture has left no significant mark on our communal structures. The disappearance of Yiddish in South Africa was no accident. It was the inevitable casualty of conflicting ideologies, a desire for rapid acculturation, and an insidious communal indifference abetted, if not overtly encouraged, by the communal leadership.

Hebrew and Zionism

Zionist ideology militantly opposed Yiddish. From its inception as a political movement, Zionism demanded the revival of Hebrew as a precondition for fulfilling Jewish national aspirations in a restored Jewish homeland. The attempts of the Czernowitz conference in 1908 to replace Hebrew with Yiddish, the language spoken by more than one-third of the world's Jews before the First World War, succeeded only in having Yiddish declared *one* of the languages of the Jewish people. Despite the best efforts of its cultural leaders, Yiddish was rejected alike by the Zionists and by the Westernised heirs of the Enlightenment. Perceived as the language of Exile, it was despised as the coarse folk tongue of the uneducated masses, denied respect as a literary medium, and deemed incapable of expressing 'higher thought', for which either the major languages of Europe or a revived modern Hebrew were judged exclusively suited. Following the destruction of European Jewry, and then the establishment of the state of Israel in 1948, Yiddish was further abhorred as the utterance of passivity in the face of genocide. Hebrew, the revived language of the Bible, was to be its virile replacement in a militarily strong Jewish nation-state that was sounding the summons to Jews to abandon the *Galut* and return to the Land.

The Zionist movement was always very powerful in South Africa. During the 1920s and 1930s most world Zionist leaders, including Reuven Brainin, Nahum Sokolow, Chaim Weizmann and Vladimir Jabotinsky, visited and found overwhelming emotional and financial support here. By contrast, the Yiddish movement in South Africa, as elsewhere in the world, was linked to the socialist ideals of the *Bund*, the Jewish Labour Organisation, which favoured – above narrow nationalistic ideals – the worldwide empowerment of the Jewish working classes through the medium of Yiddish. In South Africa, however, to be 'white' and working-class was to occupy the lowest rung on the power structure's social ladder. Hence the upwardly mobile Jewish bourgeoisie was solidly Zionist in sentiment, a commitment that probably sprang at least as much from social ambition as from nationalistic fervour. Social and racial pressures certainly exerted as much push from within as international political forces exercised pull from without to draw South African Jews towards Zionism. As a result, the Jewish language-culture struggle in South Africa was, from the start, loaded heavily in favour of only one side.

The tenets of international Zionism made themselves most strongly felt in Johannesburg, where most of South Africa's Jews were concentrated, and where the rabbinate was headed by Judah Leib Landau (1866-1942), a passionately committed Zionist born in Galicia and educated at the University of Vienna. Landau was determined to suppress, as far as was in his power, any counter-Zionist sentiments emanating from South African Yiddishists who, before the Second World War, were unsympathetic, if not wholly hostile, to Jewish national aspirations. Thus in 1931 Landau used all his influence to block the establishment of a Yiddish daily newspaper at a time most propitious for its foundation. Landau's efforts proved singularly successful, since they chimed with the widespread desire for rapid acculturation of the majority of Jewish immigrants.

Radical negation of Yiddish accelerated after the establishment of the State of Israel, particularly in the field of Jewish education. The South African Board of Jewish Education (SABJE), founded in 1928 against a background of divisiveness and conflict, was finally able, two decades later in 1948, to establish the first Jewish Day School in South Africa. Its aim was to provide a curriculum of which Hebrew was to be the central pillar, not simply for religious instruction, but for the encouragement of *aliyah* to Israel. South African Jewry thus came to offer its children a brand of 'Jewish National Education' in counterpoint to the state education model of 'Christian National Education'. Its Zionist-orientated instruction plan consciously and deliberately effaced all contact with Yiddish.

Many of the earliest pupils of the Jewish Day Schools established by the SABJE – myself among them – came from homes not committed to the destruction of the *Galut*, and rich in the resonance of Yiddish. For many such pupils and their parents, the primal role in Jewish life of Hebrew, the language of scripture, law and liturgy, was in no way threatened by a parallel devotion to Yiddish. The exclusionary emphasis the Day Schools placed on Hebrew, the *tateloshn*, over Yiddish, the *mameloshn*, seemed to many of us a linguistic encouragement to cleave to our father by spitting in the face of our mother.

Rabbi Isaac Goss, the SABJE's Director of Jewish Education from 1944 to 1979, unequivocally spelled out the Board's educational policy in repeated speeches and newspaper articles:

> Jewish education is today ... something which the Jewish child as an individual urgently requires in order that he may become a well-integrated, happy and creative personality. ... The child must be made to feel that his people are not merely living memories of a great past, but are a living entity capable of building and restoring the Jewish State. ... Hebrew is an indispensable and vital element in Jewish education as I envisage it. There is an irreducible minimum of knowledge of Hebrew, Jewish ritual, religion and history, without which one cannot even begin to understand the Jewish heritage. ... Furthermore, with the establishment of Israel, the pre-eminent importance of Hebrew today needs no stressing, and tendencies to operate with so-called Jewish-content curricula in English must be strenuously opposed, if the implication is to demote Hebrew from its central place in the curriculum.[8]

This insistence disguised several ironies, the most obvious of which was personified in the first teachers of Hebrew at King David High School in Johannesburg during the 1950s and 1960s. These men had been born and educated in Eastern Europe, mostly in Lithuania, where they had been the beneficiaries of a Jewish school system that, implementing the best principles of nineteenth-century *maskilim*, trained them as secular teachers, thoroughly conversant not only with Biblical and modern Hebrew, but also with Yiddish and, in many cases, also with Russian language and literature. Since in their classrooms they never spoke a word in or about Yiddish to their pupils, one must assume that they were prohibited by the terms of their employment from doing so. I remember vividly that any attempt I made to address my own teachers in Yiddish, or to ask questions about Yiddish literature, was brusquely dismissed. This overt denigration was particularly unfortunate, not only for us pupils, but also for our teachers, among whom were such tireless contributors to Yiddish cultural life in Johannesburg as C. Achron, J. Batnitsky, L. Goodman and M. (Ben-Moshe) Grossman. At the very time they were teaching and preaching only Hebrew in Johannesburg's Jewish Day Schools, all these men were active workers for the *Dorem afrikaner yidisher kultur-federatsye*, participating members of the editorial board of *Dorem Afrike*, and vigorous contributors to the Yiddish press both locally and abroad. As a matter of course they wrote and published in Hebrew as well. Yet this kind of Jewish bilingualism, so natural to the men of Eastern Europe who taught us, was ruthlessly discouraged in pupils like myself. The dictates of Goss determined that there was to be only Hebrew with a Zionist slant in South Africa's Jewish Day Schools. Indeed, it often seemed to members of my generation that learning modern Hebrew was more important than studying our scriptural and liturgical heritage. And since Yiddish was never mentioned, the stigma the Zionists pinned on it also stuck in the minds of many of my contemporaries.

A Hebrew set text we were required to prepare for our matriculation examination tellingly illustrates how far this ideological zeal was prepared to go. Entitled, as I recall, *Sha'ar le-sifrut* (Gateway to Literature), this book included two of Peretz's stories in Hebrew translation. Through studied omission, our Yiddish-speaking teacher cultivated the impression that Peretz was exclusively a *Hebrew* writer. Although in his earliest writing Peretz had at first moved between Hebrew and Yiddish in search of an authentic narrative voice, he soon settled firmly on Yiddish, and so ardently promoted its cause that he steadily became accepted as its final arbiter to whose judgement every major Yiddish writer of his time deferred.[9] And now here he was, barely fifty years after his death, denied in a South African Jewish Day School the cause to which he had devoted his life. Instead, he was transmogrified into a small-town *maggid* moralising in Hebrew. The stories chosen for our edification were, of course, two of those Hasidic tales that Peretz had carefully re-crafted, and never to our unformed understanding and limited reading experience was it ever suggested what is most obvious to a mature reader about Peretz's use of this Hasidic source material – the fact that in most cases it is used to make ironically negative reflections on the obsolescence of Old World pieties and the constricting limitations of traditional *shtetl* life. Instead, in Hebrew translations by another hand, Peretz's work was harnessed into service as an ideological workhorse for religious-Zionism.[10] Such teaching trickery was hardly untoward, given Goss's shallow personal evaluation of what Peretz was doing:

> Peretz's unique contribution is that, together with Berdichewski, he is one of the founders of the new genre of Chassidic stories. Peretz did more than merely tell Chassidic stories – he rediscovered Chassidism for the masses of Jews. A new world of innocence, piety and holiness is evoked in his stories. ... Peretz ... found in Chassidism what was best in Judaism, the love of life and its constant sanctification by filling its form with social justice and beautifying it by eschewing the trivial ...[11]

As though to emphasise his own limited, literalist reading of Peretz, in the two books he left Goss published his own English translations of no fewer than eight of Peretz's Hasidic *mayselekh*. Born in the 'miniature Lithuania' of Fordsburg in 1913, Goss himself unquestionably grew up speaking Yiddish.[12] That he chose to study German at university suggests that, like so many other Jews of his generation, he regarded Yiddish as a kitchen patois; by returning to its source in one of the languages of European *Hochkultur*, Goss was obviously seeking his own 'passport to European civilisation' in an idiom far removed from the cultural inadequacies of the Yiddish-speaking *shtetl*. Accordingly, as Director of Jewish Education for thirty-five years, Goss laid down a policy that denied South African Jewish children a rounded awareness of their Jewish heritage, a policy that, to echo Isaac Báshevis Singer's tart dismissal of Zionist dogma, promoted the belief that 'we jumped from the Bible to Ben-Gurion with nothing in between'. Such ideological programming guaranteed that Yiddish literature and culture would remain *terra incognita* to the majority of South African-born Jews.

That the fostering of Zionism remained the chief objective of the SABJE was confirmed in later years when it started to import as Hebrew teachers *shlikhim* from Israel. These *shlikhim* had to meet three basic requirements: they had to be observant, Hebrew speaking, and qualified teachers – of any subject, not necessarily of Hebrew. Many were trained to teach subjects as diverse as geography, history and mathematics; few were specifically equipped to teach Hebrew, least of all at the specialised level of foreign language instruction. As committed Zionists living in Israel, moreover, and coming to South Africa on a limited *shlikhut*, they were either hostile to, or ignorant of, any South African connection to Yiddish language, literature and culture.

Disesteem of our South African Yiddish heritage naturally informed the attitudes and actions of the South African Zionist Federation (SAZF), an organisation by definition committed to propagating the values of the State of Israel. This was forcefully brought home to me in 1983 when Marcus Arkin, the SAZF's Director-General at the time, was preparing for publication a volume of essays under the title *South African Jewry: A Contemporary Survey*. As the compilation of this book was nearing completion, I received a telephone call from a colleague who, knowing of my work on South Africa Yiddish literature, asked if I could supply Lionel Abrahams, then finalising his overview of South African Jewish writing, with some random names of Yiddish writers that he could 'scatter' through his piece. Astonished that a general survey of literary work in South Africa should not, from its inception, have planned to include a discrete sub-chapter of its own describing the contribution made by our Yiddish writers, I objected to such denigrating tokenism. Representations to a personal friend on the committee of the SAZF led to my being permitted by the editor to write an essay exclusively devoted to South African Yiddish writing. Having gained the grace of a few weeks more than I had initially been allowed, in consideration of the fact that I was being fitted in as a last-minute addition, I was able to conduct a number of personal interviews with Yiddish writers and teachers still alive in South Africa, and to begin the compilation of an up-to-date bibliography. Shortly after I had submitted my piece for publication, I was summoned to the offices of the SAZF to be given a fresh typescript that, I was told, comprised the 'proof pages' of my work. I was instructed to peruse this typescript 'for spelling errors only', and was pointedly informed that I would not be permitted to make any other changes whatever. Reading through what had been returned to me, I saw to my indignation that every reference I had made to the anti-Zionist polemics conducted by our Yiddishists before the Second World War – integrally part not only of South African, but also of world Jewish history – had been systematically excised. Not a single anti-Zionist sentiment, demonstration or attitude, however mildly expressed, had been permitted to appear in the pro-Zionist, censored version. South African Jewish history itself was being rewritten in order to uphold a specific political ideology. That this deliberate misrepresentation was the calculated work of an editor who had formerly been an academic added to my outrage.

I was faced with a painful choice. To have argued against the editor's doctrinaire policy would have accomplished nothing but the removal of my sub-chapter, itself a barely welcome afterthought. Although the research I had written up was now compromised by the censorship to which it had been subjected, I was nevertheless unwilling to abet the erasure of the significant role Yiddish had played in our community from a volume supposedly designed to update available data. So I returned the mutilated piece without comment, but I vowed for the future to restore South African Yiddish writing to its rightful place in our history.[13] As might have been expected, given its editor's prejudices, Arkin's book was unfavourably reviewed. More disappointing, however, was the fact that no single reviewer even mentioned its hitherto unrecorded overview of South African Yiddish writing. It was painful to discover that no one in either the academic or the popular press regarded South African Yiddish writing as of any significance. Here was conclusive proof of the success of the long campaign to expunge the Yiddish presence from the historiography and consciousness of South African Jewry. Zionist ideology, combined with dwindling Jewish historical awareness, had won its battle – but at a cost our community could scarcely afford.

Upward social mobility

Other forces were at work to deaden consciousness of Yiddish in South Africa. From the moment of their arrival, Yiddish-speaking Eastern European immigrants had been viewed with mistrust and resentment; their coming had inspired waves of open anti-semitism that reached from the popular press to legislative enactments. These immigrants, many unskilled and poorly educated, unfamiliar with our country's languages, despised on the one hand for their foreignness and working-class status, yet on the other hand automatically privileged in the wider social formation because of their 'white' skins, seemed even to South Africa's settled Anglo-German Jewish establishment an embarrassing excrescence that had to be integrated into society's mainstream 'white' culture as quickly as possible, if it were not to provoke tension within the Jewish community and hostility from without. Their language itself, scorned as outlandish and unrefined, had been the subject of heated controversy and had required impassioned representation to the government before it was accorded official recognition as an immigrant entry requirement.[14] Once having gained for Yiddish acknowledgment as a 'European' language for the purpose of entry, however, South Africa's Jewish establishment saw no reason to encourage its continuance. English was the language that assured protection under the British Crown; it was the *lingua franca* of government, business and influence in the half-century before the Afrikaner-dominated National Party swept to power in 1948; thus it was to English as the instrument of empowerment that most Eastern European immigrants were drawn. Outside pressures apart, Yiddish speakers were anxious as quickly as possible to share themselves, and enable their children to share, all the privileges of upward mobility in white South Africa. Generally lacking interest in any literature and culture, most of them declined to nurture a sentimental attachment to a language they spoke only for convenience until they were fluent enough in English. As a whole, the South African Jewish community was fundamentally Philistine in outlook, valuing language not as the vehicle of an enriching culture but as a tool for material betterment. Goss himself was compelled to recognise this:

> We may as well admit that, on the surface, it seems that the climate of opinion here (and I am only talking of our local scene) is certainly antipathetic, if not indifferent, to cultural values.
>
> Despite all the lip-service we pay to education and culture, we do not, as a community, place a premium on ideas and culture generally.[15]

Pandering to the same indifference, Goss persisted to the end in devaluing Yiddish language and culture, refusing ever to acknowledge that it could and should exist side by side with Hebrew in a country whose Jewish population had been so greatly enlarged by Yiddish-speaking immigrants:

> ... in order to increase the chances of worthwhile survival in this country, two things are imperative: (a) a more creative Zionism, and (b) the creation of a Jewish intelligentsia. ... This would mean ... the encouragement of a body of men rooted in their past, with a knowledge of the classical sources and history, or at least sufficient knowledge to give them a sense of the past and a sense of the facts of Judaism as well as the contemporary situation.
>
> It goes without saying that this body of men and women would have a speaking and (more important) a reading knowledge of Hebrew. They would be able to read Hebrew sources in the original, as well as having a knowledge of Yiddish, necessary for keeping them in contact with our articulate masses, and would also have to have a knowledge of the disciplines of literature, psychology and sociology.[16]

To pay lip service to the need for keeping Yiddish alive merely as the means of communicating with non-existent 'articulate masses' was a certain prescription for its death.

Yiddishism

Like so many of their counterparts in Europe, those committed few who did carry a torch for Yiddish in South Africa were in their turn, however, partisans of one side or another in the bitter ideological war waged around the concept of 'Yiddishism'. The battles fought in huge centres of Yiddish life in Lithuania, Poland and the Soviet Union before the Second World War were translated into a country where the numbers of Yiddish speakers were proportionally infinitesimal, and interest in Yiddish was at best tepid. As a result, through vicious infighting, South African Yiddishists largely contributed to their own destruction.

While Yiddish movements all shared a general faith in socialism, the way they defined it was a source of rancorous polemic. The socialism of the *Bund*, accepted by most Yiddishists in the West, was rejected by orthodox Communists who demanded ever more stridently that all *kulturarbet* should be oriented towards Moscow.[17] Soviet Communists joyfully pointed to the creation, by the Commissariat of Nationalities in 1926, of the autonomous Jewish region of Birobidzhan, and they called on Yiddish-speaking Jews worldwide to abandon bourgeois nationalistic aspirations and populate instead the newly designated Soviet 'Yiddishland'. The *Bund*, on the other hand, was concerned with the emancipated future of Jewish workers in the Diaspora, and most of its members were no more interested in colonising Birobidzhan than in settling in Palestine. Many Yiddishists followed the teachings of Shimen Dubnov, and later those of Khaym Zhitlovsky, striving for the creation of a *doyiker* Yiddish life in the Diaspora while accommodating themselves to the languages and cultures of the gentile nations among whom they lived.[18]

In South Africa, acrimonious quarrels dragged on between Yiddish-speakers ideologically committed respectively to the Jewish agricultural workers' association or, as it was known in Yiddish, the *Geserd (Gezelshaft far erdarbetendike yidn)*; the *Yidisher arbeter klub*, a strongly Bundist society; and *Po'alei Zion*, an ardently pro-Zionist movement. The political atmosphere of the *Yidisher arbeter klub* before the Second World War has been sharply described at first hand by Woolf Levick:

> Johannesburg from the late 1930s until after the War had a vibrant Yiddish social and cultural life. The Yidisher arbeter klub was a hive of activity: its dramatic society produced plays regularly; there were frequent lectures on a variety of topics by both guest speakers and members, all of whom

were to the political left. Their main interest was avidly following daily events in the 'socialist Sixth of the World'. ... The bright light of Marxism, which was supposedly leading the Soviet people to the millennium, and in their wake the rest of the world, diffused a strong glitter worldwide, and the Arbeter klub got its fair share. The very air one breathed there was 'Marxist', and if the actual tenets of Marx's teachings were unknown from first-hand study, slogans from the Manifesto, which were freely bandied about, took their place so adequately that several members could proudly boast of being Marxist by intuition.[19]

Like all internecine wars, these conflicts were self-destructive. Competing factions in South Africa tried to establish rival publications, without the slightest regard for the fact that the numbers of Yiddish-speaking Jews who wanted to read Yiddish at all were too small to support them. The majority saw no point in devoting themselves to a futile struggle for a language and culture utterly remote from the socio-political situation in which they found themselves. Even though they were fighting a losing battle, however, this widespread indifference did not stop South Africa's Yiddishists from fervidly pursuing their conflicting ideological programmes.

The chief ideologue of a Soviet-orientated agenda for South African Yiddishism was Leibl Feldman, a wealthy capitalist businessman who played a major role in the *Kultur-federatsye*, establishing himself as a powerful voice on the editorial board of *Dorem Afrike* and, through his financial sponsorship, making himself the policy director of Johannesburg's Yiddish *Folkshul*, which he revived.[20] There, despite strong objections from the teaching staff, Feldman insisted on downgrading the teaching of Hebrew, showing himself as wilfully blind on his side as the Hebrew ideologists of the SABJE were on theirs. Feldman totally ignored – for it is inconceivable that he could have been ignorant of – the extent to which a central range of Yiddish discourse depends on Hebrew words and phrases. His damaging attitude was dictated by a slavish adherence to the Party line on Yiddish enforced by the *Yevsektsia*, the 'Jewish Section' attached to the Department of Propaganda of the Soviet Union's Central Committee. In its attempt to purge

Yiddish of its 'petty bourgeois religious' elements, the *Yevsektsia* not only frowned upon the use of Biblical and Talmudic idioms, but also reconstructed the orthography of Yiddish, decreeing that words of Hebrew origin be spelled phonetically.[21] Feldman undeviatingly followed this *diktat* in all his own writing, and he demanded the same conformity from everyone else. In their antithetical but equally narrow dogmatism, both Yiddishist and Zionist educators instituted Jewish instruction policies for South African children that consciously cut them off from half their heritage. Both groups were deaf to the insistence of the great Yiddish poet Avrom Sutzkever: 'Yiddish and Hebrew are the two eyes of Jewish life; take one away and we are blind.'

So fanatically did many South African Yiddishists idolise Stalin that even after the publication of Khrushchev's 'secret speech', delivered in February 1956 to the Twentieth Party Congress in Moscow, denouncing the 'cult of personality' and unmasking Stalin's massacres, they refused to believe it.[22] In the wake of that speech, at the end of May 1956 David Wolpe, who had assumed the editorship of *Dorem Afrike* a year before, received a dispatch from the Jewish Telegraphic Agency (JTA) reporting the wholesale murder of leading Soviet Yiddish writers and scholars four years earlier. Appalled by this news, Wolpe immediately decided to broadcast it by rewriting his leading article for the June issue, then at the printers, and he sought the sanction of the *Kultur-federatsye*'s executive to do so. The account of their refusal given in Wolpe's memoirs is chillingly informative:

> To begin with I read out the information filed by the JTA: the general revelations of Stalin's mass-murders and, as their consequence, the unrestrained killing off of Yiddish writers and Yiddish culture, although not yet specified nor officially confirmed. ... Very soon I stepped on the landmine – as soon as I mentioned the name Stalin and his murderous deeds, an enraged voice roared out: 'No! No! Not that far!' It was Zalmen Levy. Leibl Feldman leapt up after him. The noisy chorus of 'No!' exploded. [Misha] Szur [then chairman of the Yidisher kultur-federatsye] rapped his bony fingers on the table ... the tumult was stilled. But I was completely shaken, and I felt ... anger and shame. ... [Then] Szur asked:

'Who wants to participate in the discussion about the article?' Almost all of the left wing declared themselves. ... The first who moved to stifle the 'counter-revolution' was, naturally, Zalmen Levy. Achron and Goodman sat silent, as though it were not their concern. Feldman turned his head towards me. ... And the attack began. The commander of the 'Red Front' was Zalmen Levy. He spoke heatedly so that that his patron [Feldman] and their 'comrades' might see how faithfully he defended their position ... He began from ... the title as I had presented it and as he had jotted it down. No one else would even have noticed it, but he did: 'We dare not entitle it, as its heading does, "A Murder Tragedy", because as yet we do not have any official confirmation of such a thing as "murder".'

An uncontrollable rage welled up in me, and impulsively I strode over, stood opposite him, and with all my strength yelled into his face: 'You're a toady and a cynic! What else is it but murder? Tell us!' The colour drained from his face. It was obvious that he had taken fright. ... I stood with a clenched fist and his pallor gave me pleasure. Had he not remained silent, something would have happened.

As though in expectation, dead silence reigned. The people here would gladly have preferred a brawl between the two of us than this heated polemic. Szur said, 'sit down and don't excite yourself. I have an emendation that is a good substitute. Instead of "A Murder Tragedy", let it be "A Culture Tragedy".' And before I could refuse, Achron gave his consent: 'Yes, there's no distinction.'

All at once I felt as though I had been shoved out of the battle arena. ... I had done my share; I had written about it. Now I passively observed the cheap huckstering that followed, as though in a market trade-off: here a word changed, there a sentence deleted, until they came to the explosive point: the paragraph containing the inviolable name ... Again Zalmen Levy raged. 'We won't permit it!' and Leibl Feldman, with furious bulging eyes repeated after him, 'Definitely not! That is utterly impermissible!' And as before, the chorus muttered aloud, 'No! No!' And Szur again beat on the table and was barely able to quieten the mood of hostility. Finally he said: '... In order to save unnecessary talk and time and noisy arguments, which will convince no one ... I propose that we ... put the whole paragraph to the vote ...' ... It was decided to conduct a secret ballot ... When the slips in the box had been counted, those in favour of not publishing had a considerable majority. Satisfied, they rejoiced.[23]

Given the time it occurred, the irony of this *contretemps* is savage indeed. From the time the National Party government had passed the Suppression of Communism Act in 1950, Red-hunting had become a national preoccupation. Mindful of the National Party's long history of antisemitism, the wider Jewish community was particularly alarmed because a number of named Communists, actively fighting for black rights, were Jewish by birth. With such Communist activists virtually none of South Africa's committed Yiddishists would have allied or identified themselves. So the scene Wolpe describes is mere play-acting. It presents a cast of Yiddish-speaking bourgeois, all profiting from a racially discriminatory capitalist system, striking ideological attitudes behind the closed doors of a limited-membership club.

For others outside this club, though, fear of the government's anti-Communist witch-hunt was real enough, and led to other pitiful absurdities. Leibl Yudaken, a quiet man of letters who had acquired a number of Yiddish books published in Moscow, was scared enough personally to deface them so as to remove all evidence of their place of origin. I discovered this when I obtained Yudaken's library for the University of the Witwatersrand. Among its rare books was Yekhezkel Dobrushin's critical study of the work of Dovid Bergelson.[24] When I read Yudaken's copy of this insightful study – made especially interesting as a consequence of Dobrushin's obligatory adherence to Stalin's fiat that all writers be judged strictly according to the dictates of 'socialist realism' – I was amazed to find that the publisher's logo had been cut out of its cover with a razor blade, and that the book's title and imprint pages had been torn away. Compelled as a result to seek the volume's place and date of publication in an international library catalogue, I came upon another tragic irony in the worldwide Yiddishist enslavement to ideology. Dobrushin's study, published in Moscow by the newspaper *Emes* in 1947, was among the very last Yiddish books issued in the Soviet Union before Stalin launched his murderous purge of Jews; Dobrushin, like Bergelson, was himself among its victims. Yet here in South Africa, at the very time when government-led anti-Communist hysteria was daily gaining ground, our own Yiddishists were playing out a hollow farce: privately clinging to Communist theory while publicly living by capitalist practice; publicly silent about the racist policies of South Africa's government, but privately vocal in defence of a Soviet regime in the process of being discredited in Moscow itself.

Unlike the Zionist *shlikhim* who were at least specifically engaged to *teach* here, the *Kultur-federatsye*'s *kulturarbeter*, despite supposedly being 'cultural workers' for a great internationalist Jewish cause, saw no part of their duty as interesting young people in Yiddish. So far from attempting to counterbalance the powerful Zionist influence in South African Jewish education, these *kulturarbeter* behaved as though Yiddish were their personal property. It soon became obvious that Johannesburg's Yiddish *Folkshul* could never hope to compete with the SABJE's Jewish Day Schools for the support of South African parents. Yet members of the *Kultur-federatsye* did nothing whatever to strike a balance, to promote Yiddish cultural activities, or attempt to foster interest in the Yiddish language and its literature, among young people. Instead these 'cultural workers' went on preaching to one another. As should have been obvious from the outset, this was virtually a programme of planned self-destruction. Perhaps it was. Nearly 30 years later, when I interviewed the few *kulturarbeter* left alive, it became depressingly obvious that these ageing people were perfectly content to let Yiddish die with them. With few exceptions, they were actively hostile to any incursion by younger, non-native speakers into what they circumscribed as their private world. Furthermore, although they created no long-term programmes to teach Yiddish themselves, they maliciously undermined such efforts made by others. The attempt to build a Yiddish library at the University of the Witwatersrand – ultimately thwarted by that university's expulsion of Jewish Studies from its Humanities curriculum – was greeted with apathy by those Yiddishists left alive in Johannesburg who could have contributed most towards it.

Significantly, the majority of Jewish parents here were little interested in seeing their children acquire a rounded Jewish education. The proposal to establish a network of Jewish Day Schools, firmly mooted in 1945, from the first encountered vigorous opposition from a significant sector of Johannesburg's Jews, who argued that they did not want to 'ghettoise' their children, but rather to send them to schools where they could 'mix with all types'.[25] Baldly put, this meant that they wanted their children to mix with peers whose parents could facilitate their advancement. The SABJE was obliged to mount a strenuous propaganda campaign to persuade Jewish parents that their children would gain, not lose, by attending a Day School, where, apart from receiving a first-rate secular education, they would study Hebrew during school hours, and so be able to take a normal part in extra-mural activities. To judge from the number of times Isaac Goss was obliged to repeat this enticement in his public addresses, it was plainly a marketing strategy that continued to meet with parental resistance:

> There is a need for more intensive Jewish education, which a supplemental school [the *kheyder*] cannot for obvious reasons give. The difficulties which face the teacher in the latter school are inherent in the circumstances of our environment. ... The Jewish Day School was therefore an inevitable development, if a greater qualitative Jewish education was the aim. Since in these Jewish Day Schools, Hebrew and Judaism are taught in the morning as a normal subject and the child is not deprived of his sport, no artificial dichotomy is created between his secular studies and his Jewish studies. Further, since he does not need to make so many sacrifices and he has no sense of frustration, it is here that one can hope for a more balanced Jewish education and more qualitative scholastic results. More than that, the Day School provides a wholesome synthesis of Jewish studies and Jewish living; it affords the child a vital, inspiring Jewish environment.[26]

Steadily, however, Israel's military successes did much to encourage indifferent South African Jews to accept Hebrew-Zionist education as a positive benefit. So did periodic outbursts of antisemitism from the Afrikaner government, notably in 1961 when Prime Minister Verwoerd cut off South African Jewish funds to Israel in reprisal for Israel's United Nations vote against South African racism. None of this, however, improved the attitude of South African Jews towards Yiddish. On the contrary, it intensified their hostility. If they mentioned the language at all, English-speakers tended to miscall it 'Jewish', presumably to avoid contamination with the antisemitic pejorative 'Yid'. This shamefaced euphemism marked a stage more than halfway between embarrassment and erasure. The anti-Yiddish, anti-*Galut* attitude of the Zionist State was soon accepted here as the only valid orthodoxy. Any attempt to address a wider dimension in Diaspora Jewish life was deemed manifest blasphemy.

What is to be done?

Yiddish in South Africa is now dead, and cannot be recalled to life. Lack of sufficient teachers has vitiated all attempts in both Johannesburg and Cape Town to build up a body of new readers who might research our indigenous Yiddish literature. The loss, as I have indicated, is enormous. The corpus of Yiddish writing published in this country offers far more than a casual encounter with a vanished culture. It provides a unique insight into the historical, political and socio-cultural forces that shaped our life here. There can never be a rounded picture of the South African Jewish community without a thorough knowledge of what was written about it in Yiddish. Now that South Africa's socio-political structure has undergone radical change, it is crucial that such a picture be acquired and analysed. Every ethnic minority – and every people within the black majority – now requires a revaluation of its own history. There is a pressing need to place in adjusted perspective each of the diverse population groups that constitute our nation.

Since we have library holdings of the key books and periodicals published in Yiddish in South Africa, what we need at this stage of our history is an ongoing project, sponsored by our leading research institutions, to translate and publish in English most of this material. A small though encouraging beginning has been made – at least three South African Yiddish books have appeared in English translation to date; additionally many short stories have been translated and published in our cultural journal, *Jewish Affairs*. Much more needs to be done, however. Most obviously, Leibl Feldman's two major chronicles, *Yidn in dorem afrike* and *Yidn in yohannesburg*, urgently need translating, for Feldman has recorded a mass of information unavailable elsewhere. Feldman, it is true, was not only a cramped ideologue but was also very much an amateur, and far from meticulous in citing his sources. But Feldman's claims can be a spur to more professional scholars to seek their verification; his books will mark out a richly rewarding road for future analysis. Postgraduate students in Jewish Studies, history, sociology and politics should be encouraged to pursue their primary research from Yiddish texts, and once these have been translated, published and put into the public domain, they will offer appreciably refocussed angles on our community. In literature, moreover, most of our best Yiddish writers were determined to leave their mark on international Yiddish letters by vivifying their experience of life in Africa in both poetry and prose. Their view of this African life differs considerably from the responses of other immigrant groups, for having been themselves the victims of racial discrimination in Eastern Europe, as 'whites' they found themselves in a shocking role reversal in racist South Africa. Their poetry movingly sets their longing for the values, climate and rootedness of the Old Home in contrast with their shock, courage and determination in the new world they had entered. This work is a noteworthy addition to the body of general South African culture, and has been neglected for too long, to the great injury of our fullest self-awareness as an ethnic minority.

In South Africa's new dispensation, it is not longer possible to rest content with old clichés about our Jewish life here. Revaluation is essential, and its greatest impetus will come from a thorough study of our homegrown Yiddish writing. Not to accept this challenge, especially at this decisive time in our history, is to renege on a duty we owe both to our forebears and to ourselves.

The Boer War, The Great War, and the Shaping of South African Jewish Loyalties

RICHARD MENDELSOHN

RICHARD MENDELSOHN has taught for many years in the History Department of the University of Cape Town of which he is currently the head. His research interests lie in South African Jewish history. He is the author of *Sammy Marks: The Uncrowned King of the Transvaal*, a biography of the pioneering Jewish industrial and mining entrepreneur, which was awarded the University of Cape Town's annual book prize in 1991. He has published extensively on various aspects of the history of turn-of-the-twentieth-century Transvaal, and is currently completing a book on Jews and the Anglo-Boer War.

The South African Jewish community at the start of the new millennium is a mature Jewish community – perhaps even a post-mature Jewish community. Despite widespread anxiety about crime rates, and fears for the future, the Jewish community currently experiences relative tranquility and prosperity. A highly acculturated, socially homogenous, essentially middle-class community, it enjoys a large measure of acceptance within South African society at large.

Casting back a century though, to the start of the twentieth century, we find a very different South African Jewish world: a Jewish community, young and unshaped, largely new-immigrant in composition and only very shallowly rooted in the society, a socially and culturally heterogeneous community with as yet only a very limited sense of collective identity. A fledgling community, which within just two decades endured two seismic disturbances, two earthquakes, both of which originated outside the Jewish community but both of which were felt within the Jewish community, albeit at different levels of intensity.

These two seismic events – the Boer War and the Great War, to give them their now unfashionable older titles – impacted very differently on the Jewish community. But both, it will be argued, played a critical role in the shaping of the community's relationship with the wider society, in particular the locus of its members' broader political loyalties.

Of the two conflicts, the South African War – to revert to political correctness – was the more obviously and more immediately disruptive. The outbreak of the war in October 1899 precipitated a wholesale exodus, in overcrowded open railway trucks, of the urban Jewish population of the Highveld to the coast, where most would remain till the end of the war in 1902. This disruption of the new Jewish urban communities of the interior, of the Witwatersrand and Pretoria, this displacement of South African Jewish life from the interior to the coast, seemingly so drastic and consequential, was, arguably, of only limited historical significance. Exile at the coast was uncomfortable and impoverishing for many.[1] It was also far more prolonged than originally expected – it may be safely assumed that most of the refugees, like the complacent British generals themselves, had anticipated a rapid British victory and that they would be home on the Highveld by Chanukah.

Yet for all its discomfort and impoverishment, and despite its unexpectedly extended duration, the coastal exile was only of a strictly temporary nature, and of limited consequence. By late 1902 most of the refugees had returned to the Highveld to resume their lives. They returned to a community which had continued to function right through the war, albeit at a much reduced pace. The essential structures of Jewish life in the Transvaal (and in the Orange Free State) – the religious and service institutions – remained substantially intact throughout the war, albeit they were operated by skeleton staffs.[2] In a Jewish communal sense at least, the Boer War was less than destructive, and communal continuity was largely maintained. In the Boer War case there was none of the root-and-branch dislocation of Jewish communal life of later European conflicts.

While Jewish life in the urban centres of the interior was disrupted rather than destroyed, Jewish life in the countryside suffered more substantial damage. With the exceptions of the few towns that were besieged – Kimberley, Mafeking, Ladysmith – South Africa's sizable urban centres largely escaped serious damage in the Boer War. The war was fought mainly in the countryside. Here warfare assumed the scale of awfulness of much of modern war. Recent research has shown that rural Jews were, together with their Boer and black neighbours, the victims of the brutal British clearance of the countryside, of the scorched-earth tactics adopted by Kitchener, the British commander, to bring the Boer commandos to heel. Alongside the well-known burning of farms, there was the burning and dynamiting of the elaborate honeycomb of hotels, homes and stores that Jews had established throughout the rural Transvaal and Free State during the 1880s and '90s.[3] But even here, despite the high level of destruction, there was a post-war restoration and the rapid re-establishment of the Jewish rural network – a successful reconstruction that was achieved without the aid of the compensation monies for war damage to property paid to many of their displaced Boer neighbours and to other foreign subjects by Britain, for the British found a legal loophole to unfairly deny both rural and urban Jews such compensation.[4]

One critical way in which the rural Jewish wartime experience differed from that of their Boer and black neighbours was that, as foreign subjects in the main, they avoided, for the most part, being herded into the concentration camps the British created throughout the interior of South Africa to house those displaced by the clearing of the countryside. Instead, Jews forced off the land either made their way into the towns of the Free State and Transvaal, or went off to the coast. The result, historically, was that Jews in the aftermath of the war did not share the residual bitterness that helped to fuel the rise of an exclusivist, anti-British Afrikaner nationalism in later decades. Crucially, their wartime experience had parted company with that of the Boers at the gates of the notorious camps.

Besides the relatively temporary and limited nature of the

damage inflicted on Jewish individual and communal life other than in the countryside, the South African War also placed few strains on Jewish loyalty. Unlike the First Word War as will be seen, very little was demanded of Jews in South Africa during the South African War. Unlike the First World War, it was possible to sit out the South African War without attracting unfavourable public attention. Neutrality was a perfectly acceptable course of action, and one the majority of recently arrived Jews quite sensibly chose. Most Jews opted for this perfectly natural and rational choice that offended neither side in the conflict.

Their abstention drew little comment, for there was no obvious civic reason why they should risk their lives for either side. By and large they were neither naturalised British subjects nor burghers – for the Transvaal had raised the bar on *burgerschap* (citizenship) to a height that few Jews had cleared by the outbreak of the war. Those few who had cleared the bar were compelled as burghers to fight. Some did so willingly and stayed the course. Others did so more reluctantly, and opted out as soon as they could. Still others joined the Boers voluntarily, and fought courageously, some to the 'bitter-end'.[5]

Many more Jews fought – or at least served – on the other side. A few South African- resident Jews joined up with the much larger numbers of Jews who came from Britain and elsewhere in the Empire to serve in the imperial field forces, while many more joined the town guards, the volunteer forces raised in mid-war to repel Boer attacks on the towns of the Cape Colony, which never came.[6]

But while some fought or at least donned a uniform, most Jews remained on the sidelines and did so without earning any popular opprobrium. This had much to do with the nature of the war. In a deeply polarised South Africa, abstention from the war was a common and publicly acceptable choice Jews shared with many others. Many of the Cape Dutch, for example, caught between their formal allegiance to the Queen and their emotional solidarity with their Boer kinsmen, chose to sit out the war. (Other Cape Afrikaners, of course, risked the firing squad by taking up arms with the Queen's enemies.)

While neutrality was an acceptable – and comfortable – option, and while Jewish 'loyalty' consequently never became a public issue, the outcome of the war did finally resolve where Jewish allegiances in South Africa would lie in future. The British victory stamped British authority over the whole of the country. Jews readily accepted, and indeed welcomed this. They did so easily and smoothly because even before the war the Jews in the Boer republics had already affiliated to the commercial, Anglo-centric culture of the towns; they did so also because they valued the religious tolerance of English society where there was none of the residual religious restrictiveness of Calvinist Boer society. (The South African Republic, though not the Orange Free State, had still discriminated consitutionally in 1899 against its Jewish inhabitants, in minor but offensive ways.)[7] As a result, there was no nostalgia amongst Jews, unlike among the Afrikaners, for the defeated republican order, no yearning for the restoration of the republics. This was to be expected, for Jews in the Transvaal had always been Uitlanders in Boer society, despite the intimate friendships that some, like the industrialist Sammy Marks, had enjoyed with the Boer leaders, including President Kruger.[8]

It is perhaps idle to speculate what might have been had the war never occurred, and had the Boer republics consequently retained their independence. Would we have had the development of a Transvaal Republican Jewish identity and loyalism distinct from the Jewish identity of those who lived in the British coastal colonies? Or would the outcome have been much the same, a common South African Jewish identity and set of loyalties, simply because Jews, whether in the Transvaal or in the Cape, settled mainly in the English-dominated towns?

But for the enforced unification of the country through war, would the Jewish communities of the coastal colonies and of the republican states of the interior have gone their separate ways and developed distinctive characters; or would the common origins of these communities and their shared immigrant experience – their common 'cultural baggage' – have transcended the political boundaries and created a common South African Jewishness irrespective of whether they were subjects of the Crown or republican burghers?

The South African Jewish experience in the Great War was very different from the Jewish experience in the South African War. Most obviously, the First World War was a distant war, a remote war rather than one directly experienced. There was none of the physical disruption, discomfort and dislocation of the earlier war. Daily life continued undisturbed, as did the yearly round, with Jews migrating every December to the Cape coastal resort of Muizenberg just as they had done before the war.

Yet for all that the Great War probably generated as much Jewish angst as – if not more than – the earlier war had done: anxiety this time not about one's own safety and future, not about how one was to make ends meet while waiting impatiently at the coast to return to the Transvaal, but about the fate of one's family and friends who had remained behind in *der Heim*. South African Jews were acutely aware that the Eastern Front straddled their home districts in Eastern Europe. Cut off from communication with their kin, all they knew was that their families were caught in the crossfire of a destructive and terrible conflict, and most likely had been forced to flee their homes and reduced to penury. Raising relief funds for these refugees became the principal focus of South African Jewry during the war. Money was collected through endless concerts, balls, bazaars, street collections, house-to-house collections, and collections even at *bris milahs* (circumcisions).[9]

The amounts collected were impressive, especially given the limited resources of what was still very largely a struggling immigrant community. By September 1917, for example, the Western Cape alone had sent what was then the enormous sum of £44 000 to Russia.[10] But while the overall response to the plight of Russian Jewry was impressive, not all South African Jews responded equally enthusiastically. The uneven response of South African Jewry highlights the continuing divisions within the South African Jewish community during the Great War, continuing divisions between Russian and English Jews, between more acculturated and less acculturated Jews. There were vociferous complaints, for example, that Jews living in what were then the middle-class suburbs of Johannesburg were much less engaged in the campaign to raise relief funds, and much less generous, than their Russian Jewish brethren in the meaner streets of Johannesburg.[11]

These divisions within South African Jewry were even more apparent when it came to the issue of broader loyalties beyond the strictly Jewish.

The First World War threw into much sharper relief than had the South African War the issue of Jewish public loyalties. It did so because the First World War, even more than the South African War, generated nationalist passions of great intensity, accompanied by chauvinism and xenophobia of a sort that left minority communities like South African Jewry very uncomfortably exposed.[12] As South African Jewry discovered to its cost, the Great War left very little space for the cosy neutrality of the earlier war.

The focal issue, the burning issue that brought the question of Jewish loyalty to the fore, was that of recruitment. Unlike Britain, South Africa did not fall back on conscription during the First World War but relied instead on volunteering, stimulated by great public recruiting drives, to man the contingents that South Africa sent to German East Africa and to the Western Front.[13]

Jewish responses to these recruiting drives were very mixed it would seem, reflecting the stark social and cultural divisions within the community. English Jews and anglicised Jews volunteered enthusiastically and in substantial numbers, both for the campaign in German East Africa and for the Western Front. The *South African Jewish Chronicle* carried regular news of these Jewish volunteers, often of a very poignant kind. Thus in July 1917 it reported the deaths at the front in France of Leonard Platnauer, a 'brilliant' former student of the South African College in Cape Town, who had enlisted before taking up a Rhodes scholarship, and of the 26-year-old Lieutenant Benjamin Cohen, educated at Wynberg High School and at Glasgow University, where he had qualified as a doctor.[14] (On a happier note, the *Chronicle* reported the Cape Town Jewish community's fêting of Private S Rosenthal, who had returned wounded from Delville Wood.)[15]

While the less visible English Jews and anglicised Jews volunteered enthusiastically and in substantial numbers, the more publicly visible, less anglicised Russian Jews showed much less enthusiasm, or at least so it was alleged. If this was indeed the case – we lack reliable figures and are forced to rely instead on subjective perceptions – it is easily explained. The more recently arrived Russian immigrants had not yet had time to take on the English patriotic coloration of their more anglicised brethren.

Besides, the war itself, or rather the awkward alliances it generated, were more than problematic for the Russian Jewish immigrants. Liberal Britain's alliance with an oppressive, antisemitic Tsarist Russia did nothing to inspire Russian Jewish enthusiasm for the war effort.[16] Russian victory over Germany and Austria would do nothing, they feared, to improve the lot of Eastern European Jewry; indeed it might well do exactly the opposite by bringing the Jews of Galicia under Tsarist rule.[17]

The apparent failure of Russian Jews to respond to the recruiting appeals became problematic for all Jews in South Africa, including the anglicised. It did so because it focused a spotlight of intense public disapproval on the Jewish community as a whole. Jewish shirkers were denounced from public platforms, and in the letter and editorial columns of newspapers, with young Jewish males working in stores along the Rand or holidaying peacefully at Muizenberg singled out for particularly acerbic comment. Thus, for example, 'A Patriot at Heart' complained in a letter to the *East Rand Express* about 'so many healthy and strong types of manhood [,] so-called Jews, "stiffing" it about Johannesburg', and asked whether anything could 'be done to force these shirkers to do their bit for their King and country'.[18] Similarly, the *Standerton Advertiser*, berating the 'slackers' of the district, wondered rhetorically: 'And the Jews of South Africa, where are they? Very few have yet risked loss of life or property by leaving their homes to assist the Empire of their adoption in her hour of agony and need.'[19]

This hostile attention, at a time of dangerous and potentially violent nationalist passion, both alarmed and divided the Jewish community. Lionel Goldsmid, the English Jewish editor of the *South African Jewish Chronicle*, accepted that the charges were not wholly unjust, and laid into the Russian Jewish shirkers. Thus, for example, in an editorial titled 'The Call to the Jew', he wrote:

> … we feel sure that there are few of our co-religionists who hail from Great Britain who have not answered the call. … But what of the Russian Jews? It is all very well for them to argue 'If it were not that Russia is an ally I would go.' The excuse is that of a man who lacks the courage of his own conviction. Let them say outright 'I am afraid' and they will be believed but to urge that because a country which has been step-motherly to them is allied with a country which

has been more than a mother to them is an excuse for refraining from doing their duty which shows a cowardice that is worthy of the greatest condemnation.[20]

Other leaders vigorously denied the charges, and sought to prove that Jewish volunteering was at least on a par with gentile volunteering. Thus, for example, Reverend Bender and Morris Alexander, the two most prominent figures in contemporary Cape Jewry, wrote jointly to the *Cape Times*, asserting that they '…had ample evidence that the Jews of South Africa, in proportion to their numbers, had come forward as readily, as earnestly, and as fully as any other section of the community for patriotic service in the cause of the Allies. We admitted that there were slackers among the Jews, but not in greater numbers than among other denominations. …'[21] This conflict of view within the Jewish community led to the astonishing spectacle of the editor of what was then the leading South African Jewish journal being accused of antisemitism (for excoriating his Russian co-religionists for their reluctance to volunteer for military service), and of the even more extraordinary spectacle of the editor suing his accuser, S Vogelson, the editor of a rival Jewish paper, the *African Jewish World*, in open court for libel.[22]

This embarrassing public spat points both to the deep divisions within the community and to the angst the Great War generated, anxiety of a sort that was not experienced by Jews in South Africa during the South African War a dozen or so years before. It might indeed be argued that while the South African War clearly created more of a physical disturbance for South African Jewry, it was the First World War that created more of a psychic disturbance with, it might be speculated, some important if subterranean consequences.

It could be argued that while the South African War settled the issue of where their public loyalty should lie, the First World War taught South African Jewry the necessity of embracing these loyalties enthusiastically and unconditionally, lest the Jewish community be singled out for unflattering and uncomfortable public attention; that the South African Jewish experience of the Great War helped to encourage a more active engagement with and commitment to the broader society by raising the spectre of the cost of non-commitment. That the alarming Jewish communal experience of the Great War was responsible to a significant degree for the enthusiastic embrace by South African Jewry during the interwar period of new local loyalties which were so manifest by the outbreak of the next war in 1939; that the intense South African patriotism that became so much part of the South African Jewish identity in the mid-twentieth century was at least in part a defensive reaction to the agonising hostility that Jews had experienced during the First World War.

Insiders on Outsiders:
Some South African Jewish Writers

MARCIA LEVESON

MARCIA LEVESON is an Honorary Research Fellow in the Department of English at the University of the Witwatersrand and was Associate Professor in that department. She is a member of the Editorial Board of Jewish Affairs. She has published widely, especially in the field of South African literature. Her book, *People of the Book: Images of the Jew in South African English Fiction 1880-1992*, was published in 1996.

She is a past president of the English Academy of Southern Africa.

In Rose Zwi's prize-winning novella *The Umbrella Tree* (1990), an elderly Jewish woman addresses a group of elderly black people. She tells them: 'We were the blacks of Europe ... like you are the Jews of Africa' (p.61). The novel is set shortly after the Soweto uprising of 16 June 1976, and would seem to be an expression of the feeling of solidarity that some Jews felt towards the oppressed black people. It seeks to capitalise on a shared heritage of vulnerability and persecution, and makes a claim for mutual understanding between two groups of historical outsiders. I believe that literature has an uncanny way of keeping a finger on the pulse of perception, and I should like to demonstrate how some of the issues of insider- and outsiderhood might be traced in some South African fiction.

Both before and after the new dispensation, South Africa has been a nation obsessed with prejudice and notions of race. The chief polarities of group dynamics in the country are between the black and white groups. For the historically dominant white group, due to racial, cultural, historical, economic and mythological reasons, the black has most vividly been labelled as an outsider. The dichotomies of black and white are sustained by the rational and irrational dynamic of fear and prejudice.

Social scientists differ in their understanding of the origins of prejudice. Those holding the psychodynamic view believe that hostility, wrongful generalisation and prejudice are natural conditions of the human mind, fulfilling instinctive, irrational and self-gratifying purposes – chiefly the assertion and maintenance of a privileged status. They believe that tolerance, if it exists at all, is a learned response. Racism and prejudice are therefore regarded as expressions of human nature's instinctive need to seek solidarity and confirmation from the in-group and in so doing to denigrate, oppose and threaten the out-group. Defensiveness, fear and anxiety play a role in this complex of emotions since the out-group, by definition, is constantly seen as a threat. Also, racism is complicated by the notion of ethnicity, which encompasses language, religion and culture. An ethnic other can also most potently function as an image of outsiderhood.

In South Africa, in the writing of both Jews and gentiles, both whites and blacks, the Jew has been portrayed, either positively, but more often negatively, as an outsider. At times, in the work of some key writers, the figure of the Jew and that of the black have been coupled, or the writer has used the figures of black and Jew to make a point about the relationships between different groups.

One of the first Jewish writers to treat the subject of group dynamics was Sarah Gertrude Millin. She was highly regarded in her time, especially for the novels written during the 1920s, but the increasingly right-wing views she expressed during the latter part of her life retrospectively damaged her reputation. I feel, however, that Millin has some interesting insights to offer on problems of insiderhood and outsiderhood, which are pertinent historically and, because human nature does not change so very much, are still currently valid.

Millin's novel *God's Stepchildren* (1924) is notorious as an apparently racist denigration of the coloured people, a treatment of the way in which the 'stain' of coloured 'blood' taints the generations and causes suffering. In 1977 Martin Rubin[1] exposed what he considered the inherent racism both of Millin's thinking and of the novel. In 1980 JM Coetzee[2] argued further that Millin's ideas seemed to be underpinned by German National Socialist race theories. However, more recently Lavinia Braun[3] has recommended another reading. She suggests that the concept of the 'stepchild' referred to in the title can possibly be traced to a phrase used by Heinrich Heine, a great favourite in Millin's childhood home, in which Heine refers to the stepchild status of Jews in nineteenth-century Germany in relation to their German heritage. Despite its ambivalences, *God's Stepchildren* can as easily be read as a dramatisation, not of the ascription of stigma, but of the consciousness of stigma – a very different thing. It might be that Millin's own 'stepchild-like' status as a Jew in South Africa has led her to a sympathetic identification with the pain and shame experienced by members of another minority group. Millin herself grew up on a remote stretch of the diamond diggings, 50 kilometres from Kimberley. Her Jewish family was almost isolated among the Coloured people. She deprecated the miserable conditions in which the Coloured people lived, and deplored the way in which miscegenation had caused them to be despised, but, as a Jew, she was able to identify with and empathise with their marginality and vulnerability and with the stigma attached to them.

The 1920s were a time when Jews were increasingly visible. The large Jewish immigration at the turn of the century and the resulting anti-immigration legislation, coupled with growing resentment turned against the upward mobility of many Jews, were only some factors which ensured that negative perceptions of Jews were strongly encoded in the popular discourse. Therefore, long before the influence of Nazism was felt in South Africa, traditional antisemitism, which exists always and everywhere, was entrenched and given a peculiarly local emphasis.

When she came to write *The Coming of the Lord* (1928), another novel dealing with minority groups, Millin concentrated on the relationship of the Jew with wider society. The novel is once again an attempted analysis of the problems of prejudice and marginality, an exploration of group relations and a vivid portrayal of the consciousness of Jewish alienation. One of the main characters is Old Nathan, an elderly Jewish small-town shopkeeper. Although the community views him with kindly tolerance, he is aware of the stigma of difference – 'He had not taken part ... in the social life of Gibeon ... (he says) I am here popular like the idiot of the village' (p.4).

Saul, Old Nathan's son, is a portrait of a Jew uncomfortable with his identity as a Jew. This is one of the very few treatments of this problem in South African Jewish fiction. It is certainly the earliest. Millin wrote:

> Saul Nathan was two men. One of him lived among the people in the big world, and had their interests and their conventions, and even their thoughts and traditions and standards and prejudices. And the other lived in a little ghetto, and suffered and enjoyed with his own, and looked out on the big world, and himself with it, with shame and amusement and satisfaction and sorrow and contempt. That really doubled his life (pp.96-97).

Here is a powerful evocation of the sense of outsiderhood and self-division that Millin claimed as a characteristic of her own thinking and which would seem in part to have given rise to her novels of the 1920s.

Saul is a prototype of a secular and even an assimilated Jew. He has not been taught Hebrew, he has studied overseas, and his most earnest wish is to escape from 'the undesirable society of his fellow-Jews' (p.99). In his isolation he is drawn to the company of a black doctor: '[Saul] was lonely, and once he strolled into Dr Tetyana's waiting-room, and sat down, as man to man, to talk to the Kaffir' (p.108). Millin shows how, because of his own sense of outsiderhood, Saul empathises with the black man's social embarrassment. Tetyana is so filled with gratitude that he offers to take him to the camp of the Levites on the Heights of Gibeon where a group of black men defy government instructions to disband from celebrating a sabbatical year. This is based on an historical incident at Bullhoek in 1921 where the sect calling themselves the Israelites (their religion combining elements of Christianity and Judaism) was massacred. Saul remains with them out of a sense of duty when government troops attack, and meets his death from a stray bullet. In constructing Saul as a type of martyr, who sacrifices himself in the cause of black-white friendships, Millin evokes the image of the 'Kaffirboetie' (negrophile), a figure which had already appeared in South African discourse generally and even in early fiction.

In Millin's later unpublished writing, in considering her own relationship with blacks, which echoes the self-conscious emotions she ascribes to Saul, she makes what seems to be a perceptive statement about the relationship between Jews with themselves and with blacks in the South African context. She wrote that she perceived herself to belong to the ranks of those 'negrophiles' who are '[s]eeking to escape from their ranks of the inequal ... of the pitiable ... into the ranks of the pitying, escaping from their own plight as sort of untouchables ...' She wrote: 'I should imagine the high percentage of Jewish negrophiles of our day has to do with (1) their understanding of racial separateness (2) their desire to escape it themselves.'[4] Hence her desire to 'exorcise something in [her]self' which she later called 'the not-quite element'[5] which would seem to determine her empathy with the same consciousness in many of her characters. In constructing the character of Saul, and in this particular aspect of her non-fictional writing quoted above, Millin highlights what she calls 'negrophilia', which she identifies as a 'Jewish' trait. She links it to a characteristic of Jewish identity. She comments on the 'high percentage of Jewish negrophiles' in the country.

This image of the Jew as a 'Kaffirboetie' is one of those multiple and contradictory strands of perception of Jews in South Africa which has a strong basis in reality. It would become one of the most popular stereotypes of the Jew in South Africa, especially after the middle of the century, and would balance that of the immensely wealthy and exploitative capitalist, enshrined in the Hoggenheimer cartoons, which appeared in Cape newspapers after 1903. Of course, the vast majority of South African Jews were neither Hoggenheimers nor 'Kaffirboeties'. The majority sought conformity in South African society, often as a relief from a history of European persecution, or simply to ensure a peaceful existence for themselves and their families. In varying degrees most were content to accept the norms and even the prejudices of the wider white society and to concentrate on communal and personal issues.

However, it would be true to say that many Jews who emigrated from Eastern Europe to South Africa at the beginning of the twentieth century had indeed had exposure to leftist movements, in particular to the *Yiddisher Arbeter Bund*, the powerful socialist workers' movement of Eastern European Jewry in Poland and Lithuania. In South Africa many joined organisations such as *Po'alei Zion* (workers of Zion) and the *Yiddisher Arbeter Klub* (Jewish Workers' Club) which had an affinity with the Communist Party. Many Jews were prominent in the radical wing of the Labour movement and in trade union work, later in the African Resistance Movement, the Communist Party, the Congress of Democrats and the Liberal and Progressive Parties.

Since stereotypes are often caricatures, which are constructed not from the average figure but from the striking one which catches the fancy, the stereotype of the Jewish leftist was one that fired the imagination, particularly of the Afrikaners. Over the years, a number of political detainees have referred to the way in which this idea was widespread among their captors. Denis Goldberg, imprisoned after the Rivonia Trial of 1964, related:

> ... a sergeant greets in the morning, to each political prisoner, 'good morning Jew, good morning Jew, good morning Jew,' whether they were Jewish or not. ... If you are a Jew you must be a communist, and if you are a communist you must be a Jew. If you are opposed to apartheid you must be both, whether you are or not.'[6]

In his account of his own imprisonment (*Bandiet, 1974*), Hugh Lewin – not a Jew – wrote in almost identical words: 'The warder said "Jew – you're a communist because you are a Jew – you're a Jew so you must be a communist"' (p.215). In fiction this perception is echoed in Bryce Courtenay's *The Power of One* (1987). A policeman catches a Jewish boy while he is teaching blacks at a night school. The policeman says, 'Okay, Jewboy ... don't think you seen the last of me. I know a communist when I see one' (p.451).

In a collection of interviews with South African Jewish activists, *Cutting through the Mountain* (1997)[7], Immanuel Suttner attempts to explore the deeper roots of the impetus that many Jews felt and continue to feel to identify with the underdog. Citing Biblical references and referring to 'atavistic cultural memories' (p.2) Suttner proposes that '[p]erhaps the Jewish role as harbingers and guardians of a unique social vision began with the ancient Jewish tribes' and 'continu[ed as] a tradition of social concern, and criticism, articulated long ago by the Hebrew prophets ...' (p.603). This particular role, he suggests, became entrenched when Jews became minorities among Christian or Muslim majorities, and became a habit reinforced by antisemitism. It shaped and motivated attitudes, and provided for an imaginative empathy with those more directly oppressed. Among the Ashkenazi Jews in the Pale of Settlement where persecution, prejudice and marginality were internalised, there was arguably, he says, 'an openness to radical positions and a capacity for emotional empathy with those most directly oppressed' (p.2).

This attitude would seem to be confirmed by Antony Sher, South African actor and writer who emigrated to England in the 1960s. In *The Guardian* of 2 September 1988 he wrote of his own experiences of outsiderhood:

> I suppose the Jewish and the gay thing, although still very kind of unformed, must have given me some sense of being an outsider myself and must have connected, even subconsciously, with knowing to some extent what the black and coloured people were experiencing. Knowing what it was like to be the disliked group, the disapproved of group. But purely subconsciously, in no logical way.

The subject of inter-group relationships, one that since Millin's day had hardly been touched by South African writers of fiction, surfaces again in the short stories of Dan Jacobson written during the 1950s. The period after the National Party's victory in 1948 brought about the statutory hardening of racial and group prejudice. Jacobson records that he was at this time involved in a process of self-examination. He claimed himself as a 'liberal' but was highly self-aware, castigating his own residual prejudice as a 'blur of ignorance' and 'failure of imagination' (*Commentary*, 15 May 1953, p.456).

Jacobson's fictional method is subtle and ironic. In *The Zulu and the Zeide* (1958) the relationship between the three characters – Grossman (the name suggesting gross) – a racist, prejudiced, middle-aged Jew, his senile, dependent father, and a young Zulu, Paulus, who is employed to look after the old man, are prototypes of wider societal relationships. Grossman revels in his sense of power over Paulus, who belongs to a race that he considers inferior to his own. The irony of the Jew enacting racial prejudice and even a barely restrained sadism during a period just after the Holocaust and the Nazi-type antisemitism in South Africa itself which had threatened the community, is not over-emphasised but is delicate, left to work powerfully as a subliminal accusation. On the other hand, the parallel between the marginalisation of the Zulu and the disempowered old man is stressed.

> The young bearded Zulu and the old bearded Jew from Lithuania walked together in the streets of the town that was strange to both of them. ... They could not sit on the bench together, for only whites were allowed to sit on the bench ... when they crossed a street hand in hand ... there were white men who averted their eyes from the sight of this degradation, which would come upon a white man when he was old and senile and dependent (pp.110-111).

The Zulu physically supports and protects the old man, who comes to need and love him. Grossman is obsessed by the relationship and jealous of his father's attachment to the Zulu. His resentment at having in the past had to spend money to bring his father from another country explodes in anger and frustration when he realises how the Zulu has looked after his father with care while at the same time saving to bring his own family from the rural areas to Johannesburg. At the end of the story Grossman experiences an epiphany of guilt and shame. In this story the irony suggests that South African Jewry, in the relatively affluent 1950s, may have become too entrenched in its own group position and lost sight of compassion. They have wilfully ignored the bonds that bind human beings together regardless of race, and are motivated by hatred, fear and prejudice, which the old man, because of his senility, transcends. Here the story is cast in the oblique and ironic mode. There is no character portrayed as a 'Kaffirboetie', but the story as a whole is a wake-up call from a writer who considered it a moral imperative[8] to deal with issues of prejudice, to interrogate stereotypes, to dramatise and censure group animosities and expose what he considers a failure of imaginative sympathy.

Gillian Slovo, daughter of two well-known Jewish communists, was born in South Africa but went into exile with her parents in 1964. Her novel *Ties of Blood* (1989) greatly develops the theme first treated by Millin and Jacobson, of the parallel between the Jewish and black outsiderhood. In this novel it is the Jewish experience of immigrating from Lithuania which is paralleled with that of the blacks who come to the city from rural areas. She suggests that the Jewish commitment to the struggle of the blacks against apartheid flows precisely from the Jews' own experience of discrimination and oppression. The novel documents the intertwining lives of several generations of two families – one Jewish and one black. Throughout the novel this parallel is emphasised. 'Zelig had nothing but contempt for whites who regarded contact with blacks as polluting. After all he still remembered how he was once an outcast in the land of his birth: considered less than human because he had been born a Jew' (p.41). 'Zelig identified in Nathaniel's face the same pain that he daily struggled to suppress ... He offered Nathaniel an arm. "I'm sorry," he muttered. "I understand"' (pp.46-47).

Slovo's novel is the didactic illustration of a thesis. There is minimal characterisation; throughout nearly 800 pages she indicts the apartheid regime and highlights the parallel between Jew and black. One of the characters, Jacob Swiece, after a lifetime of working for the blacks, is blown up by a car bomb. The character is based on two Jewish martyrs, Albie Sachs, gravely injured by a car bomb, and Slovo's own mother, Ruth First, killed by a letter bomb. Here the second Jew-martyr in South African Jewish fiction – the other was Millin's Saul – becomes a fictional means of affirming the Jew's commitment to the struggle against apartheid.

In Rose Zwi's *Under the Umbrella Tree* (1990), mentioned earlier, there is a scene where the blacks relate how, in order to avoid starvation, they had had to leave the rural areas to go to town. The elderly Jewish lady replies:

I understand. ... When we were small children in Russia, my father didn't have work, so he went to Africa to look for gold. He didn't find any, and it took seven years before he could save enough money to bring us to Africa. My mother had a hard time in the old country. She had five children to feed. She got up at four o'clock every morning to bake yeast buns and bread for a bakery. ... You're thinking how can white people be so poor? You should have seen the ghettoes and villages where the Jews lived in Eastern Europe. Some of them looked even worse than Alexandra township (pp.60-61).

The parallels are underscored in a heavy-handed way.

It has not only been Jews who have highlighted the quality of Jewish 'understanding'. Peter Abrahams was a Coloured writer who wrote several seemingly autobiographical short stories, published in 1942 in a volume entitled *Dark Testament*, which feature caring and 'understanding' Jews. His novel *A Path of Thunder* (1948) is an attack on racial prejudice in South Africa. Once again a parallel between the Jew and the coloured man is used as a tool of protest. A Jewish shopkeeper and his dreamy, intellectual son challenge the common South African stereotypes of the cunning and avaricious merchant and the upwardly mobile generation of South African-born Jews. The kindly shopkeeper is shown adding 'a little shovelful to the proper quota' (p.114), and performing similar acts of charity. It is possible that Abrahams had read Millin's novel, *The Coming of the Lord*, since the situation parallels that of Old Nathan and his son, Saul. However, in Abrahams's novel the young Isaac is a portrait of an early Zionist and discusses with the Coloured people their problems of identity, colour and nationalism as well. Abrahams powerfully conveys the sense of stigma attached to and experienced by Jews and blacks, all of whom feel themselves to be 'outsider[s], like [people] living between two worlds' (p.135).

The phenomenon of identification becomes reversed in other cases, where the discomfort with their own group position may lead to Jewish writers taking a different position. This discomfort was first articulated by Millin herself in her non-fictional writing, and expressed by Saul Nathan in *The Coming of the Lord*, where he spoke of feeling rejected by the gentiles and being 'filled with resentment that he belongs to a race that so hampered the simplicity of progress' (p.101). The word 'progress' ought to be probed. Although society was closed to the Jew in Europe, and considerably more open in South Africa, this was not always how Jews viewed the situation. There was often a residual fear of racial discrimination, of being denied the full enjoyment of their lives and the fullest expression of their political and social inclinations, indeed, in the worst instance, of being collapsed into the outsiderhood of the non-dominant black class. In the case of some Jewish writers this might have led to an unconscious rejection of Judaism, even to a form of antisemitism. Perhaps this is the impetus behind the way in which, particularly in her early writing, Nadine Gordimer, for example, has denigrated Jewish experience and consistently, in interviews throughout her career, has distanced herself from Jewish identification.

In her short story *My Father Leaves Home* (1991), Gordimer deals with the relations between blacks and Jews. The 'father', a Jewish immigrant to South Africa, is less assimilated than his wife, who taunts him about the experience of Jews in the 'old country'. She says:

> You slept like animals round a stove, stinking of garlic, you bathed once a week. The children knew how low it was to be unwashed. And whipped into anger he knew the lowest category of all in her country, this country.
> *You speak to me as if I was a kaffir* (p.634).

The father's anxiety – '*You speak to me as if I was a kaffir*' – expresses the Jew's abhorrence of the linkage between himself and the black, and his concomitant fear of social slippage. As a group Jews were particularly vulnerable to losing what they perceived to be their fragile purchase on the white hegemony. And this is not without a real basis in South African attitudes towards Jews. It is expressed most forcibly in the legislation from 1902 with the passing in the Cape of the *Immigration Act*, aimed at controlling the influx of Asiatics but excluding anyone who could not sign his or her name in 'European' characters; the image of the 'Peruvian' regarded as 'the equivalent of Chinamen and

Coolies'[9]; the *Immigration Quota Act* of 1930; and Greyshirt racist agitation against Jews. All these contributed to what in some instances could become an inferiority complex hedged with defensiveness and anxiety. Indeed, the negative coupling of Jews with blacks entered South African gentile fiction with the colonial writers of the diamond fields. They often associated the wily criminal IDB with a black assistant, and the physical characteristics attributed to the Jew were very similar to those which in colonial literature are ascribed to the black – being evil and sexually threatening, having protruding lips, dark skin, a cunning or shifty expression.

In Gordimer's story, the father vents his frustration on the black man who works for him. '[H]e shouted at the black man on the other side of the counter who swept the floor and ran errands and he threw the man's weekly pay grudgingly at him ... I saw that there was someone my father had made afraid of him. A child understands fear and the hurt and hate it brings' (p.66). Gordimer shows that the Jew lacks insight and compassion. Like Jacobson's Grossman he revels in a situation where he has power over someone he considers to hold a status inferior even to himself. Stigmatised on racial grounds, he becomes himself a racist.

Gordimer herself is a well-known radical. She has said: 'I have no religion, no political dogma – only plenty of doubts about everything except my conviction that the colour-bar is wrong and utterly indefensible. This I have found the basis of a moral code that is valid for me'.[10] Thus, like Jacobson, she highlights what she believes to be the moral failure of the Jew, and the subtext draws attention to the way in which the frustration which the Jew feels is complicated by the Jew's feeling of anger and especially of fear, not so much of the black man himself, but of the way in which that black man could be perceived as his *doppelganger*.

In a novel of the 1960s, *Diamond Jo* (1965), Daphne Rooke has her protagonist, Sir Emanuel Bernstein – previously a smous and diamond buyer known as Ikey Mo – refer to the Jew's consciousness of the dynamics of caste. In this instance Bernstein is an English Jew. He says:

> We came as poor people to Africa. Poverty in Africa though was different from poverty in England. Here we were not so

greatly despised, for men were judged not only by wealth and breeding but according to colour; poor Jews we might be but we were Europeans and beneath us were the Indians, the Coloured people and the Kaffirs (pp.87-88).

And most Jews wished to maintain the status quo.

Is it coincidental that in Gordimer's story the angry and racist Jew is shown as an observant Jew, one who observes the Day of Atonement and wears phylacteries, whereas figures of 'Kaffir-boeties' in other South African fiction – not necessarily by Jewish writers – are non-observant, even alienated? One thinks of Max Steinmetz in WC Scully's *Between Sun and Sand* (1898), Saul Nathan in Millin's *The Coming of the Lord* (1926), Hillela Capran in Gordimer's *A Sport of Nature* (1987), and many others.

Immanuel Suttner points out that the majority of Jewish activists, and in particular South African Jewish activists, are and have been what he terms 'Non-Jewish Jews' (Afterword p.602). These are Jews who though born Jewish, and indeed often having been the sons and daughters of Yiddish-speaking immigrants, have felt alienated from the Jewish community, who did not identify either religiously, nationally or culturally, preferring to be seen as internationalists, socialists or humanists. Suttner proposes: 'Their awareness of the historical dehumanisation of the Jews was the experiential ground in which blossomed the conviction that no one else should be dehumanised.' Dealing specifically with Jews in nineteenth-century Eastern Europe, he suggests:

> ... their knowledge of themselves as 'Jew', as the heirs to a messy, painful and ongoing history of being the devalued 'other', made the new dichotomies of communism ... seem full of hope and possibility. A Marxist worldview provided welcome relief from the wearying residual prejudices inherent in categories like Jew and gentile. Communism, by locating all racism, including antisemitism, in economic conditions, allowed for far more optimism than those tired old discourses of both the oppressed and the oppressors which located Jew hatred, and racial stratification, as inevitable and metaphysically or biologically decreed (p. 601).

Communism would seem to be a convenient dumping ground for the unresolved baggage of Jewish stigma. Suttner seems to agree. He continues:

> Undoubtedly Jews who were prominent socialists or communists believed their new religion true, and were motivated by the dream of a better future. But perhaps the new ideologies offered them something more personal than the collective redemption of humankind, namely, a way of escaping their 'Jewness', of assimilating into a universalistic non-Jewish world, without going through the intellectual and moral betrayal that conversion to Christianity (or any other order historically hostile to Jews) entailed (pp. 601-2).

Is this Millin's 'not-quite' element, the feeling of not belonging themselves, or perhaps the experience of existential outsiderhood that precipitates the need to escape from racial categories in order to free themselves from the burden of outsiderhood, as well as the longing to claim acceptance as an insider, belonging to a wider group?

Is this one of the impetuses behind the Jewish self-rejection that can be identified in the early work of Nadine Gordimer, Jillian Becker and Antony Sher, for example? Could their presentation of unsympathetic Jews be the result of a need to reject their own Jewish background, to exorcise their deeply embedded but hardly consciously acknowledged sense of inferiority by seemingly accepting the norms of the dominant culture?

In recent times there have been few identifiable Jewish characters in South African fiction. A notable exception has been Frieda Woolf in Pamela Jooste's *Frieda and Min* (1999). Jooste constructs Frieda as an ordinary Jewish girl, growing up in suburban Germiston during the 1960s, in a neighbourhood where there are few Jews. She is to a certain extent self-conscious about being Jewish and feels alienated. When the young gentile girl, Min, who comes to board with the Woolf family, seems initially withdrawn, Frieda asks, 'Is it because I'm a Jew?' (p.79) The blurb at the back of the book points out that both girls are 'outsiders', Min being a 'white kaffir', having been brought up in the bush by an idealistic father, and Frieda, known as 'The Jewish Woman's Daughter' (p.37). Frieda ruminates:

> We aren't the most Jewish Jews in the world but we have our past just the same as all Jews do and we have reason to thank God that we were spared and are still here to tell our story. We don't talk about it every day but our history has been touched by those black wings that passed over us and in that moment in some way all of our lives were changed forever.
>
> Sometimes I feel that being a Jew is like having an albatross that hangs around our necks and on days like this, hearing stories like this, I think I hear glass crashing into splinters and see yellow Stars of David floating invisible around us. I think I hear the word '*Juden*' being hissed in my ear.
>
> Whether we like it or not we know about such things and we know more than other people do because they have touched us (p.193).

But in this novel, although the sense of alienation is present, the author has resisted portraying the stereotype of the Jewish 'Kaffirboetie'. Frieda's consciousness of the Jewish heritage of oppression is not developed. The 'alienated' Jew does not become an activist. Jooste reserves that role for Min. The Jewish family is hardly touched by Min's eventual lengthy jail term and remains preoccupied with its own familial and community interests. But through her love for Min, Frieda becomes caring and more politically aware. She visits Min in jail and cares for her illegitimate child.

Although the sample is too small to make generalisations or predictions, might one not be able to observe a shift? Could one assert that, in the wake of transformation, the dynamic of prejudice in South Africa has undergone major refocusing, and the treatment of Jews has reverted to a situation that prevailed among some Jewish writers, particularly at the middle of the last century, where Jewish material had been mainly exploited for local colour and humour? M Davidson's *My Jewish Clients* (1953) and *Jewish Merry-Go-Round* (1959), Albert Segal's *Johannesburg Friday* (1954), Saul Manion's *The Greater Hunger* (1964), Barney Simon's 'Our War' in *Jo'burg Sis* (1974), Dan Jacobson's *The Beginners* (1966), Lyn Freed's *Home Ground* (1986) and Denis Hirson's *The*

House Next Door to Africa (1986) come to mind. Like some of these, Jooste's novel makes much of so-called 'Jewish' humour and ethnicity.

These considerations point to sociological and philosophical mysteries far beyond the scope of my discussion. However, it would seem that together with the changing historical and political circumstances of the 'new' South Africa, the taboo on too-explicit treatment of racial difference – other than to promote non-racialism – will no doubt alter the way in which the Jew is perceived and portrayed in literature. One should further consider the impact of the erosion of the Jewish community through emigration. With the passage of time, and despite the recent books and exhibitions on the subject, the impact of those who were involved in the freedom struggle has lost its compelling quality, so that one could claim that a specifically 'Jewish' presence in South African society has become blurred. One such instance of blurring has been the way in which in the national mourning for the death of Harry Oppenheimer, his Jewish origins have been obscured or suppressed. In fiction, it would seem that thinking and writing in the shorthand of stereotypes has given way to a treatment that demands more fully nuanced and less flamboyant images. These take their place within the wider panoply of South Africa, where legislation bans South African citizens of whatever race, colour or creed from being perceived as outsider or other.

'If It Was So Good, Why Was It So Bad?'
The Memories and Realities of Antisemitism in South Africa, Past and Present

MILTON SHAIN

MILTON SHAIN teaches Modern Jewish History and is the director of the Isaac and Jessie Kaplan Centre for Jewish Studies and Research at the University of Cape Town. He has written and edited several books on South African Jewish history and the history of antisemitism. These include *Jewry and Cape Society. The Origins and Activities of the Jewish Board of Deputies for the Cape Colony* (1983); *The Roots of Antisemitism in South Africa* (1994); *Antisemitism* (1998) and co-edited with Sander L Gilman, *Jewries at the Frontier: Accommodation, Identity and Conflict* (1999).

The historian does not simply come in to replenish the gaps of memory. He constantly challenges even those memories that have survived intact.
Yosef Hayim Yerushalm, *Zakhor*[1]

Shortly after my book *The Roots of Antisemitism in South Africa*[2] was published, I was regularly invited to discuss its contents with audiences in Cape Town and beyond. No author avoids the opportunity to spread his or her ideas and to encourage book sales. In this respect I was no different. More significantly, however, the occasions always took a similar and, for me, perplexing form. I would begin by expounding my 'revisionist' thesis which challenged the view that antisemitism in South Africa in the 1930s and early 1940s was simply a foreign import, and argue instead that it had deep roots in specific South African conditions. The audience would politely listen and express dismay when I read vulgar comments made by non-Jews about the Eastern European newcomers in the late nineteenth and early twentieth centuries. There would usually be stunned silence when I showed vulgar cartoons of corpulent and avaricious Jews in the local press, echoing the worst of European antisemitism. Murmurs of surprise were usually audible when I pointed to the widespread satisfaction of English- and Afrikaans-speaking non-Jews that the doors to Eastern European Jewish immigrants would be closed – the so-called Quota Act of 1930. Exposing the rhetoric of the Greyshirts and other radical-right movements in the 1930s and early 1940s always elicited widespread recognition, as did discussion surrounding the question of Jewish loyalty when Israel supported the Africa bloc against the apartheid government in the early 1960s. The lecture would end; there would be applause and then hands would be raised.

Invariably the entire thrust of my lecture would be undermined by personal reminiscences in which members of the audience would recall nothing but the warmth of the host population. People would remember a generosity of spirit and a cordiality between Jew and non-Jew from Louis Trichardt to Stellenbosch. They seemed completely oblivious to snide comments, negative stereotyping and ugly journalese. If it was so good, I would ask myself, why was it so bad? And why was the book – which stressed and sadly demonstrated substantial tensions between Jew and non-Jew – well received in scholarly circles? After all, it was not I who wrote in the *South African Jewish Chronicle* (SAJC) of 23 January 1914: 'South Africa as a whole – contrary to the expectations of the would-be immigrant – does not accord a very hearty welcome and apparently is already regretting that it made it possible for them to come.' It was not I but the Board of Deputies which feared that the Class Areas Bill of 1924 – designed 'to make provisions for the reservation of residential and trading areas in urban areas for persons other than natives having racial characteristics in common' – would be applied to Jews.[3] It was not I but the Board of Deputies which reported at its eleventh Congress in

May 1935 that anti-Jewish activities in South Africa had reached an unparalleled height.[4] It was not I but the radical right which introduced the 'Jewish Question' into public politics in the 1930s and fostered notions of a world Jewish conspiracy.[5]

It seems to me that this huge discrepancy between recollection and reality moves us firmly into the realm of historical memory, an area which has increasingly captured the attention of historians and cultural critics: Why is there such a huge discrepancy between memory and historical reality? Why is so much forgotten? Is it a question of generational amnesia? Is it a product of the human psyche? In the case of South African Jewry has it something to do with Jews being warmly accommodated in the 1970s and 1980s by the National Party, their erstwhile tormentors? That is to say, has memory been recast to suit particular circumstances?

Let me make it quite clear that when I refer to lapsed memory I am not talking in terms of trauma such as that experienced by Holocaust survivors.[6] I am essentially interested in the way in which a master narrative of South African Jewish history has evolved which minimises conflict between Jew and non-Jew. That narrative is one of an immigrant community, upwardly mobile and prosperous, in a land of tolerance and opportunity. It was already evident in an early South African Jewish historiography which, in turn, helped to shape what I believe is a myth of harmony between Jew and non-Jew.

Historians writing prior to the 1960s virtually turned a blind eye to anti-Jewish manifestations and instead lauded the pioneering decades as years during which Jews were accorded great respect and hospitality.[7] Afrikaners especially were singled out for their kindness and courtesy towards the 'people of the Book'. The itinerant Jewish pedlar or *smous*[8] was commonly identified as a welcome addition to society. 'My Joodje', writes George Aschman, an historian of Oudtshoorn Jewry, was a term of endearment applied by Boers to those pedlars who had for years brought news of the 'outside world' and 'gossip from the town and the rest of the countryside'.[9]

It is important to appreciate that these historians were writing in a specific context: Louis Herrman, for example, was writing just prior to the Quota Act of 1930 – a period in which Jews were increasingly defined as 'unassimilable'; Gustav Saron, Louis Hotz and

Israel Abrahams were writing shortly after serious outbursts of antisemitism in South Africa and, of course, in the wake of the Shoah. How could one treat seriously simple rhetoric and stereotyping – albeit ugly – when compared to the depravity of Auschwitz? The occasional cartoon or accusation against Jews hardly mattered when measured against gas ovens and heaps of emaciated bodies.

In similar vein, Eastern European Jewish immigrants understandably considered South Africa an enviable haven when compared with the old country. For these newcomers, hostility meant formal discrimination at best and pogroms at worst. The ferocity unleashed against Jews in 1881-82, following the assassination of Tsar Alexander II, and the outrages of Kishinev between 1903 and 1905, were benchmarks of antisemitism. A nasty comment about illicit liquor merchants in Johannesburg or Jewish trading practices in the ostrich district of Oudtshoorn could be brushed aside, especially as incipient wealth (or at least a living) made its impact. South Africa was a far cry from Ponevez and Riteve. Rhetoric that ought to have been disturbing and depressing was relegated to meaninglessness. Jews by and large enjoyed a sense of wellbeing and acceptance, and appeared to have been oblivious to burgeoning currents of anger.[10] These currents have been uncovered by *inter alia* Michael Cohen, Edna Bradlow, Gideon Shimoni and Patrick Furlong[11] in their work on the 1930s; my own work goes further, and hopefully has demonstrated the deep roots of South African antisemitism.[12]

From at least the 1870s, the Jew was depicted as a knave – dishonest, cunning and devious. In 1875, *The Era* of Richmond in the Cape Colony wrote of 'Israelitish Boereverneukers' [Jewish Boer-swindlers] being only too happy to exploit the simple Afrikaners.[13] As alien traders became more prominent in the 1880s the voices of protest grew louder. This was a period of severe economic distress following drought on the frontier and a slump in both the wool and diamond trades. In these conditions, observers were quick to note the burgeoning Jewish presence.[14] In Kimberley, where Jews had become fairly prominent, following the discovery of diamonds in the 1860s, the Eastern European newcomers attracted the type of opprobrium evident in the following comments of Lewis Michell, General Manager of the Standard Bank:

> The departure of hordes of hook-nosed Polish and Lithuanian Jews whose evil countenances now peer from every shanty and cigar divan would be a distinct gain to the community. Under cover of keeping a 'winkel' they at present flock to Kimberley from afar, like as-vogels to a dead ox, and their villainous faces enable one easily to understand the depth of hatred borne to them in Russia and elsewhere.[15]

Such sentiments, including an association of Jews with illicit diamond buying (IDB), proliferated as Jews increasingly made their presence felt. Farmers were warned, in a jocular *Cape Punch* article in 1883, to avoid the 'boereverneukers' who were a 'stiff-necked and perverse generation'.[16] Jewish and English shopkeepers were even accused of influencing the election of candidates for local office through their hold on country commerce[17] and, in the South African Republic's presidential contest of 1892, Paul Kruger was alleged to be under the influence of 'Israelites and Hollanders'.[18]

This image of the manipulative and dishonest Jew has to be seen in the context of late nineteenth-century urbanisation and modernisation. For the alienated and landless – those constituting the incipient poor-white problem – the Jewish shop was a symbol of greed and of dishonesty. Instead of being appreciated for his services, the itinerant Jewish trader and the small shopkeeper was blamed for corrupting a rustic world of innocence and harmony. Of course the legacy of European history and its intellectual traditions played a part. White South Africans, after all, are among the heirs to those traditions. And the period that saw the evolution of hostile anti-Jewish attitudes was an age of increasing literacy, improved communications and large population migrations, specifically between Britain and South Africa. The penetration of European ideas – including the deeply rooted anti-Jewish stereotype – was inevitable, and a vaguely racial definition of Jewishness ensured that those traits traditionally associated with Jews would be ascribed to their co-religionists in South Africa.

Particular antipathy towards the Jew was evident in the urban centres, especially Cape Town and Johannesburg. These impoverished immigrants – referred to in the 1890s as 'undesirables' –

attracted substantial negative comment. '… ill provided, indifferently educated, unable to speak or understand any language but Yiddish, of inferior physique, often dirty in their habits, persons and their clothing, and most unreliable in their statements' was the assessment of the Medical Officer of Health for Cape Town, Dr AJ Gregory, in 1904.[19] A cartoon in the Cape Town weekly, *The Owl*, was less guarded: 'The Coming of the Scum' was the underlying caption depicting the arrival of European Jewish newcomers at the docks. [20]

Underpinning these sentiments was the challenge posed by the immigrants to the established English-speaking mercantile class. Their trading patterns in particular proved repugnant, as evident in the following comment made in *The Owl*, regarding the East European Jewish hawkers on the Grand Parade, Cape Town:

> The fact is Cape Town at the present time is full of those Polish Jew hawkers, who live in dirtier style than kaffirs and existing on about half a crown a week rob the tradesman of his due. They don't pay rent, rates or taxes, yet they are allowed to sell goods just the same as if they kept a store. Respectable Europeans should order these people from their doors. That is the only way to put them down. Let these people do manual work.[21]

Similar sentiments were voiced in Johannesburg where the struggling Eastern European Jewish victim of Tsarist oppression acquired the pejorative label 'Peruvian'.[22] These outsiders, as Charles van Onselen has shown us, were associated with illicit liquor dealing, prostitution, and other aspects of the seamier side of Johannesburg's nightlife.[23] The 'Dirty Peruvian' was easily equated with the local 'Coolie' in the lexicon of South African prejudice.

Emerging at the same time as the 'Peruvian' stereotype, but far more sinister, was the image of the South African Jew as part of a network of international finance. This association had already taken root in Europe and found fertile ground in a country where mining magnates, among whom Jews were disproportionately represented, were such a prominent feature of society. It made little difference that these Jewish financiers had largely assimilated and were Jews in name only. Their presence ensured that the negative stereotype would be accentuated in the mounting struggle between mining magnates, with their international connections, and 'intransigent' Boer leaders in the 1890s.

The nefarious role of international finance was revealed in the abortive attempt to overthrow the Kruger regime in 1895. The so-called Jameson Raid awakened the liberal left in England to the machinations of capitalism, confirming in the minds of the radical left 'the existence of a crucial nexus joining Jewish finance with British imperialism'.[24] Although these views were not systematically articulated in South Africa, their penetration can be assumed. From the time of the Jameson Raid, an economic interpretation of political events was inescapable. The outbreak of the Boer War merely confirmed that suspicion, especially for the pro-Boers in England.[25] The argument that the British Unionists were 'the tools of financiers, mainly Jewish', gained adherents in South Africa. Letters to the press and cartoon caricatures of corpulent and semitic-looking financiers adorned the pages of *The Owl* and the *South African Review,* revealing the inroads made by English pro-Boer ideology.[26]

The conspiratorial view of international finance was most clearly enunciated by JA Hobson, the *Manchester Guardian's* correspondent in Johannesburg. Hobson, whose writings influenced the pro-Boers in England and the views of Lenin on imperialism, was vicious in his condemnation of cosmopolitan financiers. Cosmopolitan, of course, referred to Jewish capitalists. These sentiments were succinctly captured in his book *The War in South Africa,* which postulated the notion of the Boer War being fought in the interests of a 'small group of international financiers, chiefly German in origin and Jewish in race'.[27]

The notion of a Jewish-capitalist conspiracy was revived after the war, this time in connection with the controversial importation of Chinese labour to replace the dwindling reserves of African labour in the mines. Increasingly the alien plutocrats or 'Hebrew Goldbugs' were portrayed as responsible for the scheme, while poems and satirical compositions alluded to a Jewish-Chinese takeover of Johannesburg.[28] It was in this climate that Hoggenheimer, the quintessential Jewish parvenu, appeared upon the South African stage.

Hoggenheimer was not the creation of the cartoonist DC Boonzaier; nor does he have anything to do with the Oppenheimer family. He was a character in a London stageplay, *The Girl from Kays*, which toured South Africa shortly after the Boer War and struck a responsive chord in the popular consciousness.[29] By 1910 Hoggenheimer had become a household name and a visible component of the anti-Jewish stereotype, complimenting the 'Peruvian' image. In the eyes of the antisemite, it was the dishonesty of the 'Peruvian' which enabled him to achieve plutocratic prominence. Hoggenheimer, allegedly the *eminence grise* of South Africa, merely symbolised on a higher plane the machinations of the Jewish peddler and of the illicit diamond and liquor dealers.

The anti-Jewish stereotype was thus firmly in place by 1910, intimately bound up with the local stresses and upheavals engendered by South Africa's 'mineral revolution'. For many categories of the social spectrum – the impoverished farmer, the unemployed worker, the competing merchant, and the frustrated businessman – this stereotype served as a psychological cushion. It was a universal scapegoat in an age of turmoil. But very significantly, it did not engender a major anti-Jewish movement. There were ongoing calls to curtail the influx of Eastern European Jews; but there was no widespread call to limit options for Jews already living in South Africa.

During the Great War, and in the immediate post-war years, all dimensions of the stereotype were consolidated and embellished. One elaboration introduced during the war was the accusation of 'shirking' or avoiding military service. Columns of letters in the daily press berated Jews for not risking their lives for the Imperial cause. 'Jews ought to be ashamed of themselves', wrote 'Returned British East African Soldier', in the *Cape Times*.[30] Shortly after the war Jews were accused of identifying with radical political causes and Bolshevik subversion. The Bolshevik charge, of course, emerged in the wake of the Russian Revolution of 1917 and in the context of the post-war economic depression and burgeoning black radicalism. Thus a 'Russian-Jewish' conspiracy was the way leading newspapers depicted the heady days of March 1922, the so-called Rand Revolt. Newspaper after newspaper chose to characterise events as driven and orchestrated by a small group of Russian and, more specifically, Russian-Jewish immigrants.

Certainly popular opinion saw events in terms of a 'Red Revolution'.³¹

In addition to associating Jews with Bolshevism, newspapers began to question the Jewish potential for integration into South African society. 'Unassimilability' became the new catchword, an idea influenced directly by nativist literature from the United States as well as by a new domestic segregationist discourse in which race and culture were conflated.³² By introducing notions of 'racial stock' and 'racial quality', newspapers were able to mobilise well-established negative images of the Jew. At the forefront was the *Cape Times*, imbued with an exaggerated fear that British subjects were being replaced by aliens. The aliens, it noted, were 'from racial stocks which experience has shown to be unsuitable to the peculiar conditions of this country'. In the *Cape Times*'s view, a reasonable proportion of foreigners was acceptable; when that proportion rose beyond a certain point 'there was a real risk of endangering the continuity of the development of those broad ideas, upon whose conservation and general acceptance throughout the British Commonwealth the health, the solidarity and the prosperity of the Empire alike depend'.³³ In short, the newcomers were 'unassimilable'. Eugenicist-based fears of 'race mixing' and 'mongrelisation' – primarily associated with South African blacks – now informed perceptions of the Eastern European Jew.

Given these developments it is obviously no surprise that the full spectrum of the English and Afrikaans press welcomed the Quota Bill of 1930 which set out to curtail Eastern European Jewish immigration. 'The Bill will commend itself to most citizens of the Union and has not been introduced a day too soon', noted the East London *Daily Despatch*.³⁴ In the opinion of the *Sunday Times*, the newcomers were 'ignorant people of the peasant class who have neither the ability nor the experience necessary to make a living.'³⁵

In short, the Quota Bill, which soon became the Quota Act, heralded, in Todd Endelman's terms, the transformation of 'private' into 'public' or programmatic antisemitism.³⁶ By 'private' antisemitism Endelman means expressions of contempt and discrimination outside the radius of public life, as opposed to 'public' antisemitism which is the injection of antisemitism into matters of policy and the manipulation of antisemitism for partisan political ends.³⁷

The transformation was initially seen in the formation of the South African Christian National Socialist Movement – better known as the Greyshirts – under the leadership of Louis T Weichardt. At its peak the movement had 2 000 members and its success inspired a number of similar organisations to mushroom across the country. Although inspired by Nazi forms and racist or *völkish* discourse, the substantive message of South Africa's numerous fascist movements related to the South African experience: Jews had fomented the Boer War, inspired blacks against white civilization, controlled the press, exploited Afrikaners, dominated society, and so forth. Against the backdrop of drought, depression, and rapidly increasing black economic competition, these fascist clones, with a marked preference for 'the language and symbolism of Nazism', devoted themselves 'to attacking that oldest of scapegoats, the Jew'.[38] Indeed, a variation of the notorious Protocols of the Elders of Zion appeared in 1934, leading to a libel action against *inter alia* Johannes von Moltke, leader of the Greyshirt breakaway group, the South African Fascists.[39]

Hostile voices grew louder as German-Jewish refugees began to enter South Africa in the wake of Hitler's ascent to power. The groundswell of anti-Jewish feeling, especially demands for actions and threats against the existing Jewish community, now prompted the ruling United Party to introduce stiffer educational and financial requirements for purposes of immigration. These were to take effect on 1 November 1936, and resulted in an interim increase in German-Jewish immigration. By the end of October well-attended meetings, led by a group of Stellenbosch University professors, protested against the arrival of the *Stuttgart* carrying some 570 German-Jewish immigrants.[40] One month later, Purified Nationalists were calling for the unequal treatment of Jews. These arguments were predicated upon Jewish 'unassimilability' and fears of Jewish power and domination. As a political programme they wanted to curtail Jewish professional activity, limit their involvement in certain occupations, and proscribe name-changing.

In an obvious response to flourishing antisemitism, coupled with a private Bill introduced by Dr DF Malan to restrict Jewish immigration and stiffen naturalisation laws, the ruling United Party introduced an Aliens Bill in 1937, designed to restrict Jewish immigration – particularly from Germany – without mentioning Jews by name. Immigrants were to be permitted entry by a Selection Board on the grounds of good character and the likelihood of assimilation into the European population. The Bill failed to satisfy the Purified Nationalists; for them any Jewish immigration was unacceptable. The 'Jewish Question' was now a central plank in the political platform of the radical right. Malan, under pressure from the Greyshirts, focussed increasingly on the Jew as an explanation for the Afrikaners political misfortunes. It was Dr Hendrik Verwoerd, however, who stood at the vanguard of anti-Jewish agitation. In a major editorial in *Die Transvaler*, the newspaper he edited, he summarised the whole corpus of antisemitic discourse: Jewish domination in business and the professions, the unassimilability of Jews, Jewish alienation from the Afrikaners, questionable Jewish commercial morality, and the use of money by Jews to influence government through the English-language press.[41] Obviously the 'Jewish Question' was no longer the concern solely of fringe fascist groups; it was now firmly entrenched within mainstream white politics.

Malan's Purified Nationalists predictably stressed the 'Jewish Problem' in the 1938 general election campaign. Party propaganda was underpinned by an insistence on the prospect of Jewish domination. The election year also saw the emergence of a new paramilitary authoritarian movement, the *Ossewabrandwag*. Born out of the centenary celebrations of the Great Trek, the *Ossewabrandwag* attacked so-called 'British-Jewish-Masonic' imperialism and capitalism, 'British Jewish' democracy, 'Jewish money-power' and 'Jewish' disloyalty.[42] With its 'fuhrer-prinzip', authoritarian philosophy, and anti-Jewish stance, the movement was a Nazi clone. By 1941 the *Ossebrandwag* claimed to have a membership of over 300 000 drawn mainly from the Afrikaner petty bourgeoisie.[43]

The rhetoric of protest and opposition was riddled with racist assumptions and antisemitic generalisations. Jews were aliens, disloyal and bent on exploitation. Hostility was driven largely by Afrikaner intellectuals, a number of whom had studied in Germany, where they imbibed views of the corporate state, an idealist world-view, and a sense of exclusivist nationalism. These ideas propelled a powerful republicanism rooted in notions of divine election, a leitmotif within the Afrikaners' civil religion.[44] Like their European counterparts on the right, Afrikaner nationalists were opposed to liberalism, Marxism and laissez-faire capitalism. Nationalist sentiment, in other words, sharpened perceptions of the Jew as a quintessential alien. For the Afrikaner he symbolized all that was foreign and oppressive. Moreover, as English speakers for the most part, Jews were political enemies.

The Jew also helped to consolidate an all-embracing Afrikaner identity, understood in terms of cultural unity, national roots, and opposition to the foreigner. In this way antisemitism helped to cover or paper over class divisions and antagonisms within Afrikaner society. The Afrikaner's inferior status in society and his poverty could be explained in racial or national terms. By employing this discourse of race to exclude and denigrate Jews, the Afrikaner was in turn elevated. Consequently, it is no coincidence that antisemitism continued to suffuse specifically right-wing Afrikaner political discourse and programmes – this despite the upturn in the economy from the mid-1930s.

Antisemitism was given further impetus following the South African parliament's decision to support the Commonwealth war effort to resist Germany in 1939. A powerful antiwar movement was orchestrated by the *Ossewabrandwag* in which the appeal of fascism and with it the rhetoric of antisemitism was strong. A range of major National Party publications issued in the early 1940s demonstrated the formative influence of Mussolini and Hitler or the exclusive nature of an insurgent Afrikaner nationalism in which the Jew had no place.[45] However, the struggle against Hitler gradually eroded the warm reception accorded to Nazi and fascist ideas. Although the Jewish tragedy in Europe was minimised in Nationalist newspapers, ultimate knowledge of the 'Final Solution' demonstrated unequivocally the logical culmination of anti-Jewish bigotry.[46]

The 1930s had clearly witnessed a sea change in the nature and character of antisemitism. Hostility had moved from the 'private' or ideational sphere into the 'public' or party political realm. The transformation was unquestionably related to specific traumas in the 1930s: the intensification of poor whiteism following the impact upon South Africa of the world depression, the emergence of Nazism in Europe and, most importantly, the rise of an illiberal, anti-modernist and exclusivist Afrikaner nationalism. That is why 'public' antisemitism in South African was an essentially Afrikaner phenomenon, and why it appealed across the whole spectrum of Afrikaner nationalist opinion.

All these factors do not, however, explain fully why anti-Jewish rhetoric resonated so resoundingly in South Africa. Nor do they explain why antisemitism provided such a useful means of political mobilisation. To suggest that antisemitism in South Africa was simply a product of specific upheavals in South African society and of Nazi propaganda is to ignore deeply entrenched anti-Jewish sentiment before 1930. Without this preparation, Weichardt's vicious oratory, and shirtist propaganda in general, would not have been embraced at the popular level. It was in fact because of the popular response to this that Malan was forced to incorporate specifically anti-Jewish policies in the Purified Nationalist programme, and why the *Ossewabrandwag*, New Order and other fascist organisations would find such support in their anti-Jewish message.

After the war South Africa experienced a rapid decline in antisemitism. A new Afrikaner bourgeoisie – well educated, confident and more optimistic than their forebears – enjoyed the economic fruits of racist exploitation and political power. They developed very rapidly a respect for enterprise and material success. The very scaffolding that had underpinned their sense of inferiority was thus removed as they began to experience power and social mobility. A sense of competition with, and fear of, the Jew declined. A post-war consumerist culture meant the erosion of rural values and a new-found respect for the city. No longer was it an alien and inhospitable place. Most significantly, however, the impetus of exclusivist Afrikaner nationalism waned. English speakers, including Jews, were necessary for the apartheid project. Colour was the essential divide and any lingering views – heard earlier in the century – of the Jew not being 'white' soon disappeared.

Shortly after the war the Greyshirts and New Order disbanded, and in 1951 the ban on Jewish membership of the Transvaal National Party was lifted.[47] In 1953 Prime Minister DF Malan returned from a visit to Israel full of praise and admiration for the 'Jewish People'. The National Party seemed to wish to put the tensions and excesses of the 1930s and 1940s behind it. In the 'apartheid' system Jews, as whites, were to have a rightful and welcome place. Rapprochement was aided by economic growth and, more particularly, by post-war upward mobility for whites. Nevertheless, anti-Jewish sentiment persisted in certain influential quarters, directed against Jewish involvement in communist as well as anti-apartheid activities. Hitler's birthday was regularly celebrated in Hillbrow, and German songs were sung. But Jews had little cause for discomfort, despite the government questioning their loyalty in the early 1960s when Israel supported the African bloc in the United Nations against the apartheid government, and despite the government from time to time reminding Jews of their disproportionate involvement in anti-apartheid activities. Their security – at least insofar as the National Party was concerned – was further enhanced by Pretoria's very close ties with Jerusalem from the mid-1970s.[48] In 1976 Prime Minister BJ Vorster visited Yad Vashem, the Holocaust Commemorative Centre in Jerusalem. The irony of the visit by someone interned during the war for anti-government and pro-Nazi activities was not lost on liberal South African Jews. Yet the overriding message was clear: mainstream Afrikaners now accepted the reality of the Jewish tragedy.

Although antisemitism, in its crude and programmatic sense, was now apparently relegated to the past, the Jewish minority still failed to enjoy complete equal rights in Christian-dominated South African society. In education, for example, in 1967 the government introduced the notion of Christian National Education with Christian character and Christocentric religious instruction, although Jewish students could withdraw from class to attend their own programmes. Then, too, Jews were threatened by demands raised in some universities to change the Conscience Clause in the founding statutes of the nine earliest universities in South Africa, which stipulated that no test of religious belief could be imposed on any university student or teacher. Groups in the Dutch Reformed Church objected to a 'neutral' conception of higher education, but, in the end, only Potchefstroom University was able to modify its Conscience Clause in line with that institution's historic theological origins.[49]

By the early 1980s the only group propagating an exclusively Christian society was the far-right Afrikanerweerstandsbeweging

(AWB), founded in 1979 by Eugene Terre'blanche. With its swastika-like emblem, khaki military fatigues, conspiratorial views of Jewish power, and its vision of a society in which Jews would have no place,[50] the AWB ensured that Jews had a nagging sense of vulnerability. However, the initiatives of President FW de Klerk and the ANC leader, Nelson Mandela, in the early 1990s eroded prospects for the ultra-right. Their hopes were finally dashed in 1992 when the 'politics of negotiation' was supported by an overwhelming majority of the enfranchised white population in a referendum.

This is not to suggest that antisemitism on the far right is dead. When white supremacists disrupted political negotiations at the World Trade Centre in Kempton Park in July 1993, one banner held aloft read: 'Hitler was right – Communism is Jewish' – and, when Eugene Terre'blanche appeared in court for defying a summons to testify before the Goldstone Commission in 1993, a banner read 'Goldstone – King of the Jews'.[51] Every now and again the South African Jewish Board of Deputies, synagogues and Jewish day schools receive hate mail. There are always those who allege that Jews are attempting to control South Africa and the world. There are also those informed by Holocaust denial literature. The infiltration of this material into South Africa goes back to the heyday of apartheid when a German neo-Nazi such as Manfred Roëder was a welcome visitor, and his praise of Hitler widely admired in ultra-right circles. Not surprisingly, Arthur Butz's notorious *The Hoax of the Twentieth Century* was well received by SED Brown's *South African Observer*.[52] Ultra-right newspapers such as *Die Afrikaner* have also carried features questioning what they refer to as the 'gas chamber fable',[53] and in 1997 a protest at the Union Buildings in Pretoria called for freedom of speech in solidarity with Germans who had been jailed for Holocaust denial. Leon Strydom of the far-right Herstigte Nasionale Party was present at this gathering where 'Jewish financial power' was blamed for the limitations on free speech.[54] A recent book, *Volksveraad*, by Advocate Pretorius, claimed that the fall of the Afrikaner was plotted by the Illuminati, a secret society organised by Jews and supposedly in control of the world.[55]

Neo-Nazism is thus not quite dead, and conspiracy theories are not quite obliterated. Groups such as the Israelites, the Church of the Creator, the Kultur Studie Groep, the Blanke Bevrydingsbeweging, the World Preservatist Movement, the Afrikaner National Socialist Movement, the Kerk van die Verbondsvolk and the Boere Republican Army can all be relied upon to make bizarre claims about Jewish power. But their memberships are small and their influence insignificant. These extremists are concerned essentially with the politics of racial partition. Individuals preaching an anti-Jewish message are at best leaders of small disaffected groups; they are not an advance guard of an ethnonationalist movement, attempting to mould a 'people' or 'volk' by using the Jew as a classic other.

Hitherto I have discussed the white population only. Blacks (including coloureds and Indians) have never focussed specifically on the Jews when articulating grievances and aspirations. Going back to the late nineteenth century one finds that Jews hardly figure in the African press.[56] The cardinal divide in South Africa has always been one of colour. This is not to say that anti-Jewish sentiment is totally foreign to the black population. Specifically 'Jewish capitalists' have been identified in some recent industrial protests, and antisemitic placards have been displayed at a number of strikes around the country. At one strike by black Volkswagen car workers in August 1994, a pamphlet accused Jews of controlling the country and called for the killing of the 'capitalist Jew pigs'. 'Away with the Jewish settlers', 'Jews dismiss innocent workers' and 'Jews are union bashers' were displayed on another placard. 'Mr Ackerman, remember Adolf Hitler' was the comment on a placard during one Pick 'n Pay strike.[57]

Clearly some blacks have imbibed well-worn anti-Jewish stereotypes. Over two decades ago, in a study of matriculation students in Soweto, Melville Edelstein showed that blacks experienced a greater 'social distance' in relation to Jews than towards English speakers in general, although less than towards Afrikaners.[58] They told him that an African who was loth to part with his money was described as being as 'stingy as a Jew' – a trope affirmed by the black consciousness leader, Saths Cooper, in an interview conducted in the late 1980s.[59] Edelstein thought that such prejudice arose from New Testament teaching in school and church. It may well be that there is an added cause: the resentment of blacks – in the widest sense of the term – against Jewish traders in town and country.⁶⁰ Certainly one finds evidence of hostile stereotypes in fiction written by blacks,⁶¹ and a survey conducted in 1990 among urban South African 'elites' showed that black 'elites' harboured substantial antipathy towards Jews. Almost one in five said that the Jewish community 'irritated' them because, in descending order of frequency, they were parasites, snobs, racists, anti-Christ, and unpatriotic; almost the same proportion approved of right-wing antisemitic actions, and nearly one in three considered the Jewish community to be 'mostly a liability' to South Africa.⁶² It needs to be said that this was a methodologically questionable survey, and that surveys should not to be equated with actions.⁶³

Still, ideas are the bedrock of action. One sees this most clearly in the hardening of Muslim attitudes towards Jews in recent decades. Indeed in the rhetoric associated with Al-Quds Day, during the Muslim holy month of Ramadan, anti-Zionist slogans, publications and propaganda have degenerated into blatant antisemitism with an emphasis on Jewish power, cunning and duplicity.⁶⁴ Antisemitic rhetoric was particularly evident in the aftermath of a Muslims Against Global Oppression march on the Israeli Embassy in 1997 following the depiction of the Prophet Mohamed as a pig by an Israeli Jewish extremist. 'Save the World Kill a Jew', and 'Free our Country Kill the Jews' were some of the slogans that appeared on the door of the Wynberg Synagogue, Cape Town, shortly after that march. Within 24 hours a bomb had gone off in the Jewish Book Centre housed in a private Cape Town home.⁶⁵

Sadly, Holocaust denial has also crept into Islamic anger. In 1996, Radio 786, a Muslim radio station, had to apologise for airing an interview with Dr Ahmed Huber, who spoke of the 'Holocaust swindle'.⁶⁶ One year later, the same radio station interviewed a British historian, Dr Yaqub Zaki, who, besides claiming that the 'million plus' Jews who died in the Second World War had died of infectious diseases, spent much of his time engaged with elaborate Jewish conspiracies, including a bizarre connection between Jewish financiers, the Boer War, Milner and Zionism.⁶⁷ It is apparent that a significant element among the Muslim community share conspiratorial ideas of the far right. These ideas are manifested in the letter columns of the daily press and articulated in radio talk shows. In looking at this issue it needs to be stressed that anti-Zionism or criticism of the Jewish State should not be equated automatically with antisemitism. The Arab-Israeli conflict, as Bernard Lewis reminds us, 'is in its origins and its essence a political one – a clash between peoples and states over real issues, not a matter of prejudice and persecution'.[68] What is disturbing, however, is an anti-Zionist rhetoric that reveals and displays classic anti-Jewish motifs. In other words, a special hatred seems to go beyond the bounds of normal political conflict. Jews or Zionists have become, at least for some critics, diabolically evil. More recently the Internet has provided an additional source for conspiratorial thought.[69]

There can be little doubt that Muslim-Jewish relations have deteriorated in the past two to three decades. But one should not treat the Muslim community as a monolith. Various intellectual discourses operate and compete. Some are innovative and progressive, with an emphasis on Islamic humanism and universalism; others are conservative or Islamist, at odds with religious pluralism and ecumenism.[70] Qibla, an Islamist group founded in 1980, and the Islamic Unity Convention, for example, are heavily influenced by Khomeinism and some of the more radical schools of Islamic thought.[71] Common to both strands, however, is a hostile critique of Zionism. In some cases this hostility is separated from antisemitism; in others Zionism and Judaism are conflated into a combination that incorporates notions of international Jewish finance and imperialism. In the 1980's, according to Ebrahim Rasool, these ideas were often merged into an analysis of the South African struggle.[72] That struggle was informed by a powerful mood of anti-colonialism, embroiled in a third-world *weltanschauung*. Within this framework the illegitimacy of Zionism was an important component, especially given the fact that South Africa had close ties with the Jewish State.

The radicalisation of Islam in South Africa from the 1970s – rooted in anti-apartheid struggles, in the growth of black consciousness surrounding the Soweto uprising of 1976, and in revolutionary Khomenism – laid the groundwork for anti-Jewish hostility, evident with the normalisation of South African society in the 1990s. Thus the placard slogan of 'death to the Jews', 'one Zionist one bullet' and the vicious rhetoric surrounding jihad and

Middle Eastern affairs.[73] It would seem that some of the anger is underpinned by historic landlord-tenant relations in the inner city, regional encounters between employers and employees in the textile industry, radical Islamic teachings, and of course, a general anger at white privilege with which Jews are understandably associated.

Quite clearly, South Africa has not been immune to what Robert Wistrich has referred to as the 'Longest Hatred'. And yet, as indicated at the outset, memories suggest that South Africa was a haven of tranquility for Jews – a *goldene medina*. I want to make it clear that I am fully aware of the many occasions of hospitality accorded to Jews, and the many instances of people who spoke up on behalf of Jews. There is indeed a powerful strain of philosemitism in South African culture. But concurrently, and at times overlapping, was a widespread anti-Jewish stereotype, especially evident in the first half of the twentieth century. That stereotype was transformed in the 1930s into programmatic antisemitism, against a backdrop of political and socio-economic instability, and most importantly, Afrikaner ethnonationalism. The latter saw their lifestyle threatened by English-speakers who dominated the urban centres. For them the Jew emerged as a convenient symbol. An anti-modernist ethnonationalism employed the 'other' to enhance self-definition and to deflect divisions within the group. Insular and backward-looking, it focussed on the Jew, an exemplar of the modern. Such sentiments are far removed from the inclusivist and non-triumphalist character of contemporary African nationalism, exemplified in the ANC's concept of a 'rainbow nation'. Whereas the National Party in the 1930s had manipulated whatever anti-Jewish sentiment existed for political gain, the ANC has distanced itself from anti-Jewish outbursts – be they slogans pronounced by striking workers or the rantings of individuals. Antisemitism, as such, is of marginal significance in South African public life.

Perhaps most importantly, our society has generally become more conscious of the harm of stereotyping and the abuse of discernible minorities. This is a phenomenon that needs to be applauded. A Hoggenheimer cartoon on the pages of our local press today would set off alarm bells. That, it seems to me, is an important and meaningful measure of change. And yet, it may well be that most South Africans are unaware or unappreciative of this. Most Jews, I would venture to guess, believe that this country welcomed their forebears with open arms. The historical record suggests otherwise. But, as indicated at the outset, both the historical record and memory are not set in stone. They are constructed over time, and invariably these constructions serve particular interests. Since these interests are always changing, and since memory and history are inextricably intertwined, our understanding of the past is forever changing. I wish I could be present in 50 years to hear a lecture on an overview of antisemitism in South Africa to the year 2050!

Beyond The Pale:
Jewish Immigration and the South African Left

JAMES T CAMPBELL

James T Campbell is an associate professor of Africana Studies, American Civilisation and History at Brown University. Between 1996 and 1998, he was a senior research officer at the Institute for Advanced Social Research at the University of the Witwatersrand. He is the author of *Songs of Zion: The African Methodist Episcopal Church in the United States and South Africa* (1995).

I

South Africans have recently been treated to a curious debate. In 1997 *Jewish Affairs*, the quarterly journal of the South African Jewish Board of Deputies, published a special issue entitled 'Jews and Apartheid'. A collection of reviews and essays, the issue represented an attempt to come to terms with Jews' complex relationship with their nation's past, a gesture of 'remembering and renewing' in keeping with the quest for a 'new' South Africa. Contributors weighed the interplay of 'accommodation, activism, and apathy' in Jewish responses to apartheid; they described encounters with state authorities; they pondered the propriety of a collective apology for Jewish complicity with the apartheid regime. Coming from the Board of Deputies, an organisation that had traditionally maintained that Jews had no distinct interest in 'political' matters, the special issue marked a watershed in South African Jewish history.[1]

In a country like South Africa, however, one plumbs the past at one's peril. Even before the special issue hit the streets, an ugly controversy had erupted over an essay that the editors had declined to publish, a scathing denunciation of Jewish complicity written by a member of *Jewish Affairs*' own editorial board, Claudia Braude. The essay, which subsequently appeared in Johannesburg's *Mail and Guardian*, focused on Percy Yutar, the Jewish state's attorney who prosecuted Nelson Mandela and other leaders of the national liberation movement in the 1963 Rivonia trial. Yutar, Braude argued, epitomised a wider 'syndrome', in which Jews sought to deflect Afrikaner Nationalist antisemitism through conspicuous displays of loyalty to the apartheid regime. For Yutar, at least, the tactic succeeded: following the Rivonia trial, he was appointed Attorney General of the Orange Free State and later of the Transvaal, unprecedented attainments for a Jew. Braude's chief concern, however, was with the response of the wider Jewish community. At a time when Jewish anti-apartheid activists were routinely shunned, Yutar was elected president of United Hebrew Congregation, Johannesburg's largest Orthodox synagogue. Jewish leaders hailed him as 'a credit to the community', a symbol of Jews' 'contribution' to their adopted homeland.[2]

The fact that they had excluded Braude's essay did not prevent the editors of *Jewish Affairs* from publishing a blistering rebuttal, denouncing 'moral grandstanders' who sought to aggrandise themselves through 'ahistorical, utterly opportunistic polemics' appealing to 'old-style Jewish self-hatred'. The Board of Deputies and other 'representative' Jewish institutions had indeed made compromises, the editors conceded, but these needed to be seen in the context of Jewish marginality and of the accession of a violent, virulently antisemitic regime. To demand a more confrontational approach was not only to indulge hindsight, but 'wholly to mistake the role of Jewish communal leadership', whose 'duty was, and remains, in the realm of protection, not of advocacy or prescription'. Not surprisingly, such distinctions cut little ice in the climate of post-apartheid South Africa. In the weeks that followed, the Board of Deputies was assailed in the local press for a host of failings, past and present.³

By a singular coincidence, the 'Yutar debate' (as the newspapers dubbed it) coincided with the launch of Immanuel Suttner's *Cutting Through the Mountain: Interviews with South African Jewish Activists*. In contrast to Braude, Suttner emphasised not Jews' complicity in apartheid but their vital role in overthrowing it; his object, he declared in the book's introduction, was to 'recanonise' a group of 'Jewish heroes' whose contribution to South Africa's new non-racial democracy had been neglected or suppressed. He insisted, moreover, that his subjects had acted *as Jews*, that their activism was rooted in 'perspectives and qualities that are uniquely Jewish'. To be sure, the thesis was carefully qualified. Suttner acknowledged that the vast majority of South African Jews did not participate in the struggle against apartheid and often ostracised those who did; he conceded the importance of treating people as individuals rather than 'as branch offices of some collective essence'. Such qualifications did not deter him, however, from ascribing to his subjects a set of 'atavistic cultural memories', a kind of collective unconscious, compounded of such 'characteristically Jewish' values as 'solidarity for the underdog', 'hostility to all doxies', 'a capacity for imaginative empathy with those most directly oppressed', and a 'desire to programmatically implement basic intuitions about justice'. The very fact that the book focused on 'Jewish activists' (including several people who identified themselves neither as activists nor as Jews) gave the argument an ineluctably essentialist, not to say tautological, cast.⁴

One does not need to be an historian to appreciate the limitations of the current debate. Clearly the vast majority of South African Jews did acquiesce in apartheid, as did the vast majority of white South Africans generally. At the same time, Jews were massively overrepresented in the ranks of the opposition. Given the variety of anti-apartheid organisations and the obvious demands of secrecy, no precise accounting is possible, but one might reasonably estimate that Jews, who constituted about 4 per cent of the post-war white population, represented at least 40 per cent of South Africa's white left. Indeed, it was the very visibility of Jews in the left, and in the Communist Party in particular, that prompted other Jews to go to such lengths to evince their loyalty.

Seen in this light, the 'Jews and Apartheid' controversy turns less on issues of fact than on questions of perspective and emphasis – questions that, as so often in historical debates, have less to do with the past *per se* than with the exigencies of the present. In attacking the hypocrisy of the Jewish 'establishment', Braude clearly hopes to spur a reorientation of Jewish identity and politics in South Africa today. Suttner's book is even more palpably presentist. In laying claim to the activities of neglected Jewish activists, Suttner seeks not only to repair a breach within South African Jewry but to establish Jews' bona fides within the new democratic dispensation. Indeed, as Braude noted in a hostile review, the book risks indulging the same kind of 'contributionist' logic that snared Percy Yutar and his supporters, citing individual Jews' service to the nationalist cause in order to establish Jews' collective right to share in South Africa's bounty.[5]

The controversy will doubtless continue, as South Africans struggle to build a society on the wreckage of the past, and as South African Jews seek their place within it. All that historians can do is to try to ensure that the discussion unfolds in as informed and nuanced a fashion as possible. To do so requires asking a set of questions of which the current debate is almost entirely innocent – questions about the sources and character of Jewish immigration to South Africa, changing Jewish settlement patterns, class formation, experiences of work and leisure, and, perhaps most importantly, about immigrant family life. All of these questions, in turn, must be set in the context of the massive social and political upheavals unleashed by South Africa's industrial revolution, which coincided precisely with the decades of large-scale Jewish immigration. Finally, understanding Jewish political experience requires looking closely at the specific institutions through which consciousness was shaped and expressed – not only at 'representative' bodies such as the Board of Deputies, but at book clubs and boarding houses, synagogues and schools, *Landmanschaft* associations, Zionist movements, youth groups, workers' clubs, trade unions, and, last but not least, the Communist Party of South Africa.[6]

The essay that follows represents a modest step toward addressing this formidable agenda, through a close examination of the lives of four prominent Jewish activists: Hyman Basner,

Memories, Realities and Dreams

Baruch Hirson, Pauline Podbrey and Joe Slovo. Obviously these four individuals, socialists all, were not 'representative' of South African Jewry, certainly not in any easy or obvious way. Yet their stories, recounted in a series of recently published autobiographies, illuminate important patterns and processes. All four were first-generation South Africans, whose parents came to South Africa from the Baltic fringe of the Russian Empire. All came from families that were economically marginal and, in some ways, emotionally stunted. All found a refuge from loneliness in politics – in the Communist Party, in three of the four cases – only to encounter new forms of disappointment and betrayal. Taken together, their lives offer a privileged window into the travails and transformations of an immigrant community, as well as into the sometimes byzantine world of the South African left.[7]

II

During the years of Dutch East India Company rule (1652-1795), conforming Jews were legally prohibited from settling in the Cape. With the creation of the Batavian Republic, and the accession of the British a few years later, a small number of Jews, mostly of English and German descent, began to arrive. In 1841, Jews in Cape Town established South Africa's first congregation, Tikvath Israel. Despite their miniscule numbers – certainly less than half of one per cent of South Africa's white population – Jews played a prominent role in the development of the Kimberley diamond fields in the 1870s. A few – Alfred Beit, Barney Barnato, Isaac Lewis, and his cousin and partner Sammy Marks – made substantial fortunes, accumulating the capital that would help to develop the Witwatersrand gold fields a decade later.[8]

The rise of the Witwatersrand coincided with one of the most dramatic mass movements in the history of the modern world: the exodus of Jews out of the Russian Empire. In the years between the assassination of Tsar Alexander in 1881 and the outbreak of the First World War in 1914, more than three million men, women and children, a third of Russia's Jewish population, fled their homes in the Empire's 'Pale of Settlement', driven by grinding poverty, escalating legal discrimination and savage pogroms.

While the vast majority of migrants were bound for the United States, the exodus carried Jews to every corner of the globe, including South Africa, which by 1914 had absorbed over 40 000 immigrants from the Baltic. Jewish immigration continued after the war, especially after 1924, when the Johnson-Reed Act slammed shut the 'golden door' to the United States. More than 2 000 Jewish immigrants per year came to South Africa between 1924 and 1930, when the National Party enacted its notorious Quota Act, which imposed a limit of 50 immigrants per year from certain 'non-scheduled' countries, including all of Eastern Europe. Fortunately for some, the act was not airtight: it imposed no restrictions on immigration from Western Europe, while reserving an 'unallotted' quota of 1 000 immigrants per year, to be assigned at the discretion of a special board. Thanks to these loopholes, more than 6 000 Germans emigrated to South Africa between 1933 and 1936, the majority of them Jews. Even after the passage of the 1937 Aliens Act (enacted by the South African Party in order to forestall more draconian legislation proposed by the National Party), a trickle of Jews arrived, mostly family members of immigrants who already enjoyed permanent residence. (Among these fortunate few was future Minister of Housing Joe Slovo.) With the outbreak of war in 1939, the era of Jewish immigration to South Africa was over. By that time, the Jewish population numbered nearly 100 000, at least three-quarters of whom were Eastern European immigrants or their descendants.[9]

The social character of Jewish migration varied across space and time, as did the specific pathways that migrants followed. A substantial majority of the new arrivals – 70 per cent or more – hailed from greater Lithuania. The largest contingent came from the Kovno and its hinterlands, but substantial numbers also arrived from the districts of Vilna, Grodno, North Suwalki, and Vitebsk. Thousands more arrived from Poland, Latvia, Byelorussia, and as far afield as Odessa in the Ukraine. While some travelled to South Africa directly, most were transmigrants, who arrived after spending months or years elsewhere: in the East End of London, on New York's Lower East Side, in Germany, Palestine, or even the Argentine. Migrants sometimes travelled in family groups; more often they engaged in staged migration, with men embarking first and sending for wives and children (and sometimes parents and siblings) after establishing themselves. Why particular migrants chose South Africa as a destination remains a woefully underresearched question, but presumably many responded to reports from friends and kinfolk, or to the often exaggerated accounts of South African prosperity appearing in American and European newspapers in the late nineteenth century. Jews in Neustadt-Sugind, a village in the North Sulwaki district of Lithuania, were well apprised of the careers of their old townsmen, Sammy Marks and Isaac Lewis, especially after the pair donated £1 000 to repair the local synagogue. Hundreds from the village embarked for South Africa.[10]

The vast majority of Jewish immigrants to South Africa remained Orthodox. Hasidism, the sweeping pietistic movement that did so much to transform Polish Jewry, made relatively little headway in Lithuania, and never acquired a substantial institutional presence in South Africa. The same was true of Reformed Judaism, which played such a central role in the acculturation of Jewish immigrants in the United States; the first Reformed synagogue in South Africa opened only in 1933. Yet for all their Orthodoxy, the new arrivals were products of a culture in ferment. Over the last half of the nineteenth century, a host of new religious and secular ideas seeped into the Pale, introducing new possibilities and tensions into the long-settled world of the *shtetl*. With its emphasis on ethical conduct and personal asceticism, the Vilna-based Musar (Ethical) Movement steered a kind of middle path between Orthodoxy and Hasidism, rejecting traditional Judaism's elevation of detached scholarship without indulging the mysticism or anti-intellectualism of Hasidism. The *Haskalah*, the Jewish Enlightenment emanating from nineteenth-century Germany, posed an even more direct challenge to rabbinical authority. Though widely dismissed and derided, the so-called *maskilim* had a profound impact on Lithuanian Jewry, especially on younger, better-educated Jews, who shared not only their anti-clericalism but their openness to 'modern' forms of knowledge and experience, from secular science to western dress. Perhaps most importantly, the last decades of the nineteenth century witnessed the emergence of a secular Jewish literature, an extraordinary florescence of novels, short stories, poems, and plays, written in Russian and 'vulgar' Yiddish and peddling a host of 'alien' ideas, including that most corrosive of modern notions, the idea of romantic love. While less overtly polemical than the writings of the *maskilim*, this secular literature was, in its way, even more threatening to traditional authority. By turns humorous and tragic, sentimental and satirical, it spoke not to a narrow community of adepts but to a mass readership, women as well as men, who found in its pages not only recognisable characters and predicaments – jealous spouses, mendacious local officials, the endless struggle to make ends meet – but a profound 'affirmation of ordinary life' which was the very antithesis of the traditional ethic of scholars and rabbis. Not surprisingly, this literature exercised a magnetic attraction on the young: one of the ubiquitous laments of the period was of students smuggling Yiddish novels and poetry books into Yeshiva.[11]

The impact of these new ideas was magnified by the brute realities of poverty and persecution. Even by the formidable standards of Russian Jewry, the nineteenth century was a brutal time, an era of famine and epidemic disease, of recurring economic depression and ever-escalating oppression. Hundreds of thousands of Russian Jews were uprooted from their homes during the reign of Nicholas I. Tens of thousands of others were caught up in forced Christianisation campaigns, or in the notorious *Rekruchina*, which press-ganged Jewish boys into the Russian Army for terms of 25 years. Alexander II, Nicholas's successor, was a vastly more liberal figure, though ironically his greatest legacy, the abolition of serfdom, proved devastating to the fortunes of Jews, who had traditionally served as administrators and middlemen on the great estates. With Alexander's assassination and the paroxysm of pogroms that followed, the last vestiges of liberalism evaporated. Beginning with the so-called 'Temporary Laws' of May 1882, the Jewish community faced an ever-growing battery of 'edicts, laws, taxes and bureaucratic caprices ... that all but ensured that it would be a society of paupers and near paupers.' Jews were expelled from cities and villages, and barred from owning businesses or practising certain trades. By the 1890s, close to half of Jewish breadwinners in the Pale were not breadwinners at all but *luftmenschen* – people without work or resources, surviving on charity and chance. Those fortunate enough to find employment routinely worked 14, 16, even 18-hour days, toiling in cramped, filthy shops in exchange for two or three rubles a week. In the oft-quoted phrase of Karl Kautsky, the Jewish worker was 'a pariah among pariahs'.[12]

Loosed from traditional moorings, assailed by poverty, many Jews found refuge in new political movements and ideologies. By far the most influential was Zionism. Chapters of the *Chovevei Zion* (Lovers of Zion) movement sprouted across the Pale in the early 1880s, more than a decade before the publication of Theodor Herzl's epochal *Judenstaat*. Socialism also gained ground. Even before Alexander II's assassination, many Jewish students were drawn into Russia's diffuse 'populist' movement, seeking inspiration not in the lives of Talmudic scholars but in the supposed simplicity and virtue of Russian peasants, amongst whom some went to work. While little came of that particular experiment, socialist ideas continued to spread, first among the russified intellectuals of the so-called 'circle' movement and later among artisans and the small population of Jewish factory workers. The *Yiddisher Arbeter Bund* (General Jewish Workers' Union) was established in Vilna in 1897, the same year as the establishment of the Lithuanian branch of Herzl's World Zionist Federation. To most of their proponents, Zionism and socialism were antithetical. While Zionists valorised Hebrew, socialists, especially those in the Bund, embraced Yiddish, the language of daily life in the *shtetl*. While Zionists dreamed of a united Jewish homeland, Bundists accepted the realities of class differentiation and dispersal, arguing not for nationhood but for cultural autonomy within a new, socialist Russia. (Bundists' commitment to a distinct Jewish national life was vehemently rejected by Lenin, who engineered their explusion from the Russian Social Democratic Workers' Party in 1903.) Yet for all their differences in style and substance, Zionism and socialism grew from the same roots, and were often curiously intertwined in practice. Born of emiseration, both found their greatest appeal among young, economically marginal men. Self-consciously secular, both expressed a widespread rejection of the religious and cultural status quo – of the arid ritualism of rabbis, the rigid segregation of sexes, the perceived passivity and fatalism of the older generation. Both conjured a vision of a 'new Jew', who would be a subject rather than a resigned recipient of history.[13]

All of the transformations sweeping across the Pale came to a point in the arena of the family. As historian Richard Mendelsohn has written, family ties were of 'cardinal importance' in *shtetl* life. 'Jewish parent and child were bound together by an enduring web of obligations that stretched well beyond childhood, beyond even support in old age to the grave itself; a son's ultimate duty was to say *kaddish*, the mourner's prayer, on the anniversary of his parents' death.' Yet how did such obligations endure? What became of this complex behavioural repertoire in a context in which families, and the wider community in which they were embedded, were being rent asunder? Obviously this problem was not unique to Eastern European Jews – the 'collapse of the family' is a the signature lament of modernity – but certain characteristics of Jewish family life made it particularly acute. Contrary to modern stereotypes, Jewish family life in the *shtetl* was characterised by considerable emotional reticence. Open displays of affection – between parents and children, even between husbands and wives – were rare, as were overt expressions of approval. Fathers, in particular, tended to be remote figures, more invested in affairs at shul or at work than in the affairs of the households over which they ostensibly presided. This psychological separation was often compounded by long periods of physical separation, as the desperate search for work carried men away for months, even years, at a time. The figure of the remote, forbidding father, destined to become a staple of Jewish immigrant writing in both the United States and South Africa, had its roots in the Old World.[14]

Needless to say, a single paragraph cannot do justice to the complexity of family life in the Pale, much less in diverse immigrant communities, but the broad point stands: Jewish families were fragile things, complex webs of reciprocal obligations, held together by implicit understandings and unstated, or highly sublimated, bonds of affection and concern. (The classic example of sublimation, of course, was the elaborate, emotionally-fraught protocol around food and feeding.) Such an institution was peculiarly vulnerable to the upheavals of the late nineteenth century: to grinding poverty; to the deepening frustration of the young; to the rise of secular, distinctly generational movements such as Zionism and Bundism. The result, inevitably, was a steady erosion in both communal and parental authority, accompanied by increasing familial conflict. All of these pressures would be exacerbated by the wrenching experience of emigration, as parents and children grappled with an alien tongue, a changed racial landscape, an entire world that mocked inherited assumptions of value and status. Irving Howe's elegy for the Jewish immigrant family in the United States speaks equally to South African experience: 'The distance between generations came to be like a chasm of silence which neither affection nor good will could bridge. Inner shame, outer irritation, a rare coming together in grief – life ripped people apart ...'[15]

III

Jewish immigrants found their way to every corner of South Africa. A few – roughly 10 per cent, according to the first Union census – settled in the countryside, where they worked as pedlars and shopkeepers, catering primarily to Afrikaners, whose language bore a marked affinity with Yiddish. Virtually ignored by historians, these 'Boere Jode' became proverbial figures on the platteland, objects of suspicion and resentment but also of a certain respect and religious deference. A few immigrants became farmers themselves. In Bethal in the Eastern Transvaal, for example, Jewish immigrants created a profitable niche cultivating potatoes, the staple crop of Lithuania. (It was the National Party's defeat in a Bethal by-election in early 1930 that appears to have precipitated the introduction of the Quota Act.) The vast majority of immigrants, however, settled in cities, where they were drawn into the orbit of English language and culture. The lion's share came to Johannesburg, settling in the bustling Jewish enclave along Commissioner and Marshall streets, as well as in nearby working-class suburbs such as Ferreirastown, Fordsburg, Doornfontein and Yeoville. By the early years of the twentieth century, Jews accounted for more than 12 per cent of Johannesburg's white population.[16]

In class terms, Jewish immigrants covered a wide spectrum, defying later stereotypes of a comfortably middle-class community. A few found their way into the upper reaches of the bourgeoisie, where they mingled, sometimes uneasily, with gentiles and longer-settled English and German Jews. (Jews were conspicuous enough in the ranks of the Randlords for one disparaging visitor in the 1890s to describe the Golden City as 'Jewhannesburg'.) At the other end of the spectrum were the so-called 'Peruvians', unskilled, impoverished refugees, who became, in the words of historian Charles van Onselen, 'the most visible, dispossessed and unsuccessful group of workers on the Witwatersrand ... the unhappy recipients of the most vicious class and race prejudice that society could muster'.[17] As in every society, the combination of poverty and exclusion provided a perfect recipe for vice, and Jewish syndicates quickly claimed substantial shares of the local markets for illegal liquor and commercialised sex. At the pinnacle (or the nadir) of this Jewish underworld stood the 'Bowery Boys', a gang of Polish-born pimps who settled in Johannesburg after their expulsion from New York's Lower East Side. Led by the notorious Joe Silver, 'king of the pimps', the Bowery Boys turned Johannesburg into a major entrepot of the turn-of-the-century 'white slave' trade that carried thousands of women from the *shtetls* of Eastern Europe to brothels across the Atlantic world.

The vast majority of new arrivals carved out lives between these extremes, often by resorting to Old World callings. In Russia, for example, many Jews had owned or worked in canteens, catering to soldiers, railway workers, and other predominantly male (and potentially volatile) clienteles. In Johannesburg, some of these same people became *kaffireetniks*, dispensing offal to hungry black mineworkers in the fetid 'kaffir eating houses' that sprouted along the Reef. Others worked as artisans – tailors, cabinet makers, cobblers, watchmakers, plumbers, barbers – precisely the trades from which Jews in the Russian Empire were being extruded. Those with the wherewithal to acquire horse and wagon became cabbies and draymen, another familiar Old World niche. The concentration of the immigrant population in certain neighbourhoods itself created needs and opportunities – for kosher butcheries and dairies, for bakeries and boarding houses, cafes, Yiddish theatres, and for a small but growing Jewish professional class. Overall, South African Jews were conspicuously overrepresented in commercial fields. While there are no reliable figures for the early years of the migration, a 1936 social survey of Jewish Johannesburg found that 40 per cent of men over the age of 15 worked in 'commerce, finance, [and] insurance', more than three times the corresponding rate for gentiles. A national survey, published by a local Jewish organisation a few years earlier, put the figure even higher. Not surprisingly, allegations of Jewish 'commercial domination' would bulk large in Afrikaner Nationalists' demands for immigration restriction in the 1930s.[18]

Viewed in the perspective of a century, Jewish immigrants prospered, climbing the class ladder more rapidly in South Africa than in any other country in the world, save perhaps the United States. The perspective at the time, however, must have been very different. Progress was slow and uneven, and purchased at the cost of dawn-to-dusk labour in mine concession stores and family-run shops. Years of upward struggle could be wiped away at a stroke, as the local economy reeled from the impact of war or a series of sharp, gold-induced recessions. As in the Old Country, some Jews were able to prosper by sweating others, especially newly arrived 'greenhorns'. Retrospective renderings of immigrants as a 'fairly homogeneous group', characterised by 'warm-heartedness and generosity ... [and] a strong feeling of Jewish solidarity' could scarcely be more misleading. Far from homogenous or harmonious, South Africa's Jewish community was defined by diversity and conflict: conflict between Eastern Europeans and more assimilated Anglo-Germans; between small businessmen and their 'greenhorn' employees; between the 'respectable' classes and the mass of despised 'Peruvians'; between parents and children.[19]

Given the complexity of their origins, South African Jews ran the political gamut. Without question, the single most 'distinctive feature of South African Jewry' was its 'overwhelmingly Zionist character', as historian Gideon Shimoni has argued. A branch of *Chovevei Zion* was established in Johannesburg as early as 1896, presumably by Lithuanian immigrants. Additional chapters soon sprouted along the Rand and as far afield as Cape Town and Bulawayo. The Transvaal Zionist Organisation, chartered in early 1898 in response to the first World Zionist Conference in Basle, quickly enrolled over 5 000 members. By the end of the year, the Transvaal organisation had been absorbed into the new South African Zionist Federation, the first genuinely national Jewish organisation in South Africa and, more importantly, the first body to presume to 'represent' the Jewish community as a whole.[20]

Zionism's pervasiveness reflected not only the distinctive characteristics of the immigrant community – the high proportion of Litvaks, the absence of a Reformed tradition – but also the peculiarities of South Africa itself. The allegations of 'dual loyalty' that dogged Zionism in other places – allegations that caused many Jews in countries like the United States and Great Britain to shy from the movement – rarely surfaced in South Africa, where loyalty to one's *volk* was not only acceptable but praiseworthy. Prime Minister Jan Smuts was an avowed Zionist, who spoke proudly of his role in drafting the Balfour Declaration. Smuts's successor (and later his coalition partner), JBM Hertzog, likewise endorsed Zionism, both on the stump in 1924 and in a formal parliamentary resolution two years later. Even overtly antisemitic Afrikaner Nationalists accepted the legitimacy of Zionism, which they identified as the Jewish equivalent of their own struggle for national identity and self-determination. In both 1920 and 1929 National Party leaders campaigned on explicitly Zionist grounds, publishing pamphlets – in Yiddish, in one instance – assuring Jewish voters that 'our struggle is the same in principal as yours'. Ultimately, the only significant opposition to Zionism in South Africa came from within the Jewish community itself, from a small population of assimilated German and English Jews, and from a somewhat larger (and considerably more vocal) collection of socialists and communists, who regarded Zionism as a form of bourgeois nationalism.[21]

Most South African Zionists, it should be noted, were of the 'political' rather than 'practical' variety – most, that is, had no intention of undertaking *aliya* themselves. As Shimoni writes, 'For Jews in South Africa, no less than in America, confidence in the continued viability of Jewish life in their new-world home imparted a vicarious quality which enabled them to identify with the notion of a return to Zion without regarding it as directly applicable to themselves.' Yet vicarious or not, South African Zionism was pervasive and passionate. From the first appeals for Palestine in the late 1910s through the 1970s, South African Jews donated more per capita to Zionist campaigns than any other community in the world; in absolute terms, their contributions ranked second in the world, behind only the vastly larger Jewish population of the United States. Virtually every leader of world Zionism found his way to South Africa, from David Wolfssohn, Herzl's successor, who visited in 1906, to the controversial Vladimir Jabotinsky, leader of the right-wing Revisionist Zionist movement, who made three separate visits to South Africa in the 1930s. Even as the immigrant generation passed, South Africa continued to sustain a vibrant Zionist institutional life, including political associations, newspapers, and a welter of youth movements. In 1948, that most portentous of years, which saw both the birth of Israel and the introduction of apartheid, the South African Zionist Federation counted no fewer than 347 affiliated organisations.[22]

If Zionism remained the predominant influence on Baltic immigrants, the role of 'representing' the Jewish community gradually devolved upon a new organisation, the South African Jewish Board of Deputies. Like the British Jewish Board of Deputies, on which it was modelled, the board emerged during a period of intense anti-alien agitation. In 1902, with South Africa still roiled by war, officials in the Cape introduced an aliens bill excluding immigrants unable to speak a recognised 'European language'. Officials in the newly conquered Transvaal mooted similar proposals, including one bill designed to restrict business licenses to enterprises that kept their books in English. While Indians were the primary target of such proposals, they posed a clear and present danger to Jews, many of whom spoke only Yiddish. In this climate of uncertainty and fear, Jewish community leaders organised the Transvaal Jewish Board of Deputies in 1903; their counterparts in the Cape organised a similar board a year later. Through intensive lobbying, the new organisations successfully averted the threat, by securing the explicit recognition of Yiddish as a European language. In the years after 1910 the issue erupted anew, amid the struggle to draft a uniform immigration code for the newly created Union of South Africa. Prominent political leaders now called not only for immigration restriction, but for the selective deportation of 'unassimilable' aliens, especially those involved in illicit diamond buying and the liquor trade – an unmistakeable reference to so-called 'Peruvians'. Opposition to the proposal was orchestrated by the newly created South African

Jewish Board of Deputies, which was chartered in 1912 by community leaders in all four provinces. Significantly, leaders of the SAJBD, like their predecessors a decade before, chose not to challenge the principle of alien restriction per se, but focussed instead on amending the language of the proposed legislation to exempt Jews. Their success was embodied in section 4(1)(a) of the 1913 Union Immigration Restriction Act, which empowered the Minister of the Interior to deny entry on grounds of 'standards and habits of life' – legalese for Indians – rather than language or race.[23]

Many Zionists initially opposed the Board of Deputies, in fear that it would usurp the Zionist Federation's position as official 'representative' of South African Jewry. In time, however, the Federation and the Board devised an amicable division of labour, with Zionists overseeing matters related to Palestine, and the Deputies (many of whom were themselves avowed Zionists) focussing on 'domestic' affairs. Like its British counterpart, the SAJBD laboured to expunge the stigma of foreignness and unassimilability that attached to Jews, primarily through the medium of public relations. For the next half century and beyond, a steady stream of publications issued forth from the Board's Johannesburg headquarters, extolling Jews' 'contributions' to their adopted home, as well as the 'harmonious' relations that allegedly prevailed between Jews and gentiles. (The emphasis on harmony did not prevent officials at the Board from scouring newspapers and legislative records for evidence of antisemitism, or from prosecuting defamation suits.) The Board also devoted considerable energy, especially in its early days, to the cause of community reform. Spokesmen championed Jewish enterprise, attacked Jewish vice, and promoted the use of English over Yiddish, all with an eye to making South Africa a permanent home for Jews. In historian Riva Krut's words, the SAJBD was a crucial vehicle in the transformation of impoverished, immigrant Jews into 'white, urban, English-speaking and middle-class' South Africans.[24]

From the outset, the Board of Deputies adopted a posture of strict political neutrality, declining to take positions on issues that did not impinge directly on the status of Jews *qua* Jews. As early as 1910 the President of the Transvaal Board deplored attempts to draw the Board 'into the vortex of political strife'. Beyond their shared concern with antisemitism, he argued, Jews were simply individuals, 'in no way distinct from other sections of the community'. The argument would be endlessly elaborated in years to come, sometimes to the point of ruling political discussion itself out of bounds. (*The Jews in South Africa*, for example, a quasi-official history published in 1955 by Board of Deputies general secetary Gustav Saron and Louis Hotz, began with the following disclaimer: 'Whatever political causes individual Jews expressed, they acted as individuals ... and not as representatives of the Jewish group. Therefore, general political questions have no place in this history of the Jewish community.') Yet the very fact that the Board had to keep insisting on its neutrality attested to the existence of substantial disagreement within the Jewish community. As early as 1911, a group of dissenters, including several prominent Jewish supporters of Mohandas Gandhi, assailed the Transvaal Board of Deputies for its timid response to the threat of immigration restriction – for its decision, in essence, to dissociate Jews from Indians instead of joining them in opposition to the whole principle of 'alien' exclusion. In terms that uncannily anticipate the debate of our own time, these critics insisted that Jews were more than a collection of individuals, that their ethical precepts, as well as their own experience of persecution, imposed particular political obligations. Defenders of the Board, in turn, argued that Jews were but 'an insignificant minority' in South Africa, whose own position would be jeopardised if they 'threw in their lot with the Indians'. Again, the echoes of the current 'Jews and Apartheid' debate are unmistakeable.[25]

These early struggles over alien exclusion were but a prelude to perplexity, the first in a series of increasingly unpalatable choices. As antisemitism and anti-black racism grew in gruesome tandem through the 1910s and 20s, leaders of the Board of Deputies sought, almost inevitably, to deflect the former by embracing the latter. Thus Morris Kentridge, a Lithuanian-born Labour Party MP and sometime spokesman for the Board of Deputies, found himself in the awkward position of opposing the 1930 Quota Act on the grounds that South Africa needed all the European immigration it could get to prevent whites from being swamped by blacks. Such concessions to expediency, however, were not enough to stem the rising antisemitic tide. In 1936-37, with Greyshirts prowling the streets of Johannesburg and emboldened Afrikaner Nationalist leaders (including future Prime Minister Hendrik Verwoerd) threatening physically to prevent the landing of ships carrying 'these so-called refugees' from Nazi Germany, Jewish community leaders reluctantly accepted the inevitability of immigration restriction. Thus did Kentridge and the handful of other Jews in parliament join the Board of Deputies in publicly endorsing Jan Smuts's noxious (but nominally non-discriminatory) Aliens Act, hoping thereby to pre-empt the National Party opposition, which now proposed not only to curtail Jewish immigration, but to limit Jews' rights to trade, practise professions, and own property. At the same time, the Board's Executive quietly asked sponsors of the German exodus to 'bring about a drastic diminution of the immigration' to South Africa, on the grounds that it dangerously enflamed local antisemitism.[26]

IV

Last but not least, many Jewish immigrants brought with them a heritage of socialist politics, conceived in the struggle against Tsarist tyranny and nurtured in the Bund and other left-wing movements. A number of men and women later destined to play important roles in the South African left were the offspring of this community, a fact that has led some to draw a direct line of descent from the *shtetl* to the South African Communist Party. While such an interpretation contains a considerable measure of truth, it may conceal as much as it reveals. Only a small minority of immigrants came from socialist backgrounds, and many of them chose not to engage in political activity in South Africa, concentrating instead on building a better life for themselves and their children in their new home. (Several prominent Jewish activists have noted their astonishment at learning, late in their own lives, that their seemingly apathetic immigrant parents had once been interested in socialism.) Moreover, the 'tradition' that immigrant leftists carried was both particularist and notoriously sectarian. Long before the titanic struggle between Stalinists and Trotskyists, South Africa's small Jewish left was riven by debates over anarchism, Zionism, the 'language question' (i.e. the primacy of

English, Yiddish or Hebrew), and the relative merits of 'political' or parliamentary approaches versus 'direct', syndicalist action, all with an eye to explicating the particular predicament of Jews living in Tsarist Russia. Such debates and concerns were not easily or naturally adapted to South African circumstances, nor did all immigrant leftists feel compelled to do so. On the contrary, most seem to have remained far more invested in events and developments in Russia than in South Africa.[27]

The history of the short-lived Society of Friends of Russian Liberty, a Bundist organisation established in Johannesburg in 1905, offers a case in point. While the Society appears to have had some relationship with a Jewish working-men's club established in the 1890s, its object was to raise money to help Russian Jewish socialists establish self-defence organisations in the face of renewed pogroms. Fittingly, its chief accomplishment seems to have been to rekindle Old World animosities. The establishment of the society prompted local Zionists to launch a self-defence support group of their own. Irate Bundists determined to stop them. The inaugural meeting of the Zionist group, in December 1905, ended in chaos and cacophony, with Zionists waving blue and white handkerchiefs and singing 'Hatikvah' while Bundists waved red handkerchiefs and bellowed out the 'Marseillaise.' After that spectacular entrance, both groups fizzled. A visit by Sergius Riger, a leading Russian Bundist, gave the Society of Friends of Russian Liberty a brief fillip, but by 1908 it had disbanded. Significantly, the group's brief existence coincided with the first in a series of violent strike waves on the Witwatersrand, but there is as yet no evidence to suggest that the society played any role.[28]

Immigrant leftists' relatively slow engagement with South African politics reflected not only their continuing investment in Old World politics, but the inherent difficulty of 'transposing' political radicalism from one historical context to another. Immigrants everywhere confronted this problem, but the peculiarities of South Africa made it especially acute. In contrast to the United States, where the multitude of Jewish sweatshop workers provided a natural field for immigrant organisers, South Africa never produced a substantial Jewish proletariat. On the Witwatersrand in particular, industrial labour was the province not of immigrants but of African migrants; they, not Jews, were the 'pariah among pariahs'. Insofar as there was a local socialist movement, it reflected the interests of a population of English-speaking, highly skilled miners: 'soft-rock men' from the coal pits of Wales, Yorkshire, Lancashire and Cumbria, 'hard-rock men' from the tin mines of Cornwall and the gold and silver fields of Australia and the United States. These men – and nine of every ten immigrants who flocked to the Witwatersrand in the two decades after 1886 were male – brought with them craft pride, intense class consciousness, and a long tradition of trade union organisation, all of which were alloyed in South Africa by virulent racism against African workers. On three separate occasions – 1906-07, 1913-14 and 1922 – they paralysed the Witwatersrand with general strikes, each precipitated by attempts to replace skilled whites with cheaper African workers. Doubtless many Eastern European immigrants sympathised with white miners in their struggles against rapacious Randlords, but the barrier of language and their own relative insulation from the great clash of labour and capital on the goldfields ensured that they initially played little part.[29]

Outside the cauldron of the Rand, Jewish immigrant socialists seem to have enjoyed moderately more success. In the years between 1903 and 1907, a coterie of Russian Jewish socialists in Cape Town, most with Bundist affiliations, organised a series of short-lived unions and co-operatives among Jewish tailors, cabinet-makers, bakers, and cigarette makers. Not coincidentally, the conditions in these industries closely resembled those in Eastern Europe, with pitifully paid artisans working endless hours for small (and often Jewish-owned) firms. Even then, success proved fleeting, at least in part because of the priority that Bundist organisers continued to place on developments in Russia. By 1910 virtually all of the Jewish socialist unions in the Cape had either collapsed or been absorbed into mainstream British unions.[30]

The decade after Union brought a series of events that transformed the character of South Africa's white left, facilitating the participation of Jews. The Union government's flirtation with proposals to bar or even to deport Jewish immigrants in 1911-12 propelled significant numbers of Jews into the South African Labour Party for the first time. In a party in which leaders were regularly culled by deportation and appalling occupational mortality, several Jews rose to positions of party leadership; the most prominent example, Lithuanian-born Charles Clingman, became SALP secretary in 1914. Eastern European immigrants were prominent in the War on War League, established by disgruntled socialists and internationalists following mainstream Labour's capitulation to war fever, and in the League's lineal descendant, the International Socialist League, established in Johannesburg in 1915. The forerunner of the Communist Party of South Africa, the ISL is best remembered today for its pioneering efforts to organise black workers, but it also became an important pathway into the South African left for immigrant Jews. Indeed, by 1916 Jewish representation in the organisation had become so pronounced that the League began to publish its announcements in Yiddish as well as in English and Dutch.[31]

The ISL received an enormous stimulus from events in Russia. News of the Tsar's abdication in March 1917 ignited 'extravagant rejoicing in the suburb of Ferreirastown, where Jews danced in the street and embraced'. In August the League chartered a special Yiddish-Speaking Branch, based in Yeoville, with the explicit goal of attracting Eastern European immigrants, many of whom spoke little or no English. League leaders acknowledged that the initiative contradicted Lenin's injunction against ethnically-based workers' organisations, yet they justified it as a way of 'getting in touch with many new members who had hitherto taken only a spectator' interest in the ISL but who have now been fired by the Russian Revolution to link up with the organised socialist movement'. Four years later many of those new recruits became charter members of the Communist Party of South Africa. Some of them, in turn, would become leaders in South Africa's budding trade union movement, organising not only Jews but African, Indian, coloured and even Afrikaner workers in the secondary and tertiary industries emerging in the years after 1924.[32]

Not all Jews, it should be noted, welcomed these developments. Many feared that their immigrant brethren's conspicuous role in the budding socialist movement perpetuated antisemitic stereotypes and invited reprisal. An ISL election rally in Ferreirastown in June 1917 was delayed by the arrival of a deputation from the Board of Deputies, urging Jews 'to desist from proceeding with the election or at any rate from holding public meetings on the ground that there would be a riot, or worse still a pogrom of shopkeepers' windows'. In the decades that followed, such encounters would become a regular feature of South African Jewish life, especially after 1936, when a reorganised Board of Deputies created a standing committee to interview and importune people whose statements or actions cast Jews in an unflattering light. Perhaps the most amusing such interview came in the wake of the 1948 election, when a delegation of Jewish businessmen visited Sam Kahn, one of the South Africans' five designated 'Native Senators' and parliament's sole Communist Party member. Kahn, rarely at a loss for words, assured his guests that he shared their concern about antisemitic stereotypes and would retire from politics the day they sold their businesses.[33]

It is easy, from the safe vantage of the present, to mock Kahn's visitors, to deride the Board of Deputies' policy as timorous and hypocritical. Yet in the context of the time, the Deputies' fears were far from fanciful. The image of the 'Jew Bolshevik', which emerged in the 1910s and crystallised in the aftermath of the 1922 Rand Revolt – the stereotypical 'low down alien ... with his lining full of worthless rubles, his head full of anarchist ideas, and his pocket full of bullets' – had an enduring effect on the South African popular imagination, fusing as it did rising fears of social dislocation with older stereotypes of Jews as alien, subversive and disloyal. This pernicious complex of ideas would play a central role in the rise of Afrikaner Nationalism, operating in ironic counterpoint with that other antisemitic stereotype beloved of Afrikaner demonologists, the figure of the capitalist 'Hoggenheimer'. As South Africa and the world tumbled into depression and war, the frequency and virulence of antisemitic pronouncements palpably increased. The four men who served as prime minister in the decades after 1948 – Daniel Malan, JG Strydom, Hendrik Verwoerd, and John Vorster – all made their political careers in the interwar years through vicious Jew-baiting. Vorster was interned during the Second World War for pro-Nazi activities, but it was Strydom who was perhaps the most flagrantly antisemitic. Under his aegis, Jews were formally barred from membership in the Transvaal National Party, a prohibition that remained in place into the 1960s. All four men, along with untold thousands of their supporters, routinely pointed to the activities of Jewish socialists as *prima facie* evidence not only of the essential 'foreignness' of political opposition in South Africa, but of the fundamental disloyalty of Jews themselves.[34]

Small wonder, in these circumstances, that the Board of Deputies and its supporters viewed the political proclivities of their left-wing brethren with such dismay, or laboured so strenuously to remind authorities that 'every Jew is not a Bolshevist and every Bolshevist is not a Jew'. Small wonder too that some of those Jews who were Bolsheviks, or radicals of some other stripe, viewed their co-religionists with such disappointment and disdain. Clearly the 'Jews and Apartheid' debate has deep historical roots.[35]

V

Few individuals better illustrate the complex origins of South Africa's Jewish left than Hyman Basner. Basner was born in Latvia in 1905 and came to South Africa in 1912. Trained as an attorney, he is best remembered today for his service as one of the South African Parliament's five designated 'Native Senators' in the early 1940s, Hounded into exile in 1960, he died in London in 1977. Over the course of his life, he also lived in the United States, Switzerland, Lesotho, Tanzania, Ghana (where he served as an advisor to Kwame Nkrumah) and Israel.[36]

Basner's forebears came from Latvia, from Dvinsk, an important river and railway centre. Despite mounting discrimination, a remnant of Jews remained in the city, surviving as timber traders, provisioners, and keepers of the ubiquitous brothels and saloons servicing railwaymen and the Tsar's garrisons. Basner's mother's family, of whom he knew little, were Hassidic Jews. His father, the son of a fisherman, was Orthodox, yet something of a maverick, who was unable to settle back into local life after a stint in the army. Having scandalised the community by working in a non-kosher food store, he 'ran away' to South Africa in 1895. With the outbreak of the South African War in 1899, he came home, remaining long enough to leave his wife with a daughter and a son, Chaim Meir, before returning. Chaim spent his first years living with his paternal grandfather and later with an assimilated aunt in Koenigsburg, in whose home he assumed the Germanicised name Hermann Meyer, or HM. The change was but one of three Basner experienced during his lifetime – in South Africa during the First World War Hermann was anglicised to Hyman or Hymie, which later, in Ghana, became Hugh – an apt symbol of a life in which personal and national identities remained unreconciled.

The family was finally reunited in Johannesburg in 1912, when Basner was seven. He came of age in a sprawling boarding house above a Commissioner Street butcher shop, in the heart of Johannesburg's Jewish enclave. His earliest memories were of the sounds and smells of the butchery and of a parade of people: Jewish cabbies, Indian hawkers, drunken white miners, and the wraith-like figures of young Afrikaner prostitutes, who frequented an all-night café on the corner. He watched as cohorts of African mine workers, fresh recruits from the reserves, were marched double-time through the streets to compounds at Crown Mines or City Deep, though it would be decades before he understood the nature of their journey.

Like many immigrant families, the Basners moved through a succession of working-class neighbourhoods, as their fortunes rose and fell. Shortly after Hymie's arrival in South Africa, his parents opened a small dairy in Doornfontein, a mixed-race slum that served as one of the primary entry points for generations of Eastern European Jews. When business slackened, they fell back to Belgravia; when it prospered they advanced to Mayfair. Being Jewish, young Hymie was never accepted as a full-blooded white South African, yet he grew increasingly distant from his Jewish origins. He felt no religious impulse, and English soon displaced the Yiddish of his childhood, carving a chasm between him and his parents. The process of deracination accelerated at the emphatically English Jeppe Boys' School, where Basner played cricket, read wistful poems about nightingales and other creatures he had never seen, and dreamed of matriculating to Oxford.

The family itself was the very antithesis of the stereotype of the warm, emotional Jewish family. Basner's father, a diabetic, was remote and uncommunicative; his mother was worn down by the responsibilities of the family dairy and scarcely figured in his memoirs. Neither parent spoke of life in Latvia or of anything to do with politics, though as an adult Basner was astonished to learn that his father had briefly been involved with a group of radical factory workers. Even the 1922 Rand Revolt, which raged through the streets of Doornfontein and claimed the life of a next-door neighbour, did not shake the family from its torpor.

Basner's radicalisation commenced in, of all places, the United States. In late 1922 he moved to Los Angeles, joining his sister and her Russian husband, who had emigrated a few years before. He planned to finish his education and qualify as a lawyer, after which he would send for his parents. He registered at the new Los Angeles branch of the University of California, but found it to be little more than a 'glorified version of secondary school' for rich Californians, nothing like the Oxford of his boyhood fancy. 'I felt like I had blundered into an amusement arcade meaning to visit a museum', he recalled. He stopped attending class and eventually dropped out (p.12). He still dreamed of becoming an attorney, however, and enrolled in night law classes, working by day in a Hollywood law office.

For all its crashing banality, Los Angeles widened Basner's political horizons. He made black and Asian friends, and discovered HL Mencken, whose vitriolic attacks on the 'Boobus Americanus' were echoed in Basner's later assaults on Afrikaner Nationalists. A strike by Mexican workers at the San Pedro docks sparked his interest. His 'eyes were clearer now than in the days of the Rand Revolt', and he reflected on the forces that led police to baton charge peaceful strikers and to assault and arrest their supporters (p. 13). (Among those arrested was socialist novelist Upton Sinclair, whose offence was attempting to read the American Constitution at a public meeting.) Posing as an attorney, Basner visited the jail where the prisoners were being held, and watched as guards vainly tried to stop the bloodied detainees from singing. On his way out, he received a truncheon in the solar plexus from an infuriated guard. It was an oddly apt introduction to a career in South African politics.

A reversal in the dairy business aborted the Basner family's dreams of emigrating to America. Hymie returned to South Africa, where he discovered that all his American coursework and experience translated into just one year of course credit. Lacking the time or money to qualify as a barrister, he went to work for a

Jewish solicitor, under whom he served the articles necessary to qualify as a lower-court attorney. What that pathway lacked in professional prestige was more than compensated by what it offered in terms of political education. Working at the Johannesburg Magistrate's Court, Basner stood squarely at the interface of white law and black life. He came to know many of the giants of interwar African Nationalism, including ANC presidents Pixley Seme and John Dube, prisoners' advocate Charlotte Maxeke, and Industrial and Commercial Workers' Union founder Clements Kadalie. Most of his time, however, was spent with more dubious characters: slum lords, pirate taxi owners, dagga dealers, shebeen queens, and *ngakas* – traditional doctors – who had inadvertently poisoned their patients. His clients included many who had fallen foul of the 1923 Urban Areas Act, and it was here that he made his one contribution to South African jurisprudence, successfully arguing that municipalities had to establish the availability of alternative accommodation before undertaking to 'remove' black urban residents.[37]

All the qualities that would distinguish Basner's colourful political career were exhibited in his early legal career: pragmatism; a raffish regard for disreputable characters; readiness to exploit any loophole in the state's oppressive apparatus. At a time when most in the South African left indulged a doctrinaire ultra-leftism, in keeping with the prevailing winds from the Comintern, Basner made common cause with chiefs, beer brewers, independent church leaders, even African Advisory Board members, whom other white leftists derided as petty bourgeois collaborators and 'kulaks'. It was this sensibility that would later lead him to seek election as a 'Native Senator', a token office created by the 1936 Hertzog Acts as compensation for the abolition of the Cape African franchise. Basner was not naïve. He knew that the loopholes he exploited could easily be foreclosed, that offices such as Native Senator were 'toy telephones', intended to legitimate a policy of disfranchisement. Nonetheless, he remained committed, ideologically and temperamentally, to exploit whatever loopholes presented themselves.

As Basner's reputation for taking (and winning) controversial cases grew, he was drawn into the orbit of the Communist Party. By now an avowed socialist, he began undertaking work for the

CPSA in the late 1920s, and by the early 1930s he enjoyed a virtual monopoly on Party business. (The job came open after the ultra-leftists had purged CPSA founder Sidney Bunting, who had previously handled the Party's legal work.) In his memoirs, he was at pains to emphasise that he joined the Party only in 1933, after Hitler's election as chancellor of Germany, less from any real conviction than out of a belief that the Communists were the only group willing to stand up to Nazism. While the date may be accurate, the implication that he was only contingently committed to the Party probably is not, since well before Hitler's accession Basner was an active member of the Friends of the Soviet Union, a communist-front organisation founded at Party behest in 1929.[38] In any case, Basner gave his maiden political speech on the steps of Johannesburg City Hall during one of the Party's celebrated Sunday night rallies. Virtually every Party's autobiographer active in the 1930s has recounted episodes from the City Hall rallies; several retell the story of barber Issy Diamond, who stumped a heckler who asked whether he would let his sister marry a 'kaffir' by suavely replying, 'Only if I had something against the kaffir'.[39] City Hall meetings typically ended with Party supporters engaging in verbal – and often physical – battle with pro-Nazi Greyshirts.

Basner's tenure in the CPSA proved brief. While he romanticised the revolutionary struggle, dreaming of fighting fascists in Spain, he had little interest in theory or in the nuts and bolts of Party organising. And while he acquiesced in the purges and policy reversals that characterised the CPSA in this period – he lectured Johannesburg's Jewish Workers' Club on the perils of 'Trotskyism' in 1935[40] – his readiness to register reservations alarmed Party leaders. During a visit to London, he made the mistake of trying to 'discuss the dilemmas of the South African Party' with a local official, who ordered him to 'proceed forthwith to Moscow' to discuss the matter (p.97). Basner was no fool and, professing an urgent need to attend to business at home, declined what was doubtless an invitation to his own execution. Still, he remained a member of the Party, finally resigning in 1939, within hours of learning of the Nazi-Soviet Pact. Even then, he declined to criticise the Party publicly, a policy he maintained for the rest of his life. '[A]nyone who leaves the Communist Party, even for the best of reasons, and joins its opponents in order to assail the corruption of its leadership and dogma, will end up deep in the opposite camp', he later wrote. 'In time, the CIA will get him, or the Church' (p.98).

The apogee of Basner's career came in the 1937 and 1942 Native Senate campaigns. By the time the Hertzog bills finally passed in 1936, the CPSA had lurched from ultra-leftism to the ultra-pragmatism of the United Front. Yet even then Party leaders had little interest in contesting for token seats in the Senate or in the equally shambolic 'Native Representative Council'. Basner, in contrast, saw the elections as an unprecedented opportunity for the CPSA to spread its message. As candidates for office, Party leaders would enjoy free access to African locations which one otherwise needed magisterial permission to enter. Candidates were also freed of the provisions of both the 1927 Native Administration Act and 1929 Riotous Assemblies Act, which prohibited public meetings while criminalising all speech and action that tended (in the judgment of the state) 'to promote any feelings of hostility between Natives and Europeans …'. In Basner's case, the determination to contest elections also reflected his deep personal contempt for the pious white liberals for whom the Senate seats were obviously intended, especially South African Institute of Race Relations founder JD Rheinallt Jones, whose Senate bid was endorsed by the 'professional white negrophiles' (p.93) and their black 'eunuch' allies (p.73). After some debate, Party leaders decided not only to sponsor Basner's candidacy but to run a slate of Africans for seats on the Native Representative Council.

Travelling with NRC candidates Edwin Mofutsanyana and JB Marks, Basner hit the hustings, canvassing a Senate district that embraced most of the Transvaal and Orange Free State. The trio's initial efforts came to naught, thanks to electoral procedures that entrusted huge blocs of votes to domesticated chiefs and to the not-so-subtle intervention of the Union Native Affairs Department. Basner polled just 13% of votes, against Jones's 80%; Marks and Mofutsanyana lost their deposits. Yet rather than concede Basner simply kept campaigning, with an eye to the next election. In 1942, five years after his crushing defeat, Basner stunned the 'equivocal Jones' (p.76), polling nearly 60 per cent of the vote. Thus did a Latvian-born ex-communist enter parliament as sole representative of a constituency exceeding Britain in size and containing nearly a third of the South African population.

Memories, Realities and Dreams

Basner traced his electoral success to lessons he had learned as a lawyer. During the depths of the depression, the search for paying clients had carried him outside Johannesburg, to platteland towns like Pietersburg and Kroonstad and their rural hinterlands. Often he was gone for days at a time, sleeping in his car or in fly-blown hotels, defending Africans unable to obtain representation locally. His clients were largely drawn from what might be called a petty bourgeois stratum – small entrepreneurs, litigious chiefs, and leaders of independent churches such as the African Methodist Episcopal Church, whom he found to be 'consciously respectable', yet 'remarkably independent psychologically as well as materially' (pp.120-1). The experience provided Basner with an unrivalled set of political contacts on the Highveld, which he was able to harness to his campaign. More importantly, he acquired an appreciation of the untapped political potential of the countryside, an insight lost on most South African leftists, who typically dismissed rural areas as 'backward' and 'tribal'. In the late 1930s and early 1940s particularly, CPSA leaders insisted that the engine of revolution lay in the urban working class, notwithstanding the fact that it was the countryside that had produced, just a generation before, the Industrial and Commercial Workers' Union, the largest mass movement in South African history.[41]

Basner set out to fan the 'sparks among the stubble', to revive South Africa's neglected tradition of rural resistance (p.100). His task was made easier by the ravages of the 1936 Native Land Trust Act, which, together with drought and depression, had raised rural land hunger to a pitch of desperation. It was made easier still when one of his contacts produced a list of old ICU members, many of whom proved eager to rejoin the fray. There is a lesson here for South African historians, whose preoccupation with specific institutions and movements has often blinded them to the deeper continuities symbolised by the passing of that yellowed list. Clements Kadalie himself, who had founded the union in 1919, was enlisted in the campaign. Redeemed from the ravages of alcohol, the old 'Lion of the North' proved to have lost little of his fire. For a few months in 1942, the rural Highveld exhibited a political vitality not seen since the heydey of the ICU and not seen again until the rural revolts of the late 1950s.[42]

Basner's political insight was sufficient to secure his election to the Senate, but not to save him from the deeper contradictions of his position. Once in office, he confronted the dilemma faced by all radicals who seek to operate 'inside the system'. To be effective, he needed to cultivate a reputation for reasonableness, but reasonableness, in the context of the South African Parliament, meant abiding the most appalling lunacy, starting with the notion that parliament itself was a legitimate, representative institution. The dilemma was sharpened by the waxing strength of the National Party opposition, many of whose members took secret delight in Basner's slashing attacks on Prime Minister Smuts even as they publicly derided him as a 'Jew Communist' determined to 'spread his anti-Christian and anti-European and anti-white doctrine in the furthest kraals' (p.131). In time, the contradictions of his position wore Basner down. His efforts to provoke a commission of inquiry into the operation of the Native Land Trust Act came to nothing, as did his attempts to establish a new party, the African Democratic Party, as an alternative to the moribund African National Congress. Even his most conspicuous achievement – his service on the Witwatersrand Mine Natives Wages Commission, which secured an increase for African miners from fourpence to fivepence per shift – proved pyrrhic. The increase neither alleviated the poverty of migrant workers nor eroded the power of mining capital. (The state covered the increase through a remission of taxes on the industry.) Nor did it prevent the inevitable collision between African mine workers and the mining houses. Indeed, some historians have suggested that the Commission, by forestalling a strike during wartime, when workers' leverage was at its greatest, paved the way for the Mineworkers' Union's crushing defeat in 1946.

One of just five 'Native Senators', Basner also had the distinction of being one of a tiny handful of Jewish parliamentarians. The fact that he did not feel himself particularly Jewish did not shield him from antisemitic taunts nor blind him to the peculiar responsibilities of his position. In an era that saw both the horror of the Holocaust and the explosive growth of Afrikaner Nationalism, Basner understood that all his actions and pronouncements were doubly weighted. The ambiguities of his position were limpidly revealed in 1945, in an episode involving the treatment of farm labourers, a constituency whose interests Basner had long championed. Even by the standards of South Africa, black farm workers endured shocking deprivation and brutality. And nowhere were conditions more savage than in Bethal, a potato- and maize-farming district in the Eastern Transvaal that bestrode one of the main routes for Moçambican migrants travelling to the Witwatersrand. In 1945, an Anglican missionary approached Basner with reports of two particular farmers who were not only 'outstandingly brutish in a conventionally brutal environment' but also guilty of the murder of at least two African farm workers (p.179) The problem for Basner, and for South Africa's Jewish Board of Deputies, which was also called into the case, was that a significant number of farmers in the district, including the two individuals in question, were Jews. Precisely what conversations followed is not clear, but ultimately Basner and the Board elected not to publicise the case. It was left to Ruth First, a Communist Party member and herself a Jew, to lift the lid on events in Bethal in a June 1947 exposé in the CPSA's *Guardian*. That same month, a discouraged Basner resigned from the Senate.[43]

Basner's memoir, *Am I An African*, ends with his retirement from the Senate. There is virtually nothing about his continuing frustration with the ANC, his divorce and subsequent remarriage, his unavailing exile in Switzerland and Lesotho, his attempt to rebuild his legal practice in Durban, or his detention during the State of Emergency that followed the Sharpeville massacre. In late 1960 he and his wife, Miriam, made a 'trundling getaway' in an aged Land Rover, settling in Tanzania (p.196). A year later they moved to Accra, Ghana, where Basner worked as a columnist for the pro-Nkrumah *Ghanaian Times* and later as one of the Osagyefo's advisors and speech writers. These four years, according to Miriam, 'were to be the happiest, and to his mind, the most positive, of his life' (p.196-7). (Basner apparently completed the Ghana section of his autobiography, and one hopes that it too will see publication.) In 1966, however, Nkrumah was toppled in a coup, and Basner was again detained and driven into exile. After a year in Israel he spent the last decade of his life in Britain, dogged by ill-health, and, one senses, no closer to solving the riddle in the book's title than he had been as a seven-year-old boy, arriving in the City of Gold.

VI

Politically and temperamentally, Baruch Hirson stood at the opposite end of the spectrum from Hymie Basner. Hirson is a more familiar figure to South African historians, both as a political activist (a member of the African Resistance Movement in the early 1960s, he was convicted of sabotage and spent nine years in prison) and as an historian in his own right. In the decades after his release, he published a series of important historical works, each distinguished by exhaustive research, elegant prose, and an emphatically Trotskyist point of view.[44] He died in 1999, but not before completing a memoir, *Revolutions in My Life*, in which he turned his encyclopaedic knowledge and exacting theoreticism onto his own history, from his childhood in Jewish Johannesburg to his incarceration in the 1960s.[45]

Hirson was born in 1921, in circumstances uncannily similar to Basner's. His parents, Joseph and Lily, were Latvian immigrants, who came to Johannesburg with their parents in the 1890s. Hirson spent his youth in a succession of working-class neighbourhoods – Jeppe, Doornfontein, Fordsburg, Mayfair, Rosettenville – as his parents struggled to sustain a small dairy business. His home, like Basner's, was an emotional desert, overseen by a forbidding father, 'a moody man of violent temper, who would flare up quickly and then sink into a sullen silence' (p.18), and a browbeaten mother, for whom Baruch, the oldest of three brothers, became a kind of ally. The brothers appear to have been virtual strangers. (During his nine years in prison, his father and brothers never once visited, wrote, or enquired after the welfare of his wife and children.)

Historians trying to trace a tradition of Jewish radicalism carried intact from Eastern Europe to South Africa will find as little comfort in Hirson's experience as in Basner's. Hirson did have one radical relative, Charles Clingman, a maternal uncle, who served as secretary of the South African Labour Party and later helped to found the International Socialist League. But Joseph Hirson did not get on with his in-laws, and Charles does not seem to have been much of a presence in Baruch's life. Joseph himself had apparently served as a shop steward in the Municipal Workers' Union around the time of the First World War, but whatever passion propelled him had flickered out by the time of Baruch's birth. (Like Basner, Hirson learned of his father's political past only as an adult.) The family's history before coming to South Africa was scrupulously avoided as a subject. There were no oft-told tales in the Hirson household, few cherished old photographs. This 'severance with the past', Hirson concluded, was no accident; it was a signature characteristic of Jewish immigrants, for whom 'the past held few treasured memories and much of what had happened was best forgotten' (p.12). Rootlessness was compounded, in Hirson's case as in Basner's, by the absence of religious feeling in the home and by the children's lack of facility in Yiddish, which remained the language of the immigrant generation. Unlike Basner, Hirson did attend a Jewish primary school, but of a decidedly English stripe. Textbooks told of Tudors and Lancasters, of 'babbling brooks' and 'crocuses' (p.39). 'Home' was England, not South Africa and certainly not the Russian Pale.

In Hirson's childhood as in Basner's, blacks were at once ubiquitous and invisible. The dairy business employed a dozen Africans, most whom lived in the family's back yard. Hirson remembered them as kind and patient with a youngster's prattle, but he came to know few as individuals, in part because his father was forever sacking them. He recalled *Amalaita* gangs with their penny whistles parading through the streets,[46] as well as a visit to the 1936 Empire Exhibition in Johannesburg, where he saw live 'Bushmen' ostensibly 'pursuing their daily lives' in a glass enclosure (p.84). He also shared with Basner a vivid memory of newly arrived migrant workers being marched from the railway station to the mining compounds.[47] For the most part, however, Africans occupied a different world. For Hirson, as for generations of white leftists, bridging that gulf would become a lifelong quest.

All these circumstances, so similar to those of Basner's early life, produced, in that strange alchemy of character and context, a radically different personality and politics. While Basner was warm, gregarious, raffish, Hirson grew up shy and inward. While Basner was pragmatic and ideologically eclectic, not to say slipshod, Hirson studied Marxist texts with what can only be described as rabbinical devotion. On the occasions when the two men's paths crossed, they were bitter opponents. For Hirson, the efforts of Basner and his erstwhile Party comrades in the early

1940s to restrain the growing militancy of African workers in deference to the war effort represented one of the great betrayals of South African history. Basner, for his part, felt nothing but contempt for 'white Trotskyists who held seminars in which they polemicised strenuously with one another' (p.95). (It is a measure of Hirson's renowned professional generosity that, in spite of these differences, he helped in preparing Basner's memoirs for publication.)

Hirson came to radical politics through Zionism, specifically through the Zionist Youth Movement, which he joined in the year of his matriculation. The movement's appeal, he confessed, lay less in its politics than in its monthly dances, which promised a respite from his desperate loneliness. Whatever his motives, he found a political voice in the ZYM. He spoke at meetings and represented the Johannesburg chapter at a national oratory contest, winning a prize for an overwrought tribute to Zionism's founding father, Theodore Herzl. Within a year, he had graduated from the ZYM to *Hashomer Hatzair*, the Youth Guard, a Zionist socialist organisation that served as the gateway into radical politics for a generation of South African Jewish leftists. Established in 1913 in Galicia, *Hashomer Hatzair* was one of a bevy of Zionist youth movements established in the early years of the century. Though Marxist in orientation, the organisation was essentially a romantic nationalist movement, akin to the German *Wandervogel* movement, without the antisemitism or obvious homo-eroticism. The group's idiosyncratic radicalism rested on the writings of Ber Borochov, the most prominent of the young socialist-Zionist leaders emerging in Russia in the aftermath of the 1905 revolution. Borochov maintained that the Jewish class pyramid had become inverted, leaving Jews without an adequate proletariat (the necessary engine of socialist revolution) or peasantry (the necessary foundation of a nation). To remedy the situation, members of *Hashomer Hatzair* were enjoined from employing others and encouraged to work with their hands. (Agricultural labour was also valorised, as an antidote to what Zionists saw as a kind of collective 'neurasthenia' afflicting Jews.) Members were also discouraged, though not prohibited, from attending university, so as not to increase an already bloated Jewish intelligentsia. The goal, as in so many contemporary nationalist movements, was to rescue the nation from 'degeneration', decadence and demographic decline, to create, in historian David Biale's words, a 'Judaism with muscles'.[48]

This nationalist, neo-romantic impulse was reflected in the group's daily regimen. Hirson and his comrades took long hikes and sang folk songs around the campfire; they practised traditional Jewish folk dances; they lived in communal homes, adorned with prints of Diego Rivera murals. To fortify themselves for the rigours of kibbutz life, adherents eschewed tobacco, alcohol, cosmetics, ostentatious clothes and other trappings of petty bourgeois life. Sexual ideology within *Hashomer Hatzair*, as in other contemporary Zionist movements, was a 'peculiar dialectic of asceticism and sexual liberation'.[49] Deliberately flouting traditional Judaism's strict separation of the sexes, young men and women worked, studied and even showered together. Frankness, however, did not imply libertinism; on the contrary, leaders of the movement saw nudity as a way to demystify sexuality and discipline the appetites. All *Hashomer Hatzair* members pledged to remain celibate until after their arrival in Palestine.

In the long run, of course, *Hashomer Hatzair* was no place for a budding Trotskyist, but the experience left an enduring imprint on Hirson. He read the canonical works of Marx, Lenin and Trotsky, and discovered CLR James, from whom he absorbed an abiding anti-Stalinism. (Hirson, alone among the figures discussed here, never joined the Communist Party.) He followed the debate raging between Stalinists and Trotskyists over South African participation in the Second World War, and though, by his own account, his thinking remained 'uninformed and crude', he maintained a consistently antiwar position (p.112). Yet as his sophistication increased, so did his disaffection. He came to resent his colleagues' Jewish chauvinism, their political insularity, the fact that 'salad gardening' remained a higher priority than revolutionary theory. The final rupture came in an 'absurd incident' that captured well Hirson's political evolution, as well as abiding qualities of his character. Some time in 1943 he lent a cherished copy of Trotsky's autobiography to a co-worker, who returned it torn and missing pages. Enraged, Hirson tendered his resignation, announcing that he 'could no longer stay in a group in which political issues had so little meaning' (p.133).

Even before leaving *Hashomer Hatzair*, Hirson had begun to attend meetings of the Fourth International Organisation of South Africa, a Cape Town-based Trotskyist group that opened a Johannesburg branch in 1943. When the FIOSA collapsed in acrimony in 1944 he became a full-time organiser for the Workers' International League. (With a salary of £3 per week, he was forced to move back into his parents' home to make ends meet.) Hirson regarded this period as the beginning of his political maturity, the moment when he first confronted the realities of his own country, yet there was a decidedly Potemkin's Village quality to his work. Baldly stated, Hirson had embraced an analysis that defined the organised African working class as the engine of socialist revolution; yet in the context of South African society he and his comrades had very little contact with African workers. Total membership in both the FIOSA and WIL never exceeded a few dozen, of whom only a handful were Africans. (And some of them, Hirson ruefully conceded, cultivated white allies chiefly as a means to gain access to European liquor, which blacks were prohibited from purchasing.) The reality of political isolation was hammered home monthly, as Hirson and his colleagues set out for Alexandra and Sophiatown to peddle copies of the the FIOSA's *Workers' Voice* or the WIL's *Socialist Action* to indifferent Africans. Small wonder that these groups so often turned inward, dissipating energy in sectarian disputes. Hirson and his comrades anguished over whether they should patronise segregated facilities; they endlessly debated whether the Soviet Union was a 'degenerate workers' state' (Trotsky's position, in which case workers were still obliged to defend it) or a 'bureaucratic authoritarian state' (and thus past saving). The nadir came in late June 1944, two weeks after the Allied invasion in Normandy, when the *Workers' Voice* arrived bearing the headline 'Why the Second Front Will Not Be Opened'. When Hirson and his fellows complained that they could not possibly distribute the paper, back came the reply from Cape Town: 'sell the issue, the conclusion might be wrong, but the analysis is correct' (p.158).[50]

As excruciating as he found this at the time, he found it even more painful in retrospect. For the remainder of his life, Hirson continued to regard the Second World War as the left's great lost opportunity. Ground between static wages and spiralling inflation,

African workers exhibited growing militancy, at the very moment that the exigencies of wartime production endowed them with unprecedented leverage. At the same time, the repressive capacity of the state was substantially reduced, as the Smuts government sought to preserve domestic tranquility and to project South Africa's image as a liberal democracy internationally. Never before or since was the country so vulnerable to concerted industrial action by organised African workers. Unfortunately, Hirson argued, leaders of the CPSA, the party with the greatest influence over black trade unions, refused to capitalise on the situation. On the contrary, they strove to stem worker militancy, lest it endanger the 'war effort' – lest it endanger, in other words, the survival of the Soviet Union. Anti-Stalinist, antiwar groups such as the WIL naturally had no such inhibitions, but they lacked the organisation, experience, and access to act effectively. The WIL did establish brief alliances with black timbermen and with a brick and tile union, but little came of them. With the collapse of the timber workers' strike in 1945, leaders of the League resolved, over Hirson's vigorous objections, to give up trade union organising and to focus instead on 'study groups at which basic theory could be learnt' (p.198) By mid-1946 the WIL had folded. As if to pour salt in the wound, black mine workers launched, just a few weeks later, the strike 'that should have occurred in 1943' and were promptly crushed (p.200).[51]

Discouraged and lonely, Hirson retreated back to his library, scouring his beloved books for some insight into the recent debacle. Inspired by a passage in Engels on the universality of the dialectic, he commenced to read mathematics, eventually proceeding to the University of the Witwatersrand, and later to Cambridge, where he spent two lonely and unavailing years. Returning to Wits, he completed a master's degree in physics and accepted a position as lecturer. As a teacher and physicist, Hirson seemed at last to have found a vocation. It was also during these years that he courted and married Yael Sherman, a graduate student in zoology whom he had briefly known in *Hashomer Hatzair* and with whom he would have three children. But politics continued to call. After a hiatus of several years, he re-entered 'the political jungle' (p.264) (though a casual observer might prefer to call it 'alphabet soup'). Having invested his energies in the

ZYM, HH, the FIOSA and the WIL, he spent the next decade moving in and out of the PF (Progressive Forum), the NEUM (Non-European Unity Movement), the COD (Congress of Democrats), the SLA (Socialist League of Africa), the NCL (National Committee on Liberation), the AFM (African Freedom Movement), and the ARM (African Resistance Movement). His primary loyalty was to avowedly Trotskyist organisations like the SLA, but even there he was forced to accommodate considerable ideological diversity. 'The only common binding factor was a loyalty to the memory of Trotsky,' he wrote. 'For the rest there was confusion. Theory, where it existed, was scrappy, and the groups were rudderless. We avoided splits or even major disagreements by not taking decisions on most international events ...' (p.304).

As Hirson searched for a political home, the political ground which he occupied, narrow at the best of times, was fast shrinking. Even before the Sharpeville massacre and subsequent state of emergency, apartheid authorities had set out to crush political opposition. In the face of this assault, there was an urgent need for unified opposition, yet for Hirson there was nowhere to turn. Many white leftists, buoyed by events in Ghana and elsewhere in Africa, invested new hope in the forces of 'national liberation', a turn that Hirson, convinced of the fundamental 'incompatibility of nationalism and socialism', naturally rejected (p.281). In the critical years between 1959 and 1962, he met with leaders of virtually every oppositional organisation in South Africa – not only with fellow Trotskyists but with representatives of the ANC and the Congress Youth League, the South African Congress of Trade Unions, the Congress of Democrats, the reorganised South African Communist Party, even the Pan-African Congress – casting about for some way forward. All too often he was left, literally and figuratively, talking to himself.

While Hirson never really said it explicitly, one senses that he saw the turn to sabotage as a product less of tactical considerations than of intellectual exhaustion, an inability to conceive further alternatives. Once the possibility of armed resistance had been mooted, as it inevitably was after the banning of the ANC and PAC, the drift toward violence was well-nigh irresistable. Leaders of rival groups fretted that some other organisation 'might just turn to sabotage (or other violent tactics), and by virtue of their initiative, catch the public's eye ... leaving people like us behind' (p.301).⁵² In September and October 1961, an organisation calling itself the National Committee of Liberation blew up a Johannesburg pass office and several electrical pylons. On 6 December the ANC announced the formation of *Umkhonto we Sizwe*, which inaugurated its armed struggle with a series of explosions on 16 December, Dingaan's Day. In May 1962 Hirson attended the launch of a new National Committee of Liberation, later rechristened the African Resistance Movement. In its brief career the ARM launched dozens of operations, usually directed against electrical pylons, before being rolled up by the South African police. Carefully separating the organisation's black and white members, the government staged a show trial of the white, predominantly Jewish, leaders of the ARM. Convicted of sabotage, Hirson was sentenced to nine years in prison.

Even in 1962 Hirson entertained doubts about the turn to sabotage, and his retrospective assessment of the policy was scathing. While toppled pylons testified to the persistence of opposition, they in no way threatened the foundations of the apartheid state. As for the saboteurs themselves, they were embarrassingly amateurish. Organised into separate cells and supposedly known to one another only by code names, members of the ARM often saw one another socially, sometimes even confusing real and code names. While members prided themselves on tradecraft – burning notes and letters, typing manifestos on untraceable typewriters – it later became apparent that one of the leaders, Adrian Leftwich, had kept a detailed diary of meetings and operations, apparently with an eye to a future book. (Once captured, Leftwich turned state's evidence and escaped with a suspended sentence.) Hirson's own lack of tradecraft was captured in an episode from *The House Next Door to Africa*, a kaleidoscopic childhood memoir written by his son, Denis. In the book, Denis remembers going into the back yard with his father, shortly before his arrest, and burning a collection of incriminating books, the ashes of which they then spread in the compost heap.⁵³ It is a haunting image, father and young son fructifying the earth for a future harvest, but the reality was less edifying. The books in question, Hirson later confessed, were Stalinist tracts left by an acquaintance, and his object in burning them was simply 'to prevent being arrested for possessing works that I detested' (p.313). Meanwhile his own books were stored in a trunk in his university lab, where they were easily unearthed by police and introduced into evidence at the trial. Though Hirson never discussed the matter, the trial revealed that he had also used the Wits physics department labs to cache explosives, an act of recklessness that left him permanently estranged from his academic colleagues.

For Hirson, however, the chief failing of the sabotage policy was not bad tradecraft but bad politics. '[If] we had probed deeper', he later wrote, 'we might have seen that there was a basic rupture between [the policy] and the class analysis upon which we had always prided ourselves in our documents. The new course we were adopting would take us away from the workers who were essential for the building of a socialist society. The socialism to which we aspired could only be brought into being by an organised working class, and our action was taking us in the opposite direction' (p.301). For a man who prided himself on his grasp of revolutionary theory, this was a cardinal sin – one which he would have nine long years to contemplate.[54]

Baruch Hirson died in 1999. While his passing caused few ripples in political circles, it was widely observed in the academy, eliciting warm testimonials from scholars, some of whom, in years past, had been less generous in their assessments. By all accounts, including his own, Hirson was not an easy man. Prickly and opinionated, he possessed a rare capacity to sound doctrinaire even when engaging in self-criticism. Atop it all is the air of fruitlessness that pervades his life story, the deep sense of regret at errors made and opportunities lost – regrets that, for Hirson, were little eased by the triumph of an African nationalist government in 1994. Yet there is no gainsaying Hirson's courage, the breadth of his historical knowledge, or his devotion to ideas. This is a man who trained himself as an historian while sitting in a cold cell in Pretoria Central Prison, and who continued to produce important scholarship right to the end of his life, in the face of almost debilitating pain. While prone to sectarianism himself, he consistently exhibited a wholesome contempt for political expediency and 'Party line' thinking, whether in the form of the 'United Front' policy in the 1930s and 40s or the 'two-stage revolution' that is the theoretical stock-in-trade of South African socialists today. Like

Memories, Realities and Dreams

Hyman Basner, he could scarcely have been less representative of Johannesburg's immigrant Jewish community. Yet, like Basner, he was unmistakeably its child.

VII

Pessel Podbrez was born in a *shtetl* outside Kovno, Lithuania, in 1921, the same year as Baruch Hirson. Unlike Hirson or Hyman Basner, she possessed a radical pedigree: her father, Berl, was a Bundist and later a member of the Communist Party. Unlike his siblings, several of whom became Zionists and emigrated to Palestine, Berl believed that Jews should insist on all the rights and responsibilities of citizenship in whatever country they found themselves. While most Russian Jews contrived ways to avoid conscription in the Tsar's army, he chose, as 'a matter of honour', to enlist. He saw duty in the First World War, ending up in a German prisoner of war camp, where he nearly perished of starvation. Though he eventually returned home, he never seemed to recover from the experience. He had difficulty holding a job, and antagonised the customers in the small shop that his wife, Henneh, had opened to make ends meet. Finally, in desperation, he left Lithuania and came to South Africa, arriving in Durban in late 1929, just months before the imposition of the National Party's Quota Act. Pessel (who became Pauline in South Africa) and the rest of the family followed in 1932.[55]

While Hirson and Basner discovered socialism in late adolescence, Podbrey grew up browsing through her father's substantial library of socialist texts. She crept out of bed to listen to her father and other members of the Durban branch of the CPSA discuss the latest events in South Africa and the Soviet Union. Eddie Roux, who would soon leave the Party in frustration at Comintern meddling, won her lifelong affection when he did not betray her presence after catching her eavesdropping. Podbrey also met Lazar Bach – a 'time-serving bigot' from Latvia, she called him (p.29) – who steered the CPSA through its 'ultra-left' phase before being caught up himself in the Stalinist purges. She first attended a Party meeting in her own right in 1935, when she was just 14.[56]

Not surprisingly, Pauline Podbrey has become an important

exhibit for those who seek evidence of a tradition of immigrant socialism handed down from parents to children. (She is one of the interview subjects in Immanuel Suttner's *Cutting Through the Mountain*.[57]) Yet the dominant theme in her own account of her life, both in interviews and in her 1993 memoir, *White Girl in Search of the Party*, is not of generational continuity but of conflict and rupture. As a child, Podbrey developed a strong sense of Jewish identity and spirituality, instilled by a deeply religious grandmother, but her faith withered in the face of her mother's indifference and her atheist father's scoffing. Memories of *shtetl* life faded. (One childhood image Podbrey did retain was of the first black man she ever saw, in a travelling circus in Kurkl.) Her parents, taciturn at the best of times, never spoke of the old country. Only later, as an adult, did she discover the sources of their silence. In a single conversation with her mother, she learned of her father's wartime capture and near starvation, and of a subsequent brutal assault by renegade soldiers determined to steal his boots, as well as of her mother's experience seeing her parents murdered before her eyes.

All these horrors registered themselves on the character of her parents, especially on her father, who remained frustrated, uncommunicative, and almost incapable of expressing affection. He bounced from job to job, forever clashing with employers. His frustration was compounded by his lack of facility in English, which prevented him from arguing his case and left him stuttering with rage. 'He had such dreams when he was young, such magnificent hopes not only for himself, but for humanity,' Podbrey writes. 'He wrote poetry and reached for the stars but all he could grasp was a stultified, graceless existence in a strange land and a foreign tongue which never served him.' From Pauline, 'his only daughter, he had no joy' (p.140). The one thing the two of them shared – the Communist Party – became, in time, the greatest barrier between them. Having invested all his hope and passion in the Party, Berl was shattered by the Moscow show trials of 1936-37. He had abided the expulsion of Trotsky and the endless policy shifts dictated by the Comintern, but he refused to believe that so many of the revolutionary heroes he revered were traitors and saboteurs. For weeks he remained in his room, refusing to eat, a gesture tantamount, in the culture from which he sprang, to a renunciation of human fellowship, almost of life itself. 'The Party is dead,' he declared on emerging (p.29).[58]

Yet even as her father renounced the Party, young Pauline embraced it with all the ardour of adolescence. While visiting family in Johannesburg in 1937, she began to attend the Party's Sunday-night rallies at the City Hall, distributing leaflets and battling Greyshirts, to the considerable chagrin of her uncle. 'Jews must not stick their noses into what's not their business,' he warned her. 'OK, so the blacks have got a case but what's it got to do with you?'[59] Predictably, such seeming cowardice served only to strengthen her conviction. In 1939, shortly before her eighteenth birthday, she joined the CPSA. Ironically, her enrolment coincided almost exactly with two watershed events in the disillusionment of the international left: the revelation of the Nazi-Soviet Pact, and the publication of Arthur Koestler's searing *Darkness at Noon*, a thinly fictionalised account of the Moscow show trials. Neither had any discernible impact on Podbrey. She rationalised the pact with Hitler as a 'clever ploy' designed to buy the Soviets time. As for Koestler's book, she and her friends refused even to read it, dismissing it as just another instance of the 'anti-Soviet propaganda which we despised'.[60] She became, by her own account, a committed Stalinist. If Comrade Stalin endorsed Lysenko's theory on the heritability of acquired characteristics in plants, she lectured her old friend Eddie Roux, a professor of botany, then the theory was true. If Bukharin and Zinoviev had been executed as counter-revolutionaries, then counter-revolutionaries they were. When her father asked whether she would shoot him as a traitor if so ordered by the Party, she did not hesitate: 'Yes, I would' (p.30).

Shortly after joining the Party, Podbrey went to work for the Durban branch of the Trades and Labour Council. There she fell in love with HA Naidoo, founder of the Natal Sugar Workers' Union and the Party's most prominent activist. In contrast to her male comrades, whose memoirs typically say almost nothing about marriage, family or affective issues generally, Podbrey has written freely about her relationship with Naidoo. While the Immorality and Mixed Marriages Acts remained a decade in the future, there were already formidable legal and conventional obstacles to interracial liaisons. The local magistrate bluntly refused to marry them; he would not 'start the rot' by uniting 'a pure white and a pure Indian' (p.110). Eventually the couple, one Jewish and one Hindu, were married in a Christian church by a sympathetic Coloured minister.

Podbrey's marriage scandalised Durban's Jewish community. Friends and neighbours shunned her parents. When her mother went to obtain her usual ticket for Yom Kippur services, she was assigned to the rearmost pew. What most distressed Podbrey, however, was the response of her parents themselves, especially of her father. Despite his left-wing principles and his acknowledgement that Naidoo was one of the 'finest, straightest men I know', he refused to countenance the union (p.93). He even threatened to take the case to the local press, which was only too ready to report that communists encouraged miscegenation. For Podbrey, her father's behaviour stood as proof of the pervasiveness of racism in South Africa, even among the nominally non-racial left. Perhaps it was. Yet there may also have been a cultural dimension to his response. Within the universe of the *shtetl*, one of the primary burdens of a father was to ensure suitable marriages for his daughters, marriages which both ensured their security and enhanced the family's standing; it was precisely such assumptions that made the entrance of ideas of romantic love into the late nineteenth-century Pale so unsettling. Seen from this perspective, Podbrey's father's behaviour may have betokened not simply racism but the struggle of an immigrant father to defend a prerogative that his anglicised daughter did not respect or even recognise.[61]

In 1943 Podbrey and Naidoo moved to Cape Town, which had displaced Johannesburg as CPSA headquarters. Naidoo joined the Party's Central Committee; Pauline continued to work as a trade union organiser. While the racial atmosphere in the Western Cape was considerably more relaxed than in Natal, the couple struggled to find a hospital where Pauline could give birth, and later suffered the indignity of having their daughter expelled from the local Jewish school. The accession of the National Party in 1948 was a devastating blow. Naidoo was declared a prohibited immigrant in the Cape and deported back to Natal, where the family bore the full brunt of popular racism. Both HA and Pauline were 'listed' under the 1951 Suppression of Communism Act, and by the end of the year HA had been driven into hiding. With the permission of Party leaders, the couple made plans to emigrate to Britain, only to be denied passports. After vainly appealing to the British, Indian and Israeli governments for assistance, they resorted to stowing away, Pauline and the children on a passenger ship, HA in an empty oil drum on a tramp steamer. After long dockside palavers, they were admitted to Britain.

Soon after their arrival, the British Communist Party arranged for HA and Pauline to travel to Budapest, to work on the English-language broadcasts of Radio Hungary. Both embraced the opportunity 'to experience at first hand the struggles and achievements of building socialism', but disillusionment was not long in coming (p.157). No matter how desperately they sought to deny it, Podbrey writes, there was no escaping the 'hypocrisy', 'sycophancy' and 'oppressive dishonesty' of the Hungarian regime (p.192). As a Party functionary, Podbrey was among the minority who could obtain a safe abortion, but she was not sufficiently elevated to obtain penicillin for her children. At Radio Hungary, she and HA purveyed 'nonsensical rubbish', directly translated (in execrable English) from Radio Moscow (p.168). Interviewees at the local factory or chicken farm were hand-picked by Party officials, and every news bulletin included an obligatory minute of anti-Tito propaganda. Broadcasts were zealously monitored by an apparatchik in the office. Naidoo once received a severe reprimand for presuming to correct the English translation of a Stalin speech.[62]

The years in Hungary shattered Naidoo. While Podbrey is discreet on the matter, the experience clearly undermined both his physical and mental health, leaving him morose and jealous. She herself remained steadfast, exhibiting that will to believe that had long been one of her signal qualities. She told herself that Hungary's flaws were a vestige of the fascist old regime, a reflection of the lack of any democratic or socialist tradition. She angrily rejected friends' reports of antisemitism in the Soviet Union; antisemitism, she lectured them, was a morbid symptom of capitalism that could not possibly exist in a socialist society. She assured herself that Stalin – 'Daddy', the 'pivot of my ideals' (p.174) – was not aware of the distortions she witnessed daily, and would speedily correct them if he were. When the family returned to England in

1955, she remained in the Party, convinced that the revolution could yet be redeemed. To her dismay, she found that her comrades were indifferent, even hostile, to her reports on Hungarian life. 'Why, you've become a reactionary,' her friend Joe Slovo remarked (p.198).

The Hungarian Revolution of October 1956 briefly revived Podbrey's faith. Leaders of the new workers' committee at Radio Hungary invited HA and Pauline to return to their old jobs, assuring them that 'all the things you criticised have been put right ...' (p.199). (The committee also shared with the couple the contents of their Party dossiers; Podbrey's labelled her a 'premature anti-Stalinist'.) Before they could respond, however, Russian tanks rolled into Budapest. In London, Podbrey 'listened entranced' as a comrade just back from Hungary described the outpouring of art and poetry during the brief 'people's revolution', only to be shattered by his conclusion: 'The Russians were right to march in. The Fascists were preparing for a take-over' (p.200). A short time later – she does not say exactly when – she relinquished her membership of the Communist Party. Today she regards herself as a kind of progressive political agnostic, a person unable to 'offer a solution to the world's problems' but still 'determined to resist injustice where I find it'. Yet she also acknowledges 'the gaping hole where my faith had rested' (pp.200-1).

VIII

For all its novelty and insight, Pauline Podbey's *White Girl in Search of the Party* has a familiar cast. A lonely young idealist finds a home in the Party, confronts (reluctantly) the realities of Stalinism, and resigns; communism remains 'the God that failed'. The career of Podbrey's contemporary, Joe Slovo, presents a less familiar challenge: the spectacle of a brilliant iconoclast – warm, witty, ebullient – who remained an unreconstructed Stalinist virtually until his death in 1995.

If any figure earned the title of living legend, it was Joe Slovo. To the architects of apartheid, he was the arch-villain, a sinister 'KGB colonel' (always a colonel: for 15 years, National Party demonologists denied him a promotion) who exemplified communist domination of the African Nationalist Congress. To the young 'comrades' of the 1980s, he was a founding member and chief strategist of *Umkhonto we Sizwe*, a freedom fighter whose exploits were celebrated in story and song. In Slovo's last years another legend coalesced, of a benign old uncle whose warmth and irreverence (he wore his trademark red socks to Nelson Mandela's inauguration) more than compensated for his occasional dogmatism. Even in death, the legend transmutes. With the recent publication of daughter Gillian's *Every Secret Thing: My Family, My Country*, Slovo and his wife, Ruth First, have become the epitome of failed parents, touchstones for a post-apartheid society struggling to come to terms with the personal costs of political struggle.[63]

However one casts him, Slovo stands as one of the most important figures in twentieth-century South African politics. As a leading figure in the SACP, he shaped Party policy on dozens of defining issues, from the turn to armed struggle in 1961 to the decision to negotiate with the apartheid regime three decades later. As the first white person ever elevated to the ANC executive, he embodied the controversial alliance between the Party and the national liberation movement. And as a revered elder statesman and Minister of Housing in South Africa's first democratic government, he played a central role in the ANC's and SACP's bumpy transition from underground movement to political party to government.

Slovo himself first set out to assay his life in 1982, following Ruth First's assassination by South African security forces. In the aftermath of the event (which was made even more painful by a government disinformation campaign blaming Slovo and his comrades for the murder) he decided to undertake an autobiography, recording episodes in a notebook or on a small tape recorder. The tone his recollections assumed – anecdotal, wry, sometimes nostalgic, often hilarious – seemed to surprise him. As he observed in his notebook, 'My selective memories have a predilection for the ludicrous and comic which lightens and makes it possible to bear more easily the heaviness and often tragedies [sic] of the struggle.'[64] Unfortunately, as Slovo healed the autobiography languished. He resolved to return to it in 1991, when he was diagnosed with cancer, and again in 1994, but his resolution was swept away by the pressure of events and the accelerating progress of his illness. In the end, we are left with the recollections of 1982 and a few additional fragments from 1994, edited by his second wife, Helena Dolny, and supplemented by a selection of interviews, letters and tributes, all published under the somewhat portentous title, *Slovo: The Unfinished Autobiography*.

Revealingly, the book begins with a pilgrimage to Obelei, the town in north-eastern Lithuania where Yossel Moshel Slovo spent his first ten years of life. Slovo first proposed to revisit the village in 1963, shortly after he had gone into exile, but his plans were scuttled by news of the Rivonia arrests. A second attempt, in 1968, was also cancelled, this time because of troop movements occasioned by the Soviet invasion of Czechoslovakia. (Writing in 1982, Slovo still referred to the movements as 'precautionary measures' [p.4].) He finally made the journey in 1981, during a visit to Moscow. He was struck by how little he remembered; like other Eastern European immigrant families, the Slovos cherished few memories of the past. He was struck also by how few in the village remembered him. Many Jews fled Obelei in the 1930s, and most of those who did not were slaughtered in the first days after the Nazi invasion of June 1941, in some cases by *Einsatzgruppen* but more often by their Lithuanian neighbours, who responded to the outbreak of war by launching one final, bloody pogrom. With the help of Soviet officials, Slovo eventually tracked down a pair of second cousins in Vilna, with whom he had a hurried conversation, before returning to Moscow. His characterisation of the trip – 'a journey of half-completed rediscoveries' – might well serve as a subtitle for the entire book (p.11).

In 1928, when Slovo was two, his father, Wolfus, left Obelei, bound for Buenos Aires. What he proposed to do there is not clear; as with most things about his father, Slovo either did not know or chose not to say. While never as popular a destination as the United States, Argentina attracted nearly a quarter million Eastern European Jewish immigrants in the half century between 1889 and 1939, many under the auspices of Baron de Hirsch's Jewish Colonisation Society, a philanthropic organisation dedicated to resettling persecuted Russian Jews to agricultural settlements in the New World. Buenos Aires was also a major entrepot in the 'white slave' traffic; if contemporary estimates are to be believed, close to a quarter of the prostitutes in the city in the 1920s, and a substantially higher percentage of pimps, liquor sellers and petty criminals, were Eastern European Jews. As in South Africa two decades before, Jewish community leaders organised to combat the vice in their midst, excluding 'unclean' Jews from synagogues, cemeteries and theatres, occasionally staging much-publicised 'rescues' of girls. Such efforts were given additional impetus, again as in South Africa, by the rising tide of antisemitism, which swelled in the early months of the Great Depression, culminating in the right-wing coup of 1930. One of the first acts of the new government was to enact regulations requiring Jewish immigrants to pass medical and literacy tests, and to provide proof that they had been convicted of no crimes for the previous ten years.[65]

These were hardly propitious circumstances for a penniless Lithuanian immigrant, whatever his background or intentions. Wolfus wrote back to his wife and children, who were poised to follow him, and instructed them to meet him instead in South Africa. In the end, the family was reunited only in 1936. They settled in Doornfontein, the same working-class slum that had once welcomed the Basner and Hirson families. Ten-year-old Yossel sported a shaved head, a mandatory precaution against lice. He spoke not a word of English. For a time, the family's fortunes rose. They moved to Yeoville, where Wolfus and Chaya, Slovo's mother, opened a greengrocer's shop near a busy tram stop. Then tragedy struck. In 1938, Chaya died in childbirth. The shop failed. Wolfus was reduced to hawking fruit from the pavement. The family fell back to Hillbrow and then to Doornfontein, to a cheap attic room in Sher's boarding house. Yossel – now known as 'Joe' – and his older sister Sonia were forced to quit school and seek work. The baby, Reina, was consigned to an orphanage.

As with so many of Johannesburg's Jewish immigrants, the experiences of dislocation and poverty loosened family bonds. Slovo's sisters seem scarcely to have featured in his life, and he retained only the vaguest images of his mother, of a tired woman working 15-hour days behind the counter of the fruit shop. His relationship with his father never overcame the long childhood separation or the mounting barrier of language. 'Until I was ten he was a complete stranger to me,' Slovo recalled. '[I]n the remaining years of my childhood, we tried to get to know one another. But it was somehow too late and the atmosphere was one of detached formality. I don't ever recall being praised or punished by him. He could never express himself in English and, since I quickly lost my capacity to use Yiddish, the communication between us became more and more restricted.' When Wolfus Slovo died in 1957, all that his son could say in his honour was that he was 'a gentle man, a worker all his life' (p.19).

Whether the relationship between father and son deteriorated beyond detachment to hostility, Slovo does not say, but there is some suggestive evidence. Wolfus did not attend Joe's wedding to Ruth First in 1949, an absence which, in the cultural universe of Eastern European Jews, suggests the most profound rupture. Nor does he figure in any of the childhood recollections of the Slovo children, the oldest of whom was born in 1950. In her recent memoir, daughter Gillian alleges that Wolfus actually abandoned his children after his wife's death, and that Joe never forgave him. (Paternal abandonment was a ubiquitous feature of Jewish immigrant communities in the early twentieth century, as men steeped in a patriarchal culture fled the shame of being unable to provide for their families. The main Yiddish paper in New York went so far as to introduce a regular 'Gallery of Missing Husbands'.) Slovo himself said nothing about abandonment, but that should not lead one to discount the possibility. For all his legendary bonhomie, he remained intensely private about family matters, a quality that doubtless contributed to his strained relations with his daughters, all of whom have proved more than ready to discuss their family's failings. Whatever the facts of the case, Slovo clearly represents yet another instance of the kind of generational rupture revealed in the lives of Basner, Hirson and Podbrey.[66]

Slovo's formative political experiences came not in the family but in Sher's boarding house in Doornfontein. For Jews, as for all the other immigrant groups that flooded into Johannesburg after the opening of the gold fields, boarding houses were crucibles of working-class life, providing cheap accommodation and a measure of domestic stability in a city that remained rootless and disproportionately male. While the majority of boarding houses catered for English-speaking workers, those established by and for Eastern European Jews provided an especially important service, offering a base of cultural and linguistic familiarity in what must have seemed an utterly alien world. Yiddish remained the *lingua franca* at Sher's, and the atmosphere was communal and convivial. '[E]ven Bazaar, the African who helped serve at table, developed Jewish mannerisms and used Yiddish expressions,' Slovo recalled (p.20). In the evening, boarders gathered to play *klabberjas*, to trade horse-racing tips and, inevitably, to talk politics. It was here, in this largely male, distinctly secular version of *shtetl* life, that Slovo acquired the defining characteristics of his political persona: his irreverence, his self-deprecating wit, his love of storytelling (including his penchant for repeating the same story over and over). It was here too that Slovo first encountered what he called the 'bizarre and paradoxical' socialism of South Africa's immigrant Jews, which blended 'passionate devotion to the Soviet Union with Zionism and vicious racism towards the majority of the South African population' (p.22).

By his own account, Slovo's evolution from 'boarding house armchair socialism (in terms of which a "kaffir" remains a "kaffir")' to 'real radical politics' was 'a difficult one'. Part of the difficulty, he observed, lay in 'the absence of any relations with blacks other than in master-servant form' (p.22). The problem, which was shared by generations of immigrant leftists, first struck him shortly after the death of his mother, when an African delivery man from the fruit shop, Jonas, was killed in an accident. Having been obliged to say *kaddish* for his mother, young Joe wondered why no one prayed for Jonas, or seemed in any way undone by his death.[67] He found no answers to his questions during a brief stint in *Hashomer Hatzair*, the local chapter of which was led by a Trotskyist who 'harangued us about the permanent revolution and the role of the Jewish proletariat in far-off Palestine' without saying a word about South Africa (p.22). Under the influence of an Irish form master during his final year of school, Slovo began attending the junior section of Johannesburg's English Left Book Club. There he met Africans for the first time and began to develop some insight into the society in which he lived. By the late 1930s he had found his way to the CPSA's Sunday night rallies on the City Hall steps. Still in short pants, he approached Issy Wolfson, General Secretary of the Tailoring Workers' Union and a Party stalwart, and applied for membership. Initially rejected as too young, he was accepted as a probationary Party member in 1942.

Like Pauline Podbrey, Slovo embraced the Party with all the fervour of adolescence and 'the certainty (which I still have) that the revolution was just around the corner' (p.23). He happily devoted weekends to selling the *Guardian* in Alexandra and Sophiatown. He set out to organise the black workers at the Jewish-owned pharmaceutical factory where he worked as a clerk. At the ripe old age of 15, he was elected shop steward; at 16 he led his first strike. Distressed to learn that a 'nice Jewish boy' was 'making trouble with the natives', one of the firm's owners tried to reason with him. '[A]t heart we are all communists,' he said, adding that he himself had just subscribed 50 guineas to the Party's Medical Aid for Russia fund. Young Slovo defiantly replied that he belonged to the Communist Party, not an 'insurance company', and that a 50-guinea donation would not save the factory from the coming revolution. The owner sacked him (pp.24-6).

Slovo's dismissal coincided with a call by the CPSA for all able-bodied men to join the fight against the Nazis. Though only 17 he complied, lying about his age when his father refused to sign his enlistment papers. Posted to North Africa, he saw no combat, but he did see a bit of the world, including Palestine, an experience that disabused him of any residual Zionism. After his discharge he enrolled at the University of the Witwatersrand law school, thanks to an ex-servicemen's scholarship fund and to a special rule exempting veterans from normal matriculation requirements. Despite his lack of preparation – he had just two years of formal schooling – he proved a brilliant student, walking away with the top prize in the Law faculty. At the same time he poured himself into student politics. Exhibiting that mixture of pragmatism and ruthless sectarianism that would become his trademark, Slovo helped to engineer a left-liberal alliance, based on the shared ground of non-racialism. The alliance ensured Slovo and his Party comrades – Harold Wolpe, Ruth First, Tony O'Dowd, later Lionel Forman – an influence on campus disproportionate to their numbers, which they used to rout the less-well-organised Trotskyists. Decades after the fact, Slovo's portrayal of Wits's Trotskyists still dripped with vitriol: 'purists', he called them, who cultivated an 'aura of revolutionary charisma' yet always found some 'rationalisation' to avoid 'actual involvement in confrontations with the powers that be' (pp.32-3). Needless to say, such ill-feeling was reciprocated by the Trotskyists, who regarded Slovo and his comrades as manipulative Stalinists, slavishly following every twist and turn in the Soviet line.[68]

Slovo qualified for the bar in 1951, and spent the next dozen years living and working in Johannesburg. His recollections from the period centered on what he called the 'lighter side' of the South African justice system (p.59). While he and his clients were well known as political dissidents, the professional culture among advocates remained sufficiently strong that he could return from court and share a cup of tea with a colleague like John Vorster. (The future Prime Minister may have had Slovo in mind when he later famously remarked: 'Not all Jews are communists, but all communists are Jews.') The law itself retained some autonomy and meaning: police witnesses did not yet routinely perjure themselves; prisoners were not yet routinely assaulted; the 'individual trial could still be a battleground on whose terrain small and temporary social victories could be won' (p.58). Even when a case was weak, the sheer hypocrisy of the apartheid regime could offer a reprieve. Slovo recalled with relish the day a presiding judge, a staunch Nationalist, solicited his help in recovering photographs that revealed the judge in a flagrant violation of the Immorality Act. Slovo secured the photos; his clients, a group of African trade unionists, walked free.

The same air of unreality permeated daily life. On one hand, Slovo and Ruth First, whom he married in 1949, were leaders of an outlawed political party, committed to overthrowing the state. Both were among the accused in the 1956-61 Treason Trial. On the other hand, the couple and their three young daughters enjoyed all the creature comforts of white South African life. 'We had indoor servants, two motor cars, a gardener and a comfortable income, made even more comfortable by the astonishing generosity of Ruth's parents, Julius and Tilly' (p.110). (Julius and Tilly First were both Eastern European immigrants and founder members of the CPSA; Julius owned a local furniture factory that was sometimes used for Party conferences.) Ruth, in particular, had expensive tastes, turning out for Party functions in tailored dresses from her personal designer, simultaneously relishing and resenting the whispers her appearance provoked. Like generations of white leftists in South Africa, Slovo and First understood the anomalies of their position, and they occasionally grappled with self-doubt. It was just this insecurity, Gillian Slovo has suggested, this determination 'to show that she belonged', that led her mother to remain in South Africa in 1963 after Slovo had fled, despite almost certain detention.[69] Presumably, it was this same determination that led Tilly First to instruct Progressive MP Helen Suzman to stop agitating for her daughter's release. 'Many Blacks were suffering much more than my daughter,' Tilly reportedly said, 'and they must see that there were whites prepared to suffer as well.'[70] (Ruth, traumatised by months in solitary confinement, would eventually attempt suicide.)[71]

But all this lay beyond the horizon in the 1950s. Revolution still seemed possible, and whatever doubts and insecurities one felt were swallowed up in the excitement and romance of political work. As Gillian has put it, the 1950s were her parents' 'Camelot Years',[72] years of intense work and play, when the personal and political seemed to mesh, when something as simple as serving cocktails to black house guests represented a political act. For Joe in particular, social interaction with Africans provided a kind of psychic absolution, and his descriptions of African life carry an unmistakable tone of romanticism, not to say exoticism. Joining in the singing of African political prisoners, strolling the streets of Soweto (whose 'bustle, laughter and music' he contrasted with 'the joyless pallor of the deserted white streets' (p.97), Slovo escaped the guilt and gnawing feelings of complicity that were the wages of racial privilege.

To be sure, the couple paid a heavy social price for their political commitments, especially within the local Jewish community. The 1950s were peculiarly anxious years for South African Jewry, years of both unprecedented prosperity and acute political vulnerability. Daniel Malan's triumphant National Party made no secret of its antisemitism. Throughout the 1930s and early 1940s, the Party had pressed for an end of Jewish immigration; as late as 1943 it introduced legislation to restrict Jewish ownership of industrial and commercial firms. Unfazed by revelations of Nazi genocide, the government's first act on coming to power in 1948 was to issue pardons to prisoners convicted of pro-Nazi activities during the war. As in the pre-war decades, Jews' alleged proclivity for communism ranked at the top of the Afrikaner Nationalist indictment. Afrikaans politicians and newspapers noted the high proportion of Jews among white defendants in the Treason Trial, and later among 90-day detainees, asking rhetorically whether Jews were 'unhappy' in South Africa. In such a context, many Jews naturally felt threatened by families like the Slovos, whose conspicuous radicalism seemed to confirm antisemitic stereotypes and invite reprisal. While most Jewish leftists were by now inured to the importunings of the Board of Deputies, the shunning by neighbours, friends, even family members, was often much harder to bear. So complete was the ostracism of the Slovos that in 1963, with Ruth in detention and Joe and Julius First in exile, virtually no one from the community stepped forward to help care for the children, a flagrant violation of the cardinal Jewish obligation of *tsdokeh*, or charity.[73]

Only much later did Slovo and First realise how traumatic their peculiar lifestyle had been for their three daughters, who were asked, in essence, to bear the burdens of political activism without its emotional rewards. Simple prudence dictated not sharing details of illegal activities, yet secrecy was all too easily interpreted as rejection, especially in the absence of the kind of overt displays of affection and approval that both parents seem to have found difficult. ('Do you know,' First once confided to Pauline Podbrey, 'my mother was never able to show me any affection, to touch or caress or pet me, and I'm unable to show my girls how I feel about them. I regret it very much but there's nothing I can do about it. Do we all become like our mothers?'[74]) At the same time, the girls felt the sting of social exclusion, registered in the sidelong glances of classmates' parents, the birthday party invitations that never came, the dawning awareness that they lived (in the words of daughter Shawn's semi-autobiographical film) in 'A World Apart'.

Not surprisingly, all three girls experienced emotional difficulties growing up, culminating, in the case of Robyn, the youngest, in a decades-long battle with drug addiction. As adults, all have spoken openly of their resentment at the choices their parents made, and of the tangled sense of guilt and selfishness to which such feelings gave rise.[75] The burden of their anger was chiefly born by First, who was the family's primary caregiver and who, as a career woman in an era unacquainted with feminism, was cruelly stigmatised by contemporaries as a 'poor mother'. Looking back, however, all three women have directed their animus mostly at Joe, whom they remember as 'absent', preoccupied, and, for all his loquaciousness, unable to find the 'sort of words, very simple stuff' to communicate his feelings for them.[76] Such criticisms clearly stung the ageing Slovo; though he never said so explicitly, one senses that he found his daughters' rehashing of childhood traumas both unseemly and unfair. In his memoir, he devoted just two pages to the issue, acknowledging his and Ruth's failures as parents and offering an oblique apology: 'Were we, in the circumstances, morally entitled to have a family?' (p.111)[77]

It is difficult to know how to interpret the gulf between parents and daughters. The simplest solution is to dismiss the girls as spoiled, self-absorbed white South Africans, unable to appreciate the greater cause to which their parents had devoted their lives. (The consensus response of a group of ANC leaders invited to a screening of 'A World Apart' was that the daughter in the film needed 'a good slap'.[78]) A less judgemental observer might see in the rift a characteristically post-war 'generation gap', between parents taught the virtues of a 'stiff upper lip' and children steeped in a 'therapeutic culture' that invites self-revelation, not to say narcissism. There are doubtless grains of truth in both interpretations. In the present context, however, what is most striking is the way in which family members enacted, all unwittingly, a classic immigrant script. All of the qualities that Slovo and First detected in their parents and which their children, in turn, ascribe to them – emotional remoteness, a dearth of explicit approval and overt signs of affection, great wordiness combined with great reticence about intimate matters, a refusal to avow pain and fear – were drawn from a Jewish cultural repertoire only dimly understood by Slovo and First and completely lost on their more thoroughly anglicised children.

The years of Slovo's emergence as a Party leader witnessed some of the proudest accomplishments in the history of the South African left: the consummation of a formal alliance between the ANC and a reorganised SACP in the early 1950s; the adoption of the Freedom Charter in 1956; the creation of Umkhonto we Sizwe and the launching of the armed struggle in 1961, a process in which Slovo played an enthusiastic, if decidedly amateurish, role.[79]

Yet for many socialists these were also years of bitter disillusionment. Moscow's crass manipulation of the international student movement; the decadence of Soviet satellite regimes in Eastern Europe; the crushing of the Hungarian Revolution; Kruschev's revelations of Stalinist atrocities: all these events and more sowed doubt and despair. Yet if Slovo ever entertained such feelings, he never expressed them publicly. On the contrary, he remained an indefatigable defender of both the Party and the Soviet Union. In his memoir, he did concede that the SACP might have taken Krushchev's 'secret speech' to the Twentieth Party Congress more seriously, yet in the next breath he pointed to 'the strides which have been made since 1956 to restore socialist morality'. The 'perversion of socialist norms' under Stalin and Mao may have 'put back the clock of socialist achievement', he concluded, but the final victory of the Soviet-led international communist movement remained certain (p.109).

In his unshakeable faith, Slovo stands in sharp contrast not only to apostates like Hyman Basner and Pauline Podbrey but to Ruth First, his wife, who came to flout the Party line as flagrantly as he defended it. As a journalist and professional academic rather than a Party official, First naturally had greater scope for independent thinking than Slovo. She was also profoundly influenced by a four-month visit to China in the 1950s, which gave her a less Soviet-centred perspective on the global communist movement, as well as a handy way to needle her husband.[80] By all accounts, the marriage was a tempestuous one, marked by extreme competitiveness and blazing political rows, with First typically deriding Slovo as a hack and he raging against her irresponsible 'academic' view of the world. Both took solace in 'other, more or less serious, involvements', Slovo's discreet euphemism for extra-marital affairs (p.48). (Among the revelations in Gillian's family memoir was the existence of Slovo's unacknowledged son, Michael Sachs, borne by the wife of fellow exile Albie Sachs.) In his autobiographical musings after First's assassination, Slovo tried to put the best face on things, portraying their marriage as a profound 'mutuality', almost a symbiosis: 'she never allowed me to get away with the cliched catechism which tempts all who become part of an apparatus; and I never allowed her to float comfortably in the sea of criticism against so-called orthodoxy, which characterises the changing fashions of the critics on the left, particularly those with an academic background' (pp.48-9). Yet he also conceded that First bore a far heavier burden than he, enduring not only persecution by the state but rejection by her supposed comrades, who regarded her as 'deviationist' and dangerously undisciplined. Indeed, by the early 1980s, First had been completely marginalised within the SACP, a fact that did not prevent South African security forces from murdering her, nor Party members from posthumously embracing her as a martyr.

For a character so blithe, so certain of history's course, the collapse of the Soviet Union and of the broader international movement that it sustained must have been devastating. Given its provenance, the autobiography has little to say on the subject, but one can chart Slovo's reaction from the selections collected at the end of the book, as well as from his published writings from the period. In a controversial 1990 discussion paper entitled 'Has Socialism Failed?' and in a follow-up paper entitled 'Beyond the Stereotype: The SACP in the Past, Present and Future', Slovo insisted on the Party's achievements and continuing relevance, even as he candidly acknowledged its errors – 'blind adherence' to Moscow, the distortion of 'democratic centralism' into 'centralism, pure and simple', the use of other organisations as 'transmission belts for party policy'.[81] He also acknowledged, if he did not entirely resolve, the tension between the Party's avowed commitment to popular democracy and its self-proclaimed vanguardist role. In both essays, Slovo remained determinedly, defiantly optimistic: communism's errors were historically contingent 'distortions', that in no way vitiated the 'essentially humane and democratic' character of socialism; the SACP still had a vital role to play in South Africa's future, albeit in a pluralistic rather than one-party system; the 'ideological contest' with capitalism continued.[82]

On the subject of his long and vigorous defence of the Soviet Union, Slovo was contrite, if singularly unpersuasive. 'I was wrong and I am ashamed of some of the traps I was led into,' he told an interviewer in 1994. 'If you've ever been a member of an official delegation you learn less about a country than sitting in the British Museum. You don't meet the people, you don't actually see the conditions. People said there were gulags, millions of people incarcerated there. We were assured there were no such things. We didn't have the opportunity to check.' He went on to say, somewhat self-contradictorily, that he had begun to harbour doubts 'in the mid-1960s', but, having 'seen the alternative at close hand', chose to remain silent. 'The choice you face is whether you can continue to contribute to the struggle or not,' he explained. 'At that stage, independence was just not tolerated' (p.190). The problem, of course, is that Slovo himself was one of the chief architects of the SACP's political culture, including its utter intolerance of independent thinking. It was Slovo who, on hearing Pauline Podbrey's reports from Hungary, called her a 'reactionary', and who accused another comrade, Hilda Bernstein, of 'opting out of our struggle' when she confessed her concerns about the Soviet invasion of Czechoslovakia.[83] Like the proverbial orphan pleading for clemency after murdering his parents, the circumstances that Slovo offered in extenuation were much of his own making.

Ultimately, the collapse of the international communist movement is significant not just for what it meant to Slovo, but for what it meant to South Africa as it embarked, at precisely the same moment, on the path toward a negotiated settlement. Slovo's returning *bon mot* – 'As I was saying 27 years ago before I was so rudely interrupted …' – could not obscure the fact that everything had changed in the intervening years (p.193). The collapse of the Soviet Union robbed the ANC and SACP of a crucial material and ideological resource. At the same time, the armed struggle that Slovo had helped to launch three decades before had essentially failed. Even as South Africa spiralled into chaos, the apartheid regime maintained a vast preponderance of physical force and considerable will to use it. These were hardly the triumphal circumstances to which Slovo and his comrades had dreamed of returning.

Slovo's approach to these interlocking problems was frankly pragmatic. At a time when some in his party imagined that urban 'insurrection' would pave the way for an immediate transition to socialism, he insisted on the priority of a negotiated transition to democracy. When early negotiations bogged down in distrust and mutual recrimination, it was Slovo who first proposed the ANC's unilateral suspension of the armed struggle. Later, when negotiations again stalled, it was he who proposed the idea of 'sunset clauses', in effect guaranteeing National Party politicians and civil servants a substantial role in a transitional government. He exhibited the same pragmatism in his eight-month tenure as Minister of Housing. Slovo recognised housing provision as one of the new government's most important tests, and he counted among his proudest achievements his ministry's white paper, which pledged a million new houses in five years. Significantly, he accepted that the fastest and most efficient means to meet that pledge was by using 'capitalist forms', including private investment and individual ownership. Such an approach could, of course, be rationalised in terms of the prevailing 'two-stage' theory of revolution, yet there was something unsettling in the spectacle of a lifelong communist preaching the virtues of 'sweat equity' and the need for tax incentives to tempt private lenders into the township mortgage market.

Slovo clearly recognised the perils of pragmatism, the danger, as he put it, of 'snatching defeat from the jaws of victory'. He understood that change in the 'New South Africa' would come slowly, and that the longer the new government took to deliver concrete improvements in people's lives, the more vulnerable it would become to militant challenges from below. He also realised that the ANC included bourgeois elements, which, having reaped the benefits of the first-stage 'national revolution', would be only too happy to defer socialist revolution until the indefinite future.[84] It was precisely here, he believed, that a revitalised SACP could play an important role, operating both as an 'independent force' and as an integral part of the governing alliance. As 'the undisputed pioneers of genuine nonracial political organisation', communists stood as a bulwark against both narrow nationalist tendencies within the ANC and what he called the 'populist racism' of the Pan-African Congress (p.114). (Even in his final incarnation as a mellow elder statesman, Slovo remained a master of political invective.) Chastened by the collapse of the global movement to which he had devoted his life, Slovo nonetheless remained convinced that socialism was coming, and that the Communist Party would be its avatar. The alternative was simply too bleak to contemplate. 'The wretched of the earth make up over 90 per cent of humanity,' he observed in a letter to Cuba's ambassador in South Africa, written shortly before his death. 'They live either in capitalist or capitalist-oriented societies. For them, if socialism is not the answer, there is no answer at all' (p.211).

Joe Slovo died in January 1995. In an apt, though apparently unwitting, gesture, a memorial service was held in Johannesburg City Hall, where young Yossel, still clad in short pants, had joined the battle with pro-Nazi Greyshirts more than half a century before. In deference to his wishes, his body was buried in Soweto's Avalon Cemetery, an expression of his identification with South Africa's dispossessed majority and, one suspects, a final judgement against the community that had rejected his gifts. At the funeral itself, a muddy, carnivalesque affair attended by over 40 000 mourners, most of them African, the Chief Rabbi of South Africa, Cyril Harris, praised Slovo's humanism, gently chiding 'those religious people who acquiesced, passively or wrongly, with the inequalities of yesteryear'. An African speaker praised Slovo, without intentional irony, as a 'good Christian'. After the funeral, his three daughters debated whether, in the absence of a male heir, they should hire a mourner to say *kaddish*. They chose not to do so.[85]

IX

'Why are so many of you Jews?' Baruch Hirson's Special Branch interrogators demanded. Denis Goldberg, a Rivonia trialist incarcerated with Hirson at Pretoria Central Prison, recalls being awakened each day by a police warder walking down the cellblock: 'Morning Jew. Morning Jew. Morning Jew. Morning Jew.' (When one inmate protested that he was not Jewish, the warder amended the greeting to 'Morning Communist.') The first question police asked Keith Coleman, a student activist detained in the 1980s, was: 'Is jy 'n Jood?' SACP activist Raymond Suttner remembers his interrogators as 'obsessed with my being Jewish, absolutely obsessed'. Suttner's colleague, Jeremy Cronin, found it virtually impossible to persuade the Security Police that he was not a Jew.[86]

Faced with such palpable irrationality, one is tempted to dismiss the whole subject. Manifestly, the vast majority of South African Jews were not communists, or political activists of any kind. Nor were all, or even most, white leftists Jewish. Of the 25 other 'politicals' in Pretoria Central Prison with Baruch Hirson and Denis Goldberg, for example, 16, or roughly 60 per cent, were gentiles, including three Afrikaners who had grown up in the Dutch Reformed Church. And yet the question lingers. Whatever the precise proportion of Jews in the South African left, there is no question that they were significantly overrepresented. And if the values and convictions of such activists were not 'uniquely' or 'essentially' Jewish, there is no doubt that many entered radical politics along distinctly Jewish pathways – via the Yiddish-Speaking Branch of the International Socialist League, the Jewish Workers' Club, *Hashomer Hatzair*, or any of a dozen groups expressing what Joe Slovo called 'the bizarre and paradoxical' socialism of Eastern European immigrant Jews. The challenge to historians is to understand these realities, without lapsing back into the kind of sweeping generalisations that plague the current 'Jews and Apartheid' debate.

The handful of lives surveyed here cannot provide any definitive solution to the problem, but they can at least help us to refine our questions. All four individuals were not only Jews, but products of a particular immigrant community. Three were born in the Baltic; the fourth was born in Johannesburg of Latvian parents. In the context of Jewish immigration to South Africa, all were relative latecomers: the first, Hyman Basner, arrived in Johannesburg in 1906, 25 years after the assassination of Tsar Alexander, the event that set the Jewish exodus from the Russian Empire in motion; the last, Joe Slovo, arrived in 1936, at the proverbial eleventh hour. All four families had endured the wrenching poverty of Jewish life in Eastern Europe, and they remained in impecunious circumstances in their new home. In each, the wages of economic marginality were compounded by a kind of liminal social status. Jews were no longer 'the pariah among pariahs', yet their religion, dress, language, even in some cases their physiognomy, marked them as something other than fully-fledged white South Africans. In the parlance of the time, they were 'Peruvians'.

All these circumstances left their imprint on immigrant family life. Basner, Hirson, Podbrey and Slovo all grew up in emotionally desiccated homes, in which the traditional reticence between children and parents, especially their fathers, had grown into a chasm of sullen silence. Family bonds were further loosened by the experience of long separation, by the mounting barrier of language, and by immigrant children's immersion in a robustly English educational system. Organised religion, which had done so much to structure and mediate family relationships in the old country, might have helped narrow the breach, but its influence, already declining in the turn-of-the-century Pale, dwindled rapidly in South Africa. All four subjects grew up knowing virtually nothing about their parents' lives, their religious heritage, or the wider Eastern European world from which they sprang.

For such individuals radical politics, and the Communist Party in particular, represented more than just a new political affiliation. It offered community, human contact, the warmth and solidarity otherwise absent from their daily lives. Perhaps not coincidentally, all entered radical politics during adolescence or early adulthood, a period characteristically marked by the search for identity and purpose, as well as by elevated tension between parents and children. The most obvious example is young Joe Slovo, a virtual orphan, approaching Issy Wolfson on the steps of the Johannesburg City Hall and applying for membership in the CPSA, but similar elements run through the stories of Hyman Basner and Pauline Podbrey. Baruch Hirson stands as an exception in the sense that he never joined the Party, yet in other ways he offers the best example. Awkward, intense, desperately lonely, Hirson was first drawn into the Zionist Youth Movement by the promise of a dance. It was in politics, in the ZYM and later in *Hashomer Hatzair*, that he found a voice, a sense of his own value, an outlet for his long-frustrated passion.

All this helps to qualify the notion, already insinuating itself into South African historiography, of a 'tradition' of Jewish radicalism, carried intact from Eastern Europe to South Africa. It is certainly true that Jewish immigrants had greater exposure to left-wing ideas than other white South Africans; one could always find a political conversation in Sher's boarding house, in Issy Diamond's barber shop, or in the ubiquitous Jewish cafés in Ferreirastown or Doornfontein. It is also likely that the experience of discrimination in the Russian Empire had taught many immigrants to look upon constituted authority with a jaundiced eye. Yet there was nothing inevitable or automatic about Jewish radicalism. On the contrary, the burden of all the lives examined here is of discontinuity, of rupture. Joe Slovo lost his mother and was estranged from his father. Pauline Podbrey's father was a communist, but by the time she entered politics he had left the Party in disgust. Baruch Hirson and Hyman Basner only learned of their fathers' trade union backgrounds when they were adults; growing up, both regarded their parents as completely uninterested in politics. (Ronnie Kasrils, another first-generation Lithuanian-South African who made his mark in the SACP, reports an identical experience.[87]) Far from encouraging political involvement, these immigrant parents viewed their children's forays into radical politics with various combinations of indifference, disapproval and alarm.

Obviously these observations need to be offered with great circumspection, and with a frank acknowledgement of abundant counter-examples (beginning with Slovo's wife, Ruth First, whose parents were prominent Communist Party members). Yet if nothing else, the questions posed here can help us to look at familiar evidence with fresh eyes. Consider the case of the Sachs family, surely the most celebrated of South Africa's multi-generational Jewish radical families. As every South African historian knows, Albie Sachs, a leader of the ANC in exile and today a justice on South Africa's Constitutional Court, is the son of Lithuanian-born trade unionist Solly Sachs, a one-time CPSA member who won great notoriety in the interwar years for his success organising garment workers. (Fittingly, Justice Sachs was the featured speaker at the 1997 launch of Immanuel Suttner's *Cutting Through the Mountain*.) Yet if one moves back in time, to the immigrant generation itself, the image of continuity is almost completely reversed. The story of the Sachs family's passage from Lithuania to South Africa is lyrically told in *Multitude of Dreams*, the 1949 autobiography of Solly's younger brother, Bernard. 'Bennie' remembered his home as a barren, 'love-less' place, presided over by a bitter, sceptical mother and a remote, often absent father. (In addition to the eight years he spent in South Africa before sending for his family, Sachs's father was jailed for theft in both Lithuania and South Africa.) On those occasions when the family was together, an 'unnatural tension' reigned, punctuated by quarrels and 'only the minimum essential words'. Religion, which had dominated Bennie's emotional life through childhood and early adolescence, did not survive the passage to South Africa. Into this 'vacuum' Bolshevism 'rushed in like a whirlwind'. He began to attend socials and lectures of the International Socialist League, where he 'experienced a spiritual warmth that was entirely lacking in our home'. 'These people seemed to display much more interest in me than ever my father did, and the melancholy that had overcome me during my first years in South Africa soon gave way to an unbounded enthusiasm for life and its possibilities'. It is difficult to imagine a more explicit statement of the intersecting familial, political and cultural dynamics at play in the lives we have been discussing.[88]

None of this is meant to revive notions of 'anti-father complexes' or prolonged adolescence or any of the other simple-minded theories devised in the Cold War West to explain communist 'deviancy'. Nor is it to suggest that the experience of marginality led inexorably to political radicalism. Marginality, after all, can cut both ways; for every Jewish immigrant who found a refuge from loneliness in the Communist Party or identified with blacks as fellow underdogs, there were easily ten who pursued the opposite tack, fleeing isolation and the stigma of difference by conspicuously embracing the political and racial assumptions of white South Africa. The point, put simply, is that immigration was a profoundly disruptive experience, and that South Africa's celebrated Jewish radicalism may be less a product of a community 'tradition', handed down from generation to generation, than a function of historically specific processes of dislocation and conflict.

The irony, of course, is that in fleeing one kind of marginality immigrant leftists ensured another. It is difficult to imagine today, when Jewish socialists sit in parliament and on the Constitutional Court, just how isolated these people were in apartheid South Africa – how far, as it were, 'beyond the Pale'. Hounded by a brutal, authoritarian state, they also found themselves increasingly isolated and shunned by their communities. The burden of isolation was made heavier by the enormous gulf between white radicals and the black South Africans they presumed to redeem. To be sure, white leftists had some success organising Africans, particularly in the burgeoning trade union movement of the 1930s and 40s, and many participated in the multiracial bohemian culture that was such a prominent, if fleeting, feature of 1950s Johannesburg. In the main, however, the strictures of apartheid ensured that most white radicals remained remote, socially and politically, from blacks. The bitter reality was driven home weekly, as they set out to Alexandra or Sophiatown to peddle the latest copy of *The Guardian* or *Socialist Action* to indifferent passers-by.

Small wonder that white leftists indulged in destructive sectarianism. Indeed, most of the signature maladies of the South African left – elevation of seemingly minor theoretical and policy differences into momentous questions of loyalty and betrayal; the intolerance of dissent; the complete subsumption of personal into political life – were at least partly products of isolation, of working in tightly circumscribed, highly pressured circumstances. The same factors may help explain, if not entirely excuse, the SACP's notorious subservience to Moscow, and the enormous difficulty that Party members had relinquishing their faith in the Soviet Union. For South Africa's embattled white communists, allegiance to the Soviet Union offered more than mere material and ideological support – it also offered precious validation, a sense of participation in a global historical enterprise, to people who confronted daily the pain of rejection and the spectre of insignificance.

If these lives cast fresh light on some of the worst aspects of the South African left, they also illuminate some of its best features, most notably its contribution to South Africa's unlikely tradition of non-racialism. Strikingly, none of the four subjects was initially motivated by opposition to racism. Like most white South Africans, they grew up in a world in which blacks were at once ubiquitous and absent, and none seems to have found that situation particularly troubling. Only after becoming politically active did they begin to grapple with South Africa's peculiar concatenation of racial and class oppression, Basner in the context of his law practice, Hirson, Podbrey and Slovo as union organisers. There is something at once pathetic and inspiring in the spectacle of passionate young socialists, already versed in Marx and Engels and Trotsky, struggling to come to terms with the aspirations, indeed the very existence, of people who pervaded their daily lives. If their initial outreaches were sometimes awkward, if (as Hirson argues) white socialists proved too ready to accommodate narrowly nationalist aspirations, there is no gainsaying their sincerity or significance. No less a figure than Nelson Mandela has credited white leftists such as Hyman Basner (who gave him a job as an apprentice attorney), Joe Slovo and Ruth First with weaning him and his Youth League comrades from their early Africanism, by presenting them with something they had never imagined possible: white people who were not only genuinely free of racism, but prepared to commit their lives to the liberation of South Africa's dispossessed majority.

It is worth re-emphasising, in closing, the tentative nature of these conclusions, and the urgent need for further research on virtually all of the questions broached in this essay. Doubtless the questions themselves will change as Jews continue to negotiate their position within the 'New South Africa' (for surely this is the struggle which lay behind the current controversy). If nothing else, however, these lives reveal the bankruptcy of the kind of ahistorical, essentialist notions of Jewish identity and politics that are the stuff of contemporary public debate. More broadly, they show the folly of the current South African penchant for broad-stroke history, for stories of heroes and villains, crusaders and quislings. For better or worse, history rarely affords such neat resolutions or unalloyed judgments. A character like Joe Slovo devoted his life to the quest for a just, inclusive South Africa, freed from the scourges of racism and exploitation, yet he also epitomised many of the ugliest qualities of Stalinism. Arriving in South Africa as a bald, penniless ten-year-old, he remained in many respects the quintessential Eastern European Jewish immigrant, even as he disavowed (and was disavowed by) that community. As an old man ravaged by cancer, he watched, in hope and in perplexity, the near simultaneous collapses of the apartheid regime he had battled and the Soviet regime he had served. Our task as historians, writing in the early days of South Africa's new democratic dispensation, is to encompass these seemingly irreconcilable realities, to nurture an appreciation of ambiguity and paradox in a society that remains inhospitable, if not hostile, to such sensibilities. And there is no better place to begin than with the lives and legacies of those who lived beyond the Pale.

Accounting for Jewish Radicals in Apartheid South Africa

GIDEON SHIMONI

GIDEON SHIMONI was born in South Africa and is a graduate of the University of the Witwatersrand. He holds the Shlomo Argov Chair in Israel-Diaspora Relations at the Hebrew University of Jerusalem where he teaches at the Institute of Contemporary Jewry. His main fields of research and publication are the history of Zionism and the history of Jewish communities in English-speaking countries. He is the author of *Jews and Zionism: the South African Experience* (1980), *The Zionist Ideology* (1995) and has recently completed a new study of the Jewish community in South Africa's apartheid years.

The disproportionate involvement and salience of persons of Jewish birth in the radical resistance to the apartheid regime, particularly in the ranks of the Communist Party, is a highly conspicuous fact. Equally evident is the fact that the convictions and actions of these persons were deviant not only in relation to the white population but also to the Jewish community. Of course, this is not a phenomenon unique to the Jews of South Africa. In the modern history of most Jewish communities not only in Europe but also in countries of the New World, and not least of all in the USA, Jews have been ubiquitously prominent in radical leftist movements. There is no dearth of attempts by sociologists and political scientists to explain the phenomenon, but consensus on an explanatory theory remains elusive. Some theorists have speculated that certain moral and social values inhering in the Jewish religion predispose Jews to liberal or radical forms of social consciousness.[1] The supposedly pertinent values thus identified in Judaism are: its this-worldliness and the attendant messianic belief in ultimate social perfectibility; mutual responsibility for the welfare of others that translates into social justice; respect for learning, which supposedly leads to rationality in human affairs.

This theory, which might be labelled 'the Jewish values' theory, has great mythic appeal for Jews in liberal Western societies because it serves, as it were, to give Judaism a good name. It is characteristic that one finds Jews who celebrate the freeing of South Africa from apartheid, and at the same time wish to identify strongly as Jews, drawn to the 'Jewish values' approach. This is evident in the reflections of even as critical and perceptive an inquirer as Immanuel Suttner, the editor of an invaluable anthology of interviews with Jews who were in one way or another prominently involved in the struggle against apartheid. Explaining what prompted him to produce this work, Suttner admits candidly that 'by celebrating the activism of this minority and in claiming it as the positive manifestation of an essential Jewish preoccupation with "making right" the world', he seeks to reassert his 'own value as a Jew'. In his thought-provoking afterword to the book, Suttner grapples sincerely with the question whether the phenomenon of Jewish radicals can be attributed to inherently Jewish values. Although he recognises that the sociological position of Jews is an important factor in explaining the phenomenon, he yet reverts to attribution of 'atavistic religious values'. He suggests in particular that 'the aspect of Jewish tradition they link up to is the tradition of non-conformism, rebuke and solidarity with the underdog', going back to Moses' killing the Egyptian overseer and the message of the prophets.[2]

But the 'Jewish values' theory rests on simplistic if not wholly faulty assumptions concerning Judaism itself because, as any serious student of Judaism and the history of the Jews knows, there can be no doubt that countervailing conservative values also inhere in the Jewish religion and with no less potential effect on the behavior of Jews.[3] It therefore becomes necessary to explain why Judaism's 'liberal', rather than its conservative, values exert an influence on some Jews and not on others. Moreover, there is overwhelming empirical evidence of an unmistakeably inverse relationship between Orthodox religious adherence and liberal or radical activism. In South Africa, as elsewhere, the more observant of religious observance a Jew was, the less likely he or she was to be found among even the moderate adversaries of the apartheid system, not to speak of its radical opponents. If the various forms of moderate resistance to apartheid have included some observant Orthodox Jews, and even an occasional militant rabbi, these were clearly the exception rather than the rule. As for radical opponents of apartheid, without exception they were only non-religious Jews and, more often than not, self-declared atheists.

Many of the Jews who joined the struggle for liberty in South Africa espoused a dogmatic communism and slavish obedience to the Soviet line, which commanded the disavowal of any Jewish identity and engendered a self-blinding indifference to the crushing of liberty for Jews in the Soviet Union. Yet it is noteworthy that some of the Jewish radicals in South Africa maintained a positive, self-accepting attitude towards their Jewish identity even while subordinating it to their identification with what they perceived as an infinitely more important universal cause. Albie Sachs, whose radical record included important roles in the Congress of Democrats, and afterwards in the ANC in exile, during which time an assassination attempt by South African security agents left him severely wounded, has explained it in these words: 'We were Jewish, there was no doubt about it, it was never an issue.'[4] He adds however that it was never a pivotal factor in his life. In like vein he has also said: 'To this day I never let a snigger or snide remark about Jews pass and, while I hated and still hate any denial of being a Jew or any attempt to ingratiate oneself or become invisible, I did not feel in my bones that the central and dominating feature of my existence was my Jewishness.'[5] In autobiographical accounts one finds evocations of Jewish historical experience as victims of prejudice, discrimination and hatred, and especially the horrors of the Holocaust. In this context it is claimed by some, but not all, radicals that their rejection of discrimination, racism and oppression, and their striving to remake the world, is somehow rooted in a humanistic Jewish ethos and in the Jewish historical experience of suffering. This is no doubt what Pauline Podbrey meant when, having been asked to relate her Jewishness to her role in the radical resistance, she said: 'I've always felt very conscious of being Jewish, and that my communist sympathies had their roots in Jewish ethics and Jewish morality.' Adding that she was also deeply influenced by knowledge of the Holocaust in which members of her family perished, she described it as 'a living sore in her body'. 'I think that by not aligning yourself with the oppressed you are betraying the Jewish tradition,' she averred.[6]

Clearly, what these persons refer to as Jewishness is not coterminous with Judaism as religion. For in most cases the autobiographical recollections not only of the South African-born Jewish radicals but even of those born in the far more intensely Jewish milieu of Eastern Europe reveal exposure to only the most superficial and uninspiring Jewish religious experience. On the basis of the evidence, crediting 'Judaism' with a formative influence is hardly credible. A more plausible comprehension of their self-imputed Jewishness has to do with the position of Jews in society. By the same token a more adequate explanation of their proclivity for political radicalism may be posited in terms of social marginality, that is to say being outsiders in relation to the vested interests of society's established state authorities, social classes, and dominant ethnic group or groups. Of course, the radicalising potential of marginality is most acute when Jews are directly victimised, as was the case in Tsarist Russia, for example. This cannot be said to have applied in South Africa, where Jews had full civic equality and enjoyed all of the privileges of the dominant white population. Yet even there, the rigidly segmented social structure of white society and the long shadow of anti-Jewish agitation rendered Jews outsiders, to a degree sufficient to generate in many of them alienation from the established order, conventions and ideological norms of society. This facilitated the adoption of counter-normative ideologies by a disproportionate number of Jews relative to other whites.

Thus proponents of the Jewish values theory of Jewish radicalism will find no substantiation in the life of Joe Slovo, perhaps the most important personality in the entire pantheon of radical whites who committed themselves heart and soul to the struggle in South Africa. Even though he was born as Yossel Slovo in the small Lithuanian village Obelai, the attribution of his later radicalism in South Africa to specifically Jewish social values imbibed from his childhood education there would be fanciful. Witness Slovo's own uninspiring recollection: 'The synagogue was our school and an ear-twisting sadistic rabbi forced whatever he could into our heads from the Hebrew version [sic] of the Old Testament, which was our only textbook.'[7] Nor was there any Judaic substance to his adolescent life in South Africa. The poor social and economic situation of Slovo's family seems to have been a far more formative factor in his life. He spent his youth in the Jewish immigrant milieu of the Doornfontein and Yeoville suburbs of Johannesburg in the 1930s and 1940s. It was a milieu of economically struggling Jews; the first generation in South Africa, partly working class (mostly artisans or unskilled employees) and partly lower middle class. Preceded by his father, his mother and the ten-year-old Yossel had been brought to South Africa in 1936. Soon after, his mother died in childbirth and his father barely eked out a living variously as a shopkeeper or bread deliverer for the Jewish-owned Crystal Bakery and Delicatessen in Doornfontein. Much of the time they lived in a boarding house and Joe had to find work as a dispatch clerk in the firm of Sive Brothers and Karnovsky, at the cost of not completing his high school education. Slovo's elementary schooling was at the Jewish Government School. But, notwithstanding the name and the fact that the majority of its pupils were Jewish children, there was never any Jewish religious or cultural substance in the education its pupils received.[8]

It is the demonstrable situation of social marginality in relation to the dual Afrikaner-British stock white society, rather than the influence of values presumed to inhere in Judaism, that fits the case of Joe Slovo, as also of most other Jewish radicals. Moreover it was a double marginality, that is to say in addition to social marginality in relation to the established society of whites, also marginality in relation to the established Jewish community. One might spell out the specifics of the case as follows: in relation not only to institutionalised white society but also to the established, upwardly mobile Jewish community of Johannesburg and its norms of religious and Zionist identification, Slovo's was a marginal and alienated social environment. It was economically poor, irreverently non-religious, and steeped in the leftist sympathies and rhetoric – still oriented on the old world and unrelated to the South African scene – that typified many of the post-Russian revolution emigrants to the New World countries. Slovo himself described this ambience perceptively:

> My leaning towards left socialist politics was also formed partly by the bizarre and paradoxical embrace of socialism shared by most of the immigrants who filled the boarding houses in which we lived. I say bizarre because they tended to combine a passionate devotion to the Soviet Union with a Zionism and vicious racism towards the majority of the South African population.[9]

Joe Slovo's experience was similar to that of most Jewish radicals of his and the preceding generation. Judaism's putative liberal or radical values, if at all invoked, seem to have been retrospectively imagined and read into their lives, sometimes by themselves but more often by others. This is nicely illustrated in the eulogy of the writer and poet Lionel Abrahams for the 'utterly non-sectarian' Barney Simon, whose innovative theatrical work flouted the racist taboos of South Africa: 'I like imagining an invisible *yarmulke* on Barney's pate,' wrote Abrahams.[10] Chief Rabbi Cyril Harris probably came much closer to a true description in his genuine but carefully worded eulogy at Slovo's funeral when he acknowledged that 'there are two major motivations towards helping fellow human beings. One is religious ... The second motivation is humanitarian. This was Joe Slovo's way,' stated Rabbi Harris.[11] Notwithstanding Slovo's rigidly communist disaffection from Judaism, and rejection of Zionism, all who knew him attest to his unselfconscious Jewish behavioral traits, especially his buoyant flair for Jewish humour. These attributes, however, do not signify any traceable inspiration in terms of putative values of Judaism that could explain his joining the radical liberation movement in South Africa.

A marginality theory of Jewish radicalism takes cognisance of Jewishness, but in the sense of the familial and ethnic social environment that characterised a segment of the Jewish immigrant generation rather than in the sense of religion. It is in terms of such marginality that one may best account for the relative facility with which Jewish persons were able to feel disaffected from the apartheid system devised and enforced by the established ethnic groups of the white society or their political and social élites. Although such disaffection was not unknown within the established élites themselves – the communist leader Bram Fischer, scion of a famous Afrikaner national family, is a striking example – it was certainly far more exceptional and 'unnatural' than the disaffection demonstrated by Jewish persons. Albie Sachs has offered this insightful explanation of the Jewish factor in the liberal or radical political proclivity of Jews such as himself:

> A sensitivity to suffering, to discrimination ... I'm sure that was all facilitated by the Jewish background. So, yes, from that point of view, a broader sensitivity to discrimination and suffering and exclusion would have come through. But not through an organised sense of saying: 'We are Jews. We've been discriminated against, we've suffered.' It's more through the fact that you didn't automatically regard yourself as part of the ruling elite in the country where you were, in the school where you were, or in the society in which you lived.[12]

As has been suggested above, an ancillary of the marginality theory arises from the observable correlation between involvement of Jewish persons in opposition to the established societal system and their personal alienation from the Jewish communal and religious framework, or even repudiation of it.[13] Indeed, the autobiographical record of almost every Jew who became involved in the radical opposition in South Africa provides evidence of such alienation. To be sure, it is a compound alienation – usually an initial estrangement facilitates the person's deviation from Jewish community norms. This then provokes a reaction – embarrassment or disassociation or even hostility – from the institutional élites whether lay or religious, which in turn compounds the person's disaffection from Jewish institutional life, sometimes quite bitterly so.[14]

At this point of our analysis it should be noted that also the extraordinary valence of Zionism for Jews in South Africa is at least partly explicable in terms of the same basic situation of marginality in relation to established South African society. Not, to be sure, the Zionism that was expressed in sentiments and philanthropy – these were an established norm of the Jewish community – but the Zionism propounded by the youth movements. This demanded what is termed in Hebrew *hagshama*, meaning 'fulfilment'. For, in the formative period from the 1930s to the early 1960s, the same milieu of immigrant Jews and their first-generation offspring produced the majority of the young Zionists who took the path of Zionist 'fulfilment' through *aliya* (literally, 'ascending' to the Land of Israel), aspiring particularly to join the *halutz* (literally 'pioneering') form of socialist settlement embodied in the *kibbutz* commune. It was in Doornfontein and similar urban suburbs of first- and second-generation Jewish settlement, such as Oranjezicht and Vredehoek in Cape Town, that the core strength of the youth movements lay. These were: *Hashomer Hatzair*, *Habonim*, the Zionist Socialist Youth (later *Dror*), the General Zionist Youth (later *Bnei Zion*), *Hashomer Hadati* (later *Bnei Akiva*) and also *Betar*. The home and immediate social background of communists like Joe Slovo or the brothers Norman and Leon Levy or Harold Wolpe was much the same as that of most of the aspirant 'fulfilment Zionists' who, forgoing university studies and middle-class professions, underwent agricultural training in special training farms established in South Africa, and left South Africa for Israel.[15]

The appeal of Zionism as taught in the youth movements was predicated not alone on the still-strong ethnic identification of first-generation offspring of immigrants, but also on their social marginality and sense of alienation from established white society. Especially in *Hashomer Hatzair*, *Habonim* and the Zionist Socialist Youth, the incompatibility of racial apartheid and Jewish values was a cardinal and emphatic ideological premise. In essence, the ideological position of these Zionists was that complicity in the apartheid system was unconscionable but it was at least as false to authentic Judaism as well as to self-esteeming secular Jewishness to abandon – as Jewish radicals did – the Jewish people's own aspiration to freedom, national fulfilment and cultural renaissance, all embodied in the cause of Zionism. They considered it characteristic of the exilic (*galut*) situation of Diaspora Jews that out of concern for the Jewish community's safety and welfare, the communal leadership falsely denied that there was a collective Jewish imperative to oppose apartheid. Telling Jewish youth – as did the Jewish Board of Deputies – that if they felt they must oppose the evils of society they should do so not as Jews, but only as individual citizens, was virtually a renunciation of the relevance of Jewish values to the actual lives of Jews. It dichotomised 'the Jew' and 'the man' and signified Diaspora Jewry's moral bankruptcy. But equally unacceptable was the willingness of anti-Zionist Jewish radicals to place the Jewish community in jeopardy by insisting that it declare war on white supremacy. The entire dilemma was regarded as a manifestation of the post-Holocaust *galut* condition; a condition no longer of direct persecution and abject suffering, but still of vulnerability and moral deficiency. The conclusion drawn was that only in an autonomous Jewish society could Jews hope to harmonise the equally valid imperatives of Jewish particularism and universalism. Hence, joining the Zionist enterprise in Israel was the commanding Jewish imperative; not the futile and self-negating involvement of the Jewish community in opposing the apartheid system.

Herein lies both a commonality and a telling difference between the radicals and other young Jews who adopted the ideological stance of the Zionist youth movements. Like the radicals, the 'fulfillment Zionists' too evinced a degree of secondary alienation from the Jewish communal establishment, exchanging religious observances for secular ethnic identity (except in the case of the religious youth movement, *Bnei Akiva*), criticising the merely philanthropic armchair Zionism of their middle-class elders and preaching rejection of the *gola* (Diaspora). Nevertheless, the youth movements remained intrinsic to the community because affirming the primacy of their Jewishness was at the very heart of their outlook. In addition, they always enjoyed a measure of vicarious encouragement from part of the conventional Zionist establishment. The Jewish radicals, by contrast, marginalised or even effaced their Jewishness, evinced hostility toward Jewish religious and ethnicist-Zionist norms, and in so doing became wholly extrinsic to the community. For this reason they were, in turn, resented and spurned by the upholders of the community's norms, religious or ethnic-Zionist. This mutual alienation was then vastly exacerbated as the conforming majority of Jews responded to the Jewish radicals' defiance of the entire apartheid edifice with embarrassment and fear in the face of anticipated reprisals from the dominant Afrikaner regime and the white public at large.

The radicals' estrangement from the Jewish community does not, however, mean disassociation from other Jews. Indeed, clusters of social association with other Jews within the ranks of radical groups is one of the most characteristic features of the record in South Africa. It is rather a case of Jews preferring to associate with Jews who, as it were, do not associate with other Jews! Together with like-minded other Jews they found a warmly embracing cosmopolitan home; a sense of belonging and dedication, social no less than political, that they could not find either in conventional white society at large or in the sectarian Jewish community. For the generation that became politically active before 1948, taking the lead against fascism in South Africa was a profoundly meaningful part of the struggle. The real and present danger of fascism receded thereafter, but waging the colour-blind battle against apartheid and defying its racial taboos by socialising across the colour line continued to engender a virtuous and liberating feeling. These qualities of the radical political ambience were felt to be absent in the Jewish community, and more than made up for the personal sacrifices and persecution that were the lot of the radicals' political and social heresy.

Generational transmission

Of course, even if what one might now term in shorthand 'the double outsider or marginality theory' is plausible, it accounts for little more than the relative potentiality of Jews to balk at the imposition of the apartheid system on the society to which they were expected to conform as compliant whites. Clearly, this potentiality was fulfilled by very few Jews. Moreover, as described in the plenitude of memoirs and interviews that have seen publication in recent years, the great variety of paths taken by even those few Jews to the radical camp in South Africa defies attempts to explain, fully or sufficiently, why some Jews took those radical paths whereas others did not. However, one pattern or regularity in the making of Jewish radicals certainly is discernible. This is the role of the parental home or of the immigrant generation's social environment. There is considerable evidence of transmission from one generation to the next, particularly in regard to communist sympathies or affiliation.

The compound effects of outsider-marginality in the broad sociological sense and of role models in the home or its immediate social environs are observable, above all, in the lives of several important radicals who were born in Europe and were brought to South Africa by their immigrant parents. As has already been suggested, this kind of influence is evident in the life of Joe Slovo. In Slovo's case generational transmission appears to have been not directly from his parents but rather indirectly from the immigrant social milieu of his childhood and adolescence. In other cases the direct influence of the parental home is more evident. An example is Ray Alexander. She was born in Latvia in 1913 and came to South Africa in 1929, aged 16. Her autobiographical recollections point to the early formative influence of radical political consciousness in the home in Latvia. Her father was, as she recalls, 'inclined to socialist ideas', and his social circle included a local teacher who was a communist and became something of a mentor to the young Rachel Alexandrowich after her father died when she was 12 years old. While still in Latvia her own early political inclinations shifted from contemplation of Zionism to ardent communism, so that she found her way to the local communist party very soon after her arrival in Cape Town.[16] She went on to become one of the resistance movement's most militant and colourful personalities.

Pauline Podbrey is another example of a radical 'import', as it were. She was born in Eastern Europe and came to Durban, South Africa in 1933 at the age of 11. Appropriately entitled *White Girl in Search of the Party,* her autobiographical book vividly describes this search for engagement with resistance to the kind of society in which she found herself in South Africa. This search was an emanation of the radical leftist predisposition she had already formed in Lithuania. Her father, who according to her recollections had a strong influence on her, was a Bundist (socialist Jewish Worker Party supporter) in a politically conscious family environment in which others of her close relations were Zionists. Pauline found what she was seeking in the Communist Party, became heavily involved in trade union activities, and in 1950 married HA Naidoo, an outstanding Indian trade union and communist leader.[17]

Much the same background and formative influences characterise a number of other Jewish radicals. Whether born in Eastern Europe or in South Africa, leftist influences are traceable, emanating either from their parents or from other role models, also usually Jewish, to which they were exposed within their immediate social environment. What they all had in common was growing to maturity with an outsider perspective on white South African society, mostly rooted in the ambience of urban immigrant Jews still struggling to make a living.[18] As well, they had in common an increasing alienation from the institutional life of the Jewish community, whether embodied in the synagogue or in Zionist activity.

The list of these Jewish radicals, mostly communist, is quite long. It includes, for example, Esther Barsel, the daughter of Joseph and Sonya Levin who had emigrated from Lithuania and settled in Yeoville, Johannesburg, in 1936 when Esther was 13 years of age. Her husband Hymie Barsel grew up in an Orthodox observant family in the Fordsburg and Doornfontein immigrant environment from which he became estranged as he came under the influence of Dr Max Joffe (a medical practitioner), who was a major role model in the lives of quite a number of Jewish radicals. Another couple of similar background was Ray and Michael Harmel. Ray was born in Lithuania (in 1928) where at age 16 she was already involved in leftist labour union activities and hunted by the Lithuanian police. Another radical, Ben Turok, was born in Latvia in 1927 and brought out to South Africa in 1934 at age seven. According to Turok's recollection, his father was a Bundist and a member of the Jewish Workers' Club in the 1930s, although he afterwards lost interest and, not untypically, became a well-off businessman.[19] Perhaps the most clear-cut example of a 'ready made' young immigrant radical was Eli Weinberg. Born in Libau, Latvia, he came to South Africa in 1929, aged 21, with sound communist credentials – he had already been a member of the communist underground in Libau, and had even suffered arrest.[20]

Not all of the immigrant radicals came directly from the communist nurseries of Eastern Europe. There were leftist immigrant offshoots in the West. Hilda Watts (originally Schwartz), who came to South Africa from London in the 1930s (she went back and forth until settling in about 1937), was the young daughter of emigrants from Tsarist Russia and had grown up in an avidly communist home environment. Indeed, after the Bolshevik revolution her father had returned to live in the Soviet Union, leaving his family behind. In South Africa Hilda soon joined the local communists where she was a vibrant presence both before and after the party went underground.[21]

At this point in our discussion it is important to note the small but persistent presence within the Jewish community itself of a counter-normative tradition of ideologically leftist, immigrant groups. This was a formative or supportive factor in the making of some Jewish radicals. Although vastly outnumbered by the Zionists, we find these groups giving collective Jewish expression to the ideas they brought with them from Eastern Europe in a variety of forms throughout the years of Jewish immigration. Elsewhere these have been traced in some detail.[22] Here suffice it to mention only the most salient developments. The most significant was the Yiddish-Speaking Group which affiliated to the International Socialist League, forerunner of the South African Communist Party. Founded in Johannesburg in February 1917, it appears to have commanded a following of a few hundreds.[23] Its militant challenge to Zionism met a response within the same universe of discourse put up by another group formed in about 1919 – *Poalei Zion*. The members of *Poalei Zion* favored Yiddish over Hebrew. According to Leibl Feldman, who was a member of this *Poalei Zion* group, it succeeded in gaining the defection of a number of the Yiddish-Speaking Group's members, while others had to be expelled for evincing sympathy with Zionist 'chauvinism'.[24] Be that as it may, the Yiddish-Speaking Group disintegrated in 1921, its members being absorbed into the Communist Party of South Africa. As for the *Poalei Zion* group, seeking a Zionist-leftist synthesis, it occupied a position on the Jewish political spectrum somewhere between the small minority of Yiddish-speaking leftist radicals and the majority of bourgeois-aspiring Zionist immigrants. Yet even *Poalei Zion* remained well off the mainstream of Zionist sentiment. Consequently, it too faded out of existence within a few years.

More durable was the *Yiddisher Arbeter Club* (Jewish Workers'

Club) founded in 1929.²⁵ Its members condemned the 'pernicious' grip in which they said Zionism held South African Jews, and described Zionism as a shameful form of bourgeois chauvinism and danger to the working-class Jew. Its organ, *Die Proletarishe Shtimme* (The Proletarian Voice), accused the Zionists of unrealistic utopianism, sought to expose 'the great Zionist bluff', and considered the Arabs innocent victims of Zionism.²⁶ Small but persevering, the *Arbeter Club* remained an uncompromising opponent of Zionism until as late as 1948, when it quite suddenly collapsed. Its demise is explicable in terms of the accelerated upward occupational mobility of the Jewish population, particularly during the Second World War, which ran counter to its working-class sentiments and ideology. By 1948 many of its own members were already well-to-do employers of labour. Moreover, it lacked a following in the next generation, which in some cases preferred to become directly involved in the Communist Party or the Congress movement, and in other cases got caught up in the great upsurge of Zionist youth movements that took place after 1945, especially in *Hashomer Hatzair* and *Habonim*.

Of a broader nature but also providing expression for Yiddish-speaking leftists were the cultural literary organisations that emerged in South Africa. The first was the *Yiddisher Literarisher Farein* founded in October 1912 in Johannesburg. Its aim was to foster Yiddish cultural life through discussions, plays, a Yiddish library, and so on. In June 1932, after 20 years of activity, the *Farein* ceased to exist.

A parallel development of the leftist minority in the late 1920s and the 1930s was related to support for Jewish colonisation on the land in the Soviet Union.²⁷ The Zionist Federation, prodded by the World Zionist Organisation, strongly opposed these efforts. In 1932 an organisation called *Afrikaner Geserd* (Society for Settling Jewish Workers on the Land in the USSR) issued from the activities of the Russian Colonisation Fund. The *Geserd* declared its aim to be 'to render effective material and moral support towards Jewish socialist reconstruction in the Soviet Union and particularly in Birobidzhan'. It issued a printed monthly organ in Yiddish and English called *Geserdword* which also sought 'strenuously to combat Zionism in all its manifestations', and 'to shake off the harmful and illusory dream of establishing a "National

Home" in Palestine through an alliance with British imperialism'.[28] The *Geserd* represented the peak of leftist Jewish opposition to Zionism in the history of South African Jewry. It even managed to create a small youth section called *Yugend Geserd*, the only anti-Zionist Jewish youth movement ever to have emerged in South Africa. Associates of the *Geserd* also began publishing a monthly journal called *Farois* (Forward) and re-established a *Kulturfarein* (cultural federation) in 1937, and an afternoon Yiddish *folkshul*. Some of the radical Jews already mentioned in this paper took part in the work of the *Geserd*. Eli Weinberg was indeed for a time secretary of the organisation.

The last of these Yiddish leftist manifestations was a small group styled the Jewish Democratic Association, formed by Michael Szur in 1950 after the induction of the apartheid regime. This group was explicitly anti-apartheid and extremely critical of the 'political non-involvement' policy of the Jewish Board of Deputies. It invoked the memory of recent Jewish suffering in Europe, and argued that if Jews 'complained justifiably that the people of the world did not rally to our defence', then 'as a community we cannot hide ourselves behind the false slogan of neutrality and keep silent when other peoples are in distress'. It accused Zionists, among other charges, of propagating the false view that Jews were really no more than temporary sojourners in the Diaspora, thereby lulling them into passive acquiescence in apartheid.[29]

This non-normative leftist Jewish tradition informed the social environment and may have been felt in the homes of some South African-born radicals. For others, the home was already a nursery for radical ideology of a far more thorough and compelling nature that issued from the Yiddish-speaking leftist groups. The home of the formidable journalist and radical activist, Ruth First, is a striking case in point. Both her parents, Julius and Tilly, had been dedicated communists before she was born. Her father Julius was born in pre-independent Latvia and came to South Africa in 1910. He served a stint as chairman of the Communist Party of South Africa in the 1920's. As is prominently inscribed in the record of the liberation struggle, Ruth was married to Joe Slovo and met a tragic death while in political exile, the victim of assassination by agents of the South African government.

Denis Goldberg is another example of radicalism solidly rooted in the home environment quite independently of the local Yiddish-speaking leftist tradition. He was a communist who made an important contribution to the incipient *Umkhonto* underground and was arrested and imprisoned in the wake of the Rivonia arrests and trials of the mid-1960s. Both his father and his mother were communists, born in London's East End to immigrant parents from Eastern Europe. They came to South Africa in about 1929, where Denis was born in 1933 into a home which, in his words, 'was open to anybody in the [Communist] Party, in the ANC, in the liberation movement'. The Goldbergs, Denis adds, 'were not in the mainstream of the Jewish community'.[30] Goldberg senior had a little cartage contracting business, 'so his truck was used as the platform for meetings'. Goldberg attributed no part of his radical predisposition to Jewishness: 'I grew up in a communist household and was aware of political relations and realities in South Africa from a very early age. By the time I left school and went to the university in 1950, at the age of 16-17, I realised that I had to decide whether these were my own views or views I had adopted because they were my parents'.'[31] Goldberg was released from prison – after serving 22 years – through the efforts of an Israeli personage, Herut Lapid, who was dedicated to aiding political prisoners and a member of kibbutz Ma'ayan Baruch in which Denis's daughter, Hilary, had settled. Even so, Goldberg continued to firmly dissociate himself from Zionism and Israel. Although thankful for the role the Israelis played in his release from prison, he chose to live in London. In an interview published in 1997 he referred to his Jewish background in the same dismissive vein: 'I'm Jewish because my grandparents and parents were. My grandparents were Orthodox, my parents were atheists.' He said he saw no need to explain things in Jewish terms of any sort.[32]

That the daughter of a radical as negative toward Jewishness as was Goldberg could choose to live in Israel is indicative of the ongoing interplay between cosmopolitan and ethnic-Zionist propensities in Jewish families. This interplay is evident also in some other cases, for example the family of another important radical, Rowley Israel Arenstein in Durban. His daughter was active in the Zionist youth movement, *Habonim*, and several members of that movement's Durban branch came under Arenstein's influence. One was David Ernst, son of the leading Jewish educationalist in Durban, who also became active in resistance to the apartheid regime and suffered imprisonment. Arenstein himself attributed his early social consciousness to the influence of his mother, who had grown up in the Ukraine with a radical outlook of the Menshevik variety.[33]

Yet the empirical evidence does not permit of a generalisation attributing universal formative influence to generational transmission of radical proclivities in the home or immediate social environment. In the lives of those radicals who grew to maturity in the post-1948 apartheid years, it appears to be less significant than it was for their predecessors. To be sure, it remains evident in some important cases. Thus generational transmission could hardly be more obvious than it was in the experience of Albie Sachs. He was born in 1935, the son of Lithuanian-born Emile Solly Sachs, the prodigious trade unionist who had been a Communist Party member until he was expelled for not toeing the party line in the early 1930s. By contrast Ronnie Kasrils, perhaps the most prominent of all white radicals who grew to maturity in the post-1948 period, was born in 1938 to parents who were rather typical first-generation South Africans. As was typical of the adolescent experience of Jews who grew up in the Yeoville suburb of Johannesburg with its dense, lower middle-class Jewish population, Kasrils also had a brief exposure to the Zionist youth movements. He recalls having flirted briefly with membership of various youth movements and has said that as an adolescent he felt very Jewish and identified strongly with Israel's War of Independence. He recollects as an adolescent being strongly aware of the Holocaust and the history of Jewish persecution, and says that he 'drew an analogy with the suffering of black people in this country and racism'.[34] But this was a sentiment felt by many of his contemporaries who did not act upon it politically. Kasrils relates that it was only in 1961, after being shocked into action by the Sharpeville massacre, that he joined the liberation struggle in the ranks of the Communist Party. Whatever may have been the factors or role models that influenced him at that stage, they do not seem to have included significant generational transmission in the home.

A liberal home environment does appear to have played some role in the political development of Raymond Suttner, who stands out as one of the foremost white radicals involved in the liberation struggle during the post-Verwoerd period of 'reformed' apartheid. He was born in 1945 to South African-born parents who were liberals and Progressive Party supporters. His grandparents on his father's side came from Lithuania and on his mother's side from England. Having operated underground for the Communist Party and the ANC in the early 1970s, Suttner was detained without trial in 1975 and then sentenced to seven-and-a-half years in prison. Released in 1983, he undauntedly resumed his anti-apartheid activity, particularly in the work of the United Democratic Front. In the 1986 state of emergency he was again detained without trial, becoming the longest-serving white detainee – 27 months, of which 18 were in solitary confinement.

Interviewed concerning his Jewishness, Suttner has provided a particularly insightful account. He attested to a low Jewish consciousness, heightened only in the face of antisemitism, experienced particularly when he was in prison and found that the security police were obsessed with his being Jewish. 'For the people who detained me,' he commented, 'my being Jewish was an essential element of [communist] criminality.'[35] He expressed doubt that there was in reality such a thing as uniform Jewish values, because he had found that among Jews in South Africa there were contradictory values. For most Jews and Jewish organisations Jewish values were purely self-centred, and tended to be supportive of the prevailing social order. 'I don't think there's a uniform Jewish ethic which has informed people,' he opined. 'If there is, it's been capable of a variety of different meanings, and some of these meanings have been interpreted in a very ethnic, egocentric way.'[36] By his own account Suttner, who was a university lecturer in law, had begun his university studies with home-grown liberal values but formed the conviction that these were insufficient 'as a strategy for change in South Africa'; they were no more than 'a way of preserving a sense of personal rectitude'.[37] While furthering his studies in England from late 1969 to mid -1971, he had joined the Communist Party and the ANC, and on his return to South Africa began to operate underground. In sum, it seems that not 'Jewish values' but the influence of universal liberal values in the home and intellectual influences in the university environment were the major formative factors in the making of Suttner as a radical opponent of apartheid.

Passage through the Zionist youth movements

A secondary factor noticeable in the making of some radicals was exposure to the Zionist youth movements. This is seemingly paradoxical because these youth movements were something integral to the Jewish community from which Jewish radicals were so sharply alienated. But it seems that these movements provided a stimulus for political awareness and sometimes a training ground for radical activism, which were otherwise lacking in the adolescent experiences of most Jews. In a dialectical way they played some role in the ideological education of quite a number of Jewish radicals. Sam Kahn was an early case of a communist of note who had strong roots in the Jewish community's youth societies, the organisational predecessors of the uniformed youth movements. He was born in South Africa, and as a youth became very active in the Zionist 'Young Israel' movement in Cape Town, and later in the Students' Jewish Association at the University of Cape Town, where he qualified as a lawyer. But alienation from the Jewish community set in with his joining of the Communist Party in the early 1930s. He went on to gain election in the 1940s as a representative of 'non-whites' in the Cape Town City Council, and on the basis of the same typically South African racial legislation, in the 1948 elections – the elections that put the National Party into power – he became the sole communist representative in parliament. Kahn was the most fearless and acerbic critic of South African racism and oppression and its systematisation under apartheid, until he was ejected from parliament in 1952 following the government's Suppression of Communism Act. After more than a decade of further banning and harassment, Kahn took himself and his family into exile in London. In 1987, while he was on a family visit to Israel, a motor accident tragically took his life at the age of 75.[38]

The most striking testimony for Zionist youth movement

influence as a stimulator of social awareness that could lead to radical activism against South Africa's racist society may be found in the autobiography of Baruch Hirson. Hirson was born in South Africa in 1921. Although he grew up in the same 1920s and 1930s Jewish immigrant milieu of Doornfontein that was the nursery for other future radicals, his account of his own home background reveals no particular sensitivities to the injustices and oppression that pervaded the surrounding society. Quite to the contrary, both home and school conditioned him to be a typical privileged white. It was outside of the home and its conventionally superficial Jewish religious observances and rites of passage that he formed a critical perception of the social evils around him. Hirson titled his autobiography *Revolutions in my Life,* and he clearly attributes to his intense involvement in *Hashomer Hatzair*, from late 1939 until late 1943, the adoption of the Marxist *weltanschauung* that constituted the major revolution in his life. The ideas that engaged him in the course of his experience in *Hashomer Hatzair* became a catalyst for the Trotskyism that eventually became his rigorous ideological dogma and led to his sharp rejection of Zionism and dedication to promotion of the class struggle in South Africa. After he left *Hashomer Hatzair*, his political activities, which were for much of the period concurrent with his academic career as a physicist at the University of the Witwatersrand, became increasingly radical. Hirson was only one of several major radicals who issued from *Hashomer Hatzair* into the local struggle and paid the price of arrests, bannings and exile. Most were communists and active in the Congress of Democrats. Lionel Forman was an important example, and there were many other minor personalities. Hirson comments: 'The number of people who left *Hashomer Hatzair* to join the political left (as it was then conceived) indicates that *Hashomer Hatzair* was a crucible of political development.'[39]

The formative influence of early Zionist attachments is evident also in the activities of Arthur Goldreich.[40] Goldreich was born in 1929 in South Africa. His family was unusual in that, unlike almost all of his Jewish contemporaries in the radical resistance, it not only stemmed from England rather than Eastern Europe but even his grandparents were born in England. Although his father and mother were born in South Africa, they too spent some time back in England. In Arthur's recollection, when he was a child his family considered itself part of a kind of élite Anglo-Jewish segment of the Jewish community. One of his grandparents had first come to South Africa as a soldier in the Anglo-Boer War period and was a cousin of Samuel Goldreich, the first chairman of the South African Zionist Federation. Another unusual aspect of Arthur's upbringing was the completion of his high school education in the Afrikaans language in the small town of Pietersburg to which the family had moved in the 1930s. His family was traditionally religious in the Anglo-Jewish manner, and as a child Arthur was provided with a private Hebrew teacher. In the Afrikaans-medium high school that he attended in Pietersburg he was permitted to choose Hebrew rather than the usual German as a third required language. The family was also well disposed to Zionism, and the bright adolescent Arthur became the leader of a Zionist youth association in Pietersburg. In 1948 he joined a group of contemporaries in the *Habonim* youth movement who volunteered to help in Israel's War of Independence, and spent some time after the war on a kibbutz in the Galilee. After returning to South Africa in 1954 he became active in the Congress movement and later, as a front man for the incipient communist underground, he took up residence in a farm estate at Rivonia on the northern outskirts of Johannesburg, which became the underground's secret centre. It was there that the South African security police captured the leadership in July 1963 in a series of arrests that led to the incarceration of Nelson Mandela and other leaders of the *Umkhonto* underground. All five of the whites arrested at Rivonia were Jews. While detained in the Johannesburg Marshall Square prison, Goldreich, together with three other prisoners, made a dramatic escape, after which he settled in Israel.

Harold Wolpe, Goldreich's comrade and partner in the escape, settled in England where he became a university teacher in sociology and continued his anti-apartheid work. It is noteworthy that Wolpe too had passed through a period of exposure to the Zionist youth movement. Wolpe's Eastern European-born parents were not particularly politically conscious. His upbringing and education at Johannesburg's Athlone Boys' High School, whose pupils were predominantly Jewish, was very conventional. But as a boy, like many of his friends, he was for a time a member of *Habonim* and when he became a university student he participated in a Zionist Socialist youth project for teaching in a night school for blacks. In his recollection it was at that time that his mind began to open up to the cruel realities of South African society. He began to search for a passage to political engagement and was drawn into the Young Communist League.[41] He became a close comrade of Joe Slovo and Ruth First and a major personality in the Communist Party and underground.

I have suggested that an ancillary factor discernible in the paths to radicalism of a number of young Jews was awakening of social and political awareness through exposure to the Zionist youth movements, even though they were integral to the organised life of the Jewish community from which Jewish radicals were very alienated. But having noted this, a strong reservation must be registered. This is that in many cases other ancillary factors, wholly unrelated to the Jewish community, are also discernible. One that stands out is the influence of liberal and humanitarian ideas and sentiments communicated by some exceptional teachers in certain English-medium high schools and, more so, by role models – usually senior students – in the Universities of Cape Town and the Witwatersrand. In some cases, exposure to these role models was a primary factor in the stimulation of anti-apartheid convictions, in other cases they merely reinforced proclivities already generated in the home or redirected ideals and ideological tendencies toward involvement in the anti-apartheid struggle formed in the Zionist youth movements.

Rusty (Lionel) Bernstein, a major personality in the communist segment of the liberation struggle, is an example of this pathway to radical convictions and activism. Reflecting on his path to political awareness, Bernstein writes: 'I have no ready answers ... I can give no explanation for the origins of my politics.' He certainly could not trace them to his home. Born in South Africa in 1920, he was orphaned at the age of 12 and educated in Hilton College, an exclusive boarding school in Natal. But in his autobiographical book he does in fact relate how he was influenced by the anti-fascist convictions of a particular Hilton College teacher (whose subject, curiously, was Latin).[42] The struggle against fascism in the second half of the 1930s was the context in which he took his first political steps in the small Labour League of Youth in the late 1930s, but it was during his studies at the University of

Witwatersrand's School of Architecture that he became a convinced communist. He mentions in particular being inspired by 'an extraordinary third-year student', Kurt Jonas. 'It was at Florian's [a coffee house in Hillbrow frequented by leftists] via Kurt Jonas that I first learnt of the invisible world of black workers and their trade unions which existed on my own doorstep.'[43] Jonas was a Jew, born in South Africa but educated in Germany where he had qualified in law. Returning to South Africa when Hitler came to power, he switched to the study of architecture. Jonas was a profound intellectual; an avowed Marxist who influenced not only members of the Zionist Socialist Party with which he associated himself, but also left-inclined fellow students like Rusty Bernstein and Jock Isacowitz (who was to become, in turn, a Zionist-Socialist, a communist, and a leader of the radical war veterans' organisation, the Springbok Legion, and later the Liberal Party).

In conclusion

In sum, the available autobiographical evidence, examples of which have been considered above, suggests an explanation for the phenomenon of Jewish radical opponents of apartheid in terms of a primary sociological factor. That factor is marginality or outsider status in relation to the established élites and interests of white South African society compounded by alienation from Jewish religion and the normative life of the Jewish community. It has also been suggested that one ancillary factor discernible in a considerable number of cases is awakening of social and political awareness through exposure to the Zionist youth movements even though they were integral to the organised life of the Jewish community. All these factors may well be described as 'Jewish', but they derive from the social situation of Jews in South Africa, and not at all from Judaism in the sense of religion. Independently of Jewish factors or complementary to them, in many cases the influence of persons who served as inspiring role models was the decisive factor in the making of Jewish radicals. In the pre-apartheid years, these role models and the political ideas they communicated were mostly encountered in the anti-fascist arena. Later they were mostly met at the 'liberal' English-medium universities in Cape Town and

Johannesburg. In some cases, they were preceded by influences experienced in school years. Some of these role models were themselves Jewish, others were bearers of the English liberal tradition or dissidents in relation to Afrikaner norms.

Yet the factors thus identified are no more than rough regularities or common denominators. In the final analysis, one cannot conclude that these suffice to account fully for the making of Jewish radicals and the phenomenon of their disproportionate involvement in the radical opposition to the apartheid system. The individual differences between Jewish radicals are myriad, and no generalisation can cover every single case. For every Joe Slovo or Ray Alexander born in Eastern Europe there is a Rowley Arenstein or Ronnie Kasrils born in South Africa. For every Denis Goldberg or Ruth First (Slovo) whose lives were totally divorced from Jewish and Zionist associations, there is an Arthur Goldreich or Baruch Hirson who passed through one or other phase of meaningful Jewish involvement, and so on. Imponderables such as idiosyncratic personality traits, chance exposures to inspiring role models, and the warm embrace of supportive social groups enter into the equation and perhaps are the ultimate differentiating factors. Also, one cannot entirely dismiss the frustrating thought – but one which the social scientist or historian is bound to resist – that radicals, and liberals for that matter, are not made but simply born.

The Road to Rivonia:
Jewish Radicals and the Cost of Conscience in White South Africa

GLENN FRANKEL

GLENN FRANKEL is an editor and reporter for *The Washington Post*. He has served as the *Post's* bureau chief in southern Africa, Jerusalem and London, as well as editor of *The Washington Post Magazine*. He won a 1989 Pulitzer Prize for his coverage of the Middle East. He is the author of two books: *Beyond the Promised Land* (1994), which won the National Jewish Book Award, and *Rivonia's Children: Three Families and the Cost of Conscience in White South Africa* (1999). A graduate of Columbia University, he has been a Professional Journalism Fellow at Stanford University and an Alicia Patterson Fellow.

I want to begin not in South Africa but in Kidlington, a small suburb outside Oxford, England, where in the summer of 1996 I had come to visit Hilda and Rusty Bernstein, an elderly couple, originally from South Africa. We'd just finished our first cup of tea when Hilda rose and said she'd be right back. Several minutes passed – Hilda was 81 years old that summer and she moved with wisdom rather than haste. She came back with a thick manila envelope and she dumped the contents onto the kitchen table. Out came strips of white fabric, cut in the shape of shirt collars, each one covered in a man's minute handwriting. They contained letters from prison written in 1963 by Rusty, smuggled out to Hilda in laundry from an isolation cell deep in the bowels of the Pretoria Local prison in South Africa. Rusty had spent 88 days in solitary confinement there before being charged with sabotage and put on trial for his life alongside Nelson Mandela and nine other anti-apartheid activists.

While Hilda went through these notes with me, Rusty sat silently in a nearby chair. He was a quiet man, not unfriendly, not unhumorous, but not inclined to speak until spoken to. The letters on the shirt collars seemed to come from a different person altogether – a man in the grip of raw despair and on the edge of sanity, agonisingly concerned about his wife and children and his own precarious fate. Hilda read a few aloud. Then I read some. In those moments we were transported back 33 years to a prison cell and a country in the process of becoming a police state, and to a family caught in a web in which their political and personal lives were irrevocably entangled.

One of the things we discussed that day was the role that Jewish identity played for radicals such as Hilda and Rusty. They'd insisted it played no role and was of no importance whatsoever. I argued otherwise. In any event, in her book *The World That Was Ours*, which recounts those harrowing police-state days, Hilda quotes one particular message from Rusty as stating: 'What makes a man face trial for treason twice in the matter of seven years?'[1] Yet on their kitchen table I saw the original. It read: 'What makes *a nice Jewish boy* like me twice face trial?'

So what's this? I asked them both. Hilda looked just a little sheepish. It's just a phrase, she replied, just a phrase.

Well, it may have been just a phrase, but in the end I felt it was a lot more than that. It summed up, in fact, some abiding truths about white left-wing radicals in South Africa in the darkest days of the struggle against apartheid: that they were courageous and committed; that they made enormous personal sacrifices; that a sizeable majority of them were of Jewish origin; and that they didn't know exactly what to make of their own backgrounds. It wasn't so much that they were ashamed of being identified as Jews. They simply didn't know how to process the fact or what it meant, why it singled them out and what they owed to Jewish tradition and what, in turn, Jewish tradition owed to them.

Hilda and Rusty were part of a small group of white communists, many of them of Jewish origin. They had worked closely with Nelson Mandela and his comrades at the heart of the anti-apartheid movement for more than 20 years before the movement was banned and Mandela was locked away for life. These people led double lives: they were middle-class professionals, living in the comfortable white suburbs of Johannesburg, raising families, playing tennis, enjoying the good life. Yet at the same time they were doing illegal political work under increasing restrictions and police surveillance. All through the 1950s, even after the Communist Party was outlawed, these radicals continued to organise and operate underground. They were responsible for some of the most stirring moments of that era. Rusty Bernstein was the principal author of the ANC Freedom Charter.[2] He, Joe Slovo, Ruth First and many others stood in the dock alongside Mandela and the ANC's leadership during the four-year Treason Trial that began in 1956. And after the ANC was banned in 1960, they were integral members of the group that set up Umkhonto We Sizwe and established a secret headquarters in nearby Rivonia. Some of them were actively involved in the sabotage campaign that Umkhonto launched in December 1961, and many paid a heavy price for their role. When the South African security police raided Rivonia in July 1963, it crushed the movement. Hilda and Rusty escaped with their lives; others were killed or jailed for life. The cause they believed in was set back a generation. It took nearly three decades for Nelson Mandela to emerge from prison and four more years for a new, democratic South Africa to be born. It was a long wait for redemption. Many of the activists did not live to see it.

I wrote about them and the early 1960s, the era in which they faced their deepest crisis of conscience, in my recent book *Rivonia's Children*. I focused on three families – the Bernsteins, the Slovos and the Wolpes, all of them of Jewish origin. And I tried to gauge the impact of their political activities on their families and their personal lives. I called the book *Rivonia's Children* because Rivonia is the place where their dream of revolution was forged, and where it was shattered. And I use the word 'children' not to be derogatory but because I believe these people were both incredibly idealistic and very naïve.

One of the important themes of my book is the meaning of

Jewish identity for the radicals and their enemies. It's no accident, I believe, that of the six whites arrested on the day of the Rivonia raid, all were of Jewish origin. Nor is it surprising that all four of the whites who stood trial alongside Mandela, Walter Sisulu, Govan Mbeki and Ahmed Kathrada were Jews. Nor that somewhere between 60 and 80 per cent of the whites in the underground movement were Jews. But that's not all of course. One must add Helen Suzman, the Progressive member of parliament who shared a hatred of apartheid with the radicals but was despised by many of them for her liberalism – and who despised them in turn for their Marxism. It's no surprise that Helen, too, is Jewish. Nor that she was elected from a parliamentary district in Johannesburg's northern suburbs that probably had the greatest concentration of Jews in the country. And finally, to round out our cast of characters, we mustn't forget that Percy Yutar, the man who sat in the prosecutor's chair at the Rivonia trial, was also a Jew. But more about him later.

Since Hilda and Rusty couldn't answer my question, I launched my own informal inquiry into why some of South Africa's Jews had been in the forefront of the struggle against apartheid. This search inevitably took me back to the late nineteenth century and the western half of the Russian empire, to the urban areas where Jews from rural *shtetls*, or ghettoes, increasingly concentrated. The working- class associations, the Bund trade union movement and the grievance committees they forged rapidly plunged into radical politics. As they left places like Latvia, Lithuania, Belorussia, the Ukraine and Poland, they carried with them their belief in socialism, their atheism and their anti-clericalism.

The historian Irving Howe writes that their original radicalism didn't really stem from a precise analysis of modern capitalism as much as from a visceral reaction against religious Orthodoxy; it had more to do with the hope of self-transformation than with organising the working class.[3] This radicalism was still strongly tied to the world it was seeking to reject, and still deeply responsive to the fathers it meant to outrage. Thus there developed in Vilna the odd tradition of the Yom Kippur ball. On the holiest night of the Jewish year, when religious Jews and many secular ones fasted and sought to atone, these radicals staged a banquet and a dance, seeking to demonstrate their contempt for mainstream Judaism.[4]

Hilda and Rusty Bernstein were firmly part of this radical tradition. Hilda's father was a Bolshevik from Odessa, who changed his last name from Schwartz to Watts when he moved to England following the failed 1905 revolution. He married a Jewish girl from Lithuania, but no Jewish traditions were honoured in their home. There was a Christmas tree at Christmas and Simeon Schwartz was determined that his three young daughters become proper English girls.[5] When Hilda moved to South Africa as a teenager, few of her friends even knew she was Jewish. Some still didn't believe it 60 years later when I met them.

Then there were Jews like Joe Slovo. He was born in Lithuania in 1925 and when he came to South Africa at age nine, he could only speak Yiddish. Joe grew up in poverty – his mother died when he was a teenager and his two sisters were farmed out to other families, while he and his father lived in a boarding house in Johannesburg.[6] Joe never finished high school, but he managed to sneak into law school at the University of the Witwatersrand after the war. He should have become a big-time rich lawyer – he had the brains and the charm for it. Instead, Joe joined the Communist Party, championed social causes, and worked closely with the ANC. In his style and outward appearance, Joe was more consciously Jewish than many of his comrades. He told jokes with a Yiddish inflection, he liked Jewish food and he didn't seem embarrassed by his ethnic origins.

Yet Joe was just like his comrades in the sense that just about all of them viewed themselves as atheists, internationalists and revolutionaries. Identity politics were at best an ideological distraction; Jewishness was something to be transcended or even despised. As Pauline Podbrey, a trade unionist and party activist, told Steven Robins in an interview for the book *Cutting Through the Mountain*:

> Looking back on it now it seems as if everybody was Jewish. But there was no sense of Jewishness among them. Nobody ever discussed their Jewishness or brought it forward as an issue. I suspect that quite a few of us were not too anxious to be identified as Jewish, although nobody made a conscious effort to deny it. But it just wasn't allowed to impinge on Party work. It would have been seen as a concession to nationalism.[7]

Among the Jewish community, those who joined the Communist Party and various liberal organisations were the exception rather than the rule, although they were often influential – and notorious – far beyond their actual numbers. The party was dominated by Jews from its founding in 1921. Government officials blamed Bolshevik Jews for the 1922 mine-workers' strike. Partly as a result, the Immigration Quota Act of 1930 reduced the flow of Jewish immigrants from Eastern Europe to a trickle. Still, of 60 active leaders of the party's Johannesburg district on a 1946 police list, 23 were identified as Jewish, including the chairman, Michael Harmel. 'We know that a large percentage of a certain population group devote themselves to undermining activities,' stated Nationalist law-maker CTM Wilcocks before the Senate. Everyone knew which population group he was talking about.

Among blacks, there were many who appreciated the impact of Jews on South Africa. The lawyer who gave Nelson Mandela his first legal job was a Jewish liberal named Lazar Sidelsky, and Mandela never forgot the kindness. He would later write that he found Jews to be more broad-minded about matters of race and politics, perhaps because they themselves had often been victims of prejudice.[8] Black author Lewis Nkosi believed that Jewish interest in classical music, jazz, art and literature softened the crude, rock-hard urban landscape of Johannesburg, which was still in many ways an upstart mining camp. Nkosi wrote:

> It was the Jews who tempered this harsh social order of apartheid with a tenuous liberalism and humane values. If one was foolhardy enough to have girl friends across the colour line, they were likely to be Jewish; if one had white friends of any sort they were most likely Jewish; almost 80 per cent of white South Africans who belonged to left-wing and liberal organisations were Jewish; whatever cultural vitality Johannesburg enjoyed was contributed by this Jewish community.[9]

Of course, it would be wrong to think that Jews as a whole were active in the struggle against apartheid. Most preferred to keep a low profile. Fear of the National Party rendered the official Jewish community speechless when it came to apartheid. The South

African Jewish Board of Deputies studiously avoided comment when the government passed the Group Areas Act in 1950, which enshrined racial segregation in housing and commercial ventures. It did not join with Catholic and Protestant leaders in protesting the 1956 law that empowered the Minister of Native Affairs to ban racially-mixed religious services. A handful of Jewish liberals pressed the community to take a moral stance. Ronald Segal, editor and publisher of the influential quarterly *Africa South*, argued that if Jews were a race they should condemn the new racial purity laws as an echo of Hitler's Nuremberg codes; and if they were a religious community they should protest the state's attempt to interfere with the right to worship. Others, like the author Dan Jacobson, argued in defence that it was too much to ask of any community that it risk communal suicide. In any event, the Jewish establishment would not be shamed into action.[10] Officially it argued that while individual Jews could say what they liked, there was no community consensus on what it called 'political matters', and therefore nothing that could be considered the 'Jewish position' on such issues. Unofficially, Jewish leaders warned that any attempt to stand against the apartheid juggernaut would serve only to reawaken the ugly neo-Nazi brand of antisemitism that slept within the soul of the National Party.

Still, there was an ambivalence about the radicals among them. AnnMarie Wolpe recalled for me how, when she was released from detention in 1963, a two-man delegation from the King David School in Johannesburg paid a visit to her home. AnnMarie's husband Harold, a key member of Umkhonto We Sizwe, had just escaped from the Marshall Square jail, and these two men expressed deep disapproval of his deeds. At the same time, however, they said they recognised that Harold's escape had left AnnMarie in a difficult position financially, and they offered to waive nursery school fees for her two young daughters until such time as she was able to pay. AnnMarie came away with the feeling that these men were just as embarrassed by the enthusiastic championing of the state of Percy Yutar as they were by the treasonous activities of Harold Wolpe and his comrades.[11]

The Jewish weekly press steadfastly sought to ignore the Rivonia raid and its implications. But those implications did not go unnoticed by the Afrikaans press. One Sunday newspaper reported that it had received a number of letters from readers commenting on the 'high percentage' of Jews among the 90-day detainees. It asked the Jewish Board of Deputies why this was so, and whether it was an indication that Jews were not happy in South Africa.[12]

The board ducked the question in its official reply. 'The facts show abundantly that the Jewish community of South Africa is an established, loyal and patriotic part of the population,' it stated. 'The conduct of individuals of any section is their own responsibility and no part of the community can or should be asked to accept responsibility.' As for those individual acts: 'The Jewish community condemns illegality in whatever part of the population it might manifest itself.'[13]

In other words, when it came to political morality the official Jewish community took a pass. It was primarily concerned, as Jewish communities in general have been, with ensuring Jewish survival, not with challenging evil.

Nonetheless, where some Jews saw the radicals' Jewish origins as an embarrassment that they needed to conceal or distance themselves from, others saw an opportunity. Chief among these was Percy Yutar, the deputy attorney general of the Transvaal.

Yutar, who was 52 at the time of the Rivonia trial, was one of South Africa's most prominent and experienced prosecutors. He had a tough, logical mind, a flair for the dramatic and an unquenchable thirst for publicity. The mainstream press, which was often fawning when it came to government personalities, called him 'far and away the most qualified legal brain this country has ever possessed'.[14]

Now Percy Yutar was an Orthodox Jew. He was born in Cape Town of parents who had come to South Africa, like so many of the radicals he pursued, from the ghettos of Lithuania. Percy was one of eight children and money was scarce. As a young man he was expected to work in his father's butcher shop. Even though the Yutars were a religious family, his father would violate Jewish law and open the shop on Saturday morning to service the weekend trade. One Saturday Percy was jamming slick cuts of raw beef through the electric mincing machine when his left hand slipped and his fingers plunged into the blades. The fingers were mangled beyond repair, leaving Percy with raw stumps at the end of his hand and a constant reminder of the price he exacted from himself for violating the Sabbath.[15]

Yutar attended the University of Cape Town on a scholarship and eventually became the first student in South Africa in a century to be awarded a doctorate in law. Still, even with the highest of degrees, he wasn't welcome in the South African civil service. He was given a lowly position as an 'Outdoor Officer' for the office of the Telephone Manager in Johannesburg. It took five years before he was promoted to junior law clerk in the accounts department in Pretoria. The antisemitism among his co-workers was intense; there were many nights when a frustrated Yutar would return home to his lodgings in Pretoria, close the door and cry himself to sleep. But he hung on and eventually, in 1940, became a prosecutor. No one worked harder, or seemed to enjoy his power more. Eventually he became deputy attorney general for the Transvaal. But his ambition to rise even higher remained profoundly transparent. 'The office of the Attorney General is a laurel I would much like to pluck,' he told the *South Africa Jewish Times* in 1958.[16] No one doubted him.

Along the way Yutar made many compromises. He became one of the Special Branch's favourite prosecutors. They brought him big cases and helped promote his career. When the 90-day detention law came to pass, some prosecutors might have had qualms about what it meant to build a case on testimony from witnesses so thoroughly at the mercy of the worst kind of policemen. Percy Yutar was not so fastidious. He took the weapons the apartheid police state was providing and he used them to their utmost. It was, as he often solemnly said, his duty. The new police state needed jurists like Percy because they provided it with a veneer of legitimacy. And he gained prominence – he was named the first Jewish attorney general of the Transvaal as a reward for services rendered.

In many ways the Rivonia defendants and Yutar represented two traditional Jewish responses to tyranny. The radicals had chosen to oppose the state. Even though they themselves as whites were among the beneficiaries of apartheid, they sided with its victims. Those among them who identified themselves as Jews cited the moral imperative to oppose evil as well as the pragmatic argument that, in the long run, Jewish interests would best be served by siding with the oppressed majority.

Yutar's response came from a different tradition. Throughout the Middle Ages, when faced with a tyrannical ruler, an interceder would emerge to defend Jewish interests in the court of the tyrant. This person became known as the *shtadlan* or Court Jew. By paying tribute or doing other favours for the tyrant, the Court Jew sought the ruler's protection for himself and his fellow Jews. When the relationship succeeded, the *shtadlan* often gained prominence and riches for himself. For anyone in the Jewish community who had a serious problem with the tyrant's thugs, he became the man to see. Yutar in effect became the symbolic *shtadlan* for South African Jewry. By prosecuting his fellow Jews, he offered protection for the larger community.

Many Jews were not pleased about Yutar's self-appointed role; many felt moral qualms about apartheid and preferred that the community keep the lowest of profiles. When Julius Lewin, a prominent law professor and liberal, used a memorial meeting for the Warsaw Ghetto as a forum to criticise Jewish apathy on racial justice, the Board of Deputies sought to quickly to smother the debate. Lewin had said it was 'a betrayal of religion' for Jews to submit to 'political blackmail' and not speak out against apartheid. 'South Africa is a sick society and the Jews cannot hope to enjoy permanent security while other non-conforming groups feel threatened in the atmosphere created by the ruling race,' he warned.[17] But the Board responded with censure and alarm: 'Appeals to Jews as Jews to support any political program are without justification and do the Jewish community and also the country as a whole a disservice. It is particularly to be deplored when such appeals emanate from individuals or groups within the Jewish community itself.'[18]

It turned out that Percy Yutar is still alive, and I tracked him down in Johannesburg, living in a gated community only a few blocks from Helen Suzman's home. These days Percy's legacy has turned bitter. President Mandela invited him to lunch and publicly exonerated him for his role during the Rivonia trial. Still, during our many hours together Percy complained that he and his family have been subjected to countless humiliations. He now argues that he helped save Mandela's life by charging him and his comrades with sabotage rather than treason. He has conveniently forgotten that both charges were capital offences, and that sabotage was easier to prove.

Of course, many people fought in the liberation movement – blacks, Asians, whites and those of mixed race. I decided to focus on a handful of Jewish activists, not because their sacrifices were greater than anyone else's, but because they chose to make those sacrifices. It is surely not hard to understand why Nelson Mandela, Walter Sisulu and other black activists risked their lives for the liberation of their people. But for whites, and especially Jews, however small the number, to join with them was a remarkable and selfless act. I wanted to understand why.

One of the key reasons, an unavoidable truth, is that most of the Jewish radicals were indeed communists. From the time of its founding in 1921 until it was outlawed in 1950, the South African Communist Party was the only party in the country that welcomed black members. Had they lived in the United States, the gates of social justice the comrades were pressing at would have gradually opened and, like others of their generation, they would no doubt have gradually migrated away from communism to social democracy or liberalism. But in South Africa they were up against a rigid enemy with ironclad beliefs and police-state methods. Without their ideology, many of Rivonia's Children could not have found the courage to act. Norman Levy, one of the comrades, told me: 'We loved the certainty that Marxism gave us, and we needed it.'

But in the end, I believe their Jewishness was also important. Their alienation from white society, their ability to see beyond their own immediate self-interest and to empathise with others and, finally, their willingness to act upon their beliefs – all of these singled them out.

There are many critical charges that can be wielded against these folks – that they were Stalinists and totalitarians, that they were at best blind to the sins and crimes of the Soviet Union. Still, looking at them in the South African context, they look like heroes. The courage to act is what redeemed them – and what allowed them to make their distinct contribution to the forging of the new South Africa. Nelson Mandela has frequently cited their participation in the anti apartheid movement as justification for the spirit of reconciliation he has preached. The fact that even a small group of whites was willing to put aside their privileged status and fight alongside blacks meant to Mandela that people could not be judged solely by their skin color; all whites had to be given the chance to participate in the new society. In a real sense, Hilda and Rusty Bernstein, Joe Slovo and Ruth First, Harold and AnnMarie Wolpe and all of their comrades bear at least some responsibility for the surprising degree of racial reconciliation in the new South Africa.

In the spring of 1998 I went back to London to see Hilda and Rusty and many of the others. As it happened, one of the elderly comrades, a woman named Ray Harmel, died while I was in town. I attended the memorial service at the crematorium at Golders Green. It was a good communist ceremony: there was no rabbi present, no mention of God or the Torah. But the crowd was full of elderly people with names like Bernstein, Goldberg and Goldreich.

Rusty gave the main address. He made no mention of class struggle or any other part of Marxist dogma. He made no attempt to glorify Ray or the role she had played. Her life had been a hard one: her marriage had been difficult; her work for the movement had been both tedious and dangerous. She had fled Lithuania at a young age for South Africa, and in middle age she had had to pick up and flee again, this time to London.

And yet, Rusty said, Ray had been involved in something larger than herself. She had contributed in her own small way to a great movement that had turned the tide of history. It was, in fact, what all of them had been part of. They could be proud of her, and of themselves.

Soon they will all be gone, and with them a small page of history. They will die in relative anonymity, and they will have made their stand. By staying true to their cause and themselves, Rivonia's Children, despite all of their mistakes, helped keep hope alive in South Africa, and pave the hard road to freedom.

Jews and the Open Society

DENNIS DAVIS

DENNIS DAVIS was educated at Herzlia School, the University of Cape Town and Cambridge University. He taught at the University of Cape Town's law school until 1990. Between 1990 and 1997 he held the title of Professor of Law and Director of the Centre of Applied Legal Studies at the University of the Witwatersrand. Between 1995 and 1997 he held a joint appointment at the University of Cape Town and the University of the Witwatersrand. He was then appointed as Judge of the High Court in Cape Town. He has authored and co-authored 11 books and over 100 articles in academic journals as well as numerous op-ed pieces on constitutional law, jurisprudence, commercial law, criminology, politics and South African history.

'The halachah operates in the practical realm of reality, and an insular withdrawal from the creative act in the pragmatic world is contrary to the spirit of the Torah.'

Rav Soloveitchik[1]

The title of this paper echoes the theme made famous by Karl Popper who sought to distinguish between holism and individualism.[2] For Popper, holism assumes the view that human social groupings are greater than the sum of their members, that such groupings are organic entities in their own right, that they act on their members and shape their destinies, and that they are subject to their own independent laws of development.

Popper linked this concept of holism to historicism – the belief that history develops inexorably and necessarily according to certain principles or rules towards a determinate end. Popper claimed that the holist believes that individuals are essentially formed by the social groupings to which they belong, while the historicist holds that it is possible to understand such a social grouping only in terms of the internal principles that determine its development.

For Popper, adherence to this conceptual viewpoint inevitably leads to totalitarianism; that is to centralised government, control over the autonomy of the individual, and the concomitant pursuit of large-scale social planning by government.

For Popper any human social grouping is no more or less than the sum of its individual members. History is the largely unplanned and unforeseen result of the actions of individuals. Large-scale social planning to an antecedently conceived blueprint is inherently misconceived.[3]

This links to the further theory developed by Popper, namely that humankind makes progress through its fallibility. All theoretical explanations need to be subjected to critical scrutiny with a commitment that we abandon that which we find to be false. Hence, we arrive at the importance of a critical spirit in an open society – progress comes best in a society in which each individual is able to evaluate critically the consequences of the implementation of social and political policy – particularly that of government. The open society is thus one in which there is an association of free individuals respecting one another's rights within the framework of mutual protection supplied by the state and where policy is achieved through the making of responsible rational decisions.

For the purpose of the topic of this paper – a topic chosen by the organisers of this conference – I am prepared to use Popper subject to two caveats. Firstly, as the text of the South African constitution makes clear, there cannot be an open society unless there is a commitment to human dignity, equality and freedom. Disempowerment through starvation, homelessness, discrimination is not a recipe for any open society. Hence in Section 1 of the South African constitution, the values of human dignity, equality and freedom are proclaimed as the very source of an open and democratic society.

Secondly I do not want to discard the importance of the group.

The group shapes the individual just as the individual helps shape the group. I am speaking here as a Jew, born in South Africa, where my religion, colour, background, Jewish heritage and South African upbringing all combine to shape what I might say on this and every other topic.

Is Judaism compatible with such a society?

The question can be phrased differently, namely to what extent can a Jew be committed to a culture of reasoned justification?

Before I engage with this question, there is one qualification that needs to be stated. There have been many Jews who have contributed to the development of an open and democratic society in South Africa, at least to one constitutionally committed to an open society. The history of Jews who were involved in the political struggles that finally led to the constitutional state in 1994 is well documented. Few of these people appeared to find the source of their commitment within any of the competing Jewish traditions.[4]

By contrast, the Jewish community's response to apartheid was no less shameful than that of other white communities. The Board of Deputies, the umbrella body mandated to watch over the welfare of the Jewish community in South Africa, adopted the neutral stance; as the community contained many differing political opinions, it, as the representative body, could not be seen to prefer one political stance over another. Thus in 1972 the Board's president Maurice Porter gave two reasons for the Board's stance: 'At least two reasons have motivated us: first the Board of Deputies has always been governed by the principle that it is a non-political body and does not enter the arena except in matters which specifically affected the Jewish community as such: and secondly Jewish opinion on politics and racial issues is far from uniform.'[5] A similar view was expressed two years later by Arthur Suzman: '… we cannot as a body align ourselves with or against any of the existing political parties.'[6] In 1976 the Board hosted a dinner in honour of ex-Nazi sympathiser BJ Vorster after the latter's visit to Israel. Although Board President David Mann mouthed a few ambiguous phrases about the need for better race relations, the symbolic nature of the dinner was clear.[7]

The Board passed the buck to the rabbinate to articulate a moral response. Although South Africa was blessed with a far less fundamentalist and anti-intellectual rabbinate than is the case presently, it failed the moral challenge. Certainly there were glorious exceptions such as Chief Rabbi Louis Rabinowitz during the 50s and early 60s, Rabbis Ben Isaacson, David Rosen and Selwyn Franklin during the 70s and 80s, as well as reform rabbis such as Rabbis Super and Sherman, but they were in a small minority.

The record is one of moral failure, pragmatism and the expedient reclaiming of activists who had effectively been disowned by the community at that time.[8]

So the history reveals that within the South African Jewish community there is little by way of precedent for an argument that any tradition of Judaism, particularly self-proclaimed Orthodoxy, provided a set of commitments to an open society.

The debate in the post-apartheid context

The primary question to be asked is the following: to what extent can one be a committed Jew and be equally in favour of a society based upon deliberation? There would appear to be four different responses to this problem:

1. Resist any openness.
2. Openness to the outside world but not to Jews.
3. Openness to all.
4. The benefits of an open society for all but Jews. While many antisemites would appear to fall within this category, in reality they are joined in this view by the self-hating Jew.[9]

But this later group is not the target of this paper.

Before I analyse the three remaining categories, I want to engage on a small excursus of memory. When I was a child growing up in racist South Africa, and later as a student, the Jewish community appeared reasonably committed to a position of deliberation and respect for all Jews. In theory the same position held true for its attitudes to the broader community. In practice, however, the community was almost paralysed in its anxiety about the parlous position in which it perceived itself to be located. So it said little about the racist horrors that steadily engulfed our society, from the indignities of separate amenities to the Dr Mengele-type tactics that have been revealed to us in recent court cases and in the TRC reports. Two examples must suffice. When Wolpe and Goldreich escaped from prison, Yigal Allon was quoted as saying Jews could not be citizens of a country that proclaimed racism as the law. The Board of Deputies responded that this may have been the view of Mr Allon but it was not shared by the South African Jewish community.[10] For me, even as a young boy, the escape engendered great pride, a sense that justice could win out in an evil world. The establishment effectively told me that these thoughts were un-Jewish!

My second example turns on Chief Rabbi Casper who during his insipid reign as chief rabbi ruled that conscientious objection was halachically impermissible.[11] Other religious leaders lent support to the 'end-conscription campaign' – Jewish religious leadership preferred to adopt the Quisling approach.

So the examination for me of the three alternatives is shaped by a scarred history in which Jews within my community failed to show a commitment to an open society based upon compassion and justice.

1. Resist any openness

This approach resists any assertion or claim to commonality to the outside world. Jews are superior, not simply different, and hence there is no need to engage with inferior culture. Take the example of Rabbi Yitzchak Ginsburg, the former head of the Yoseph Tomb Yeshiva, who an interview said as follows: 'It is a superiority that invests Jewish life with greater value in the eyes of the Torah. If you see two people drowning, a Jew and a non-Jew, the Torah says you save the Jewish life. If every simple cell in a Jewish body entails divinity, is a part of G-d, then every strand of DNA is a part of G-d. Therefore there is something special about Jewish DNA. There is something infinitely more holy and unique about Jewish life than non-Jewish life.'[12]

This approach to the world starts from the point of superiority. It is an easy step to claim total superiority for a source of knowledge that has divine sanction. It further follows that such divine knowledge must be given its literal meaning, for any other meaning would entail the insertion of human intervention, thereby weakening the very claim upon which the entire claim to the divine sanction is based.

Within a world where the economic forces of globalisation have threatened not simply the autonomy of the nation state but the very essence of identity, it is hardly surprising that relief is sought in this fundamentalism. It provides an escape from modernity, a site of understandable struggle against the effect of globalisation together with a lexicon that provides all the answers to the rapidly changing economic and political terrain. It is thus a small wonder that the challenge posed by Rav Soloveitchik in his masterpiece *The Lonely Man of Faith* (as cited above) is not even considered by a vast proportion of Orthodoxy. To contemplate a contested tradition in which there is a respectable body seeking to reconcile Jewish autonomy with universal engagement is too difficult a task. Instead the closure of the Jewish mind continues apace. Within South African Jewry, Johannesburg has become the Kandahar of the community!

2. Openness to all but not to all Jews

This rather odd variant of the first approach has become a dominant strain within contemporary South African Jewish life, arguably because Orthodox rabbinical leadership has adopted a culture of authority within secular South African life. Thus in 2000 the Cape Jewish community invited reform rabbi David Hoffman to deliver the address at the annual Holocaust memorial service. This caused a veritable brouhaha within the ranks of Orthodox rabbis, many of whom found a range of oddly convenient reasons not to attend the annual memorial for six million victims who were never made subject to the same form of differentiation by Hitler and the Nazi extermination machine.

The theological foundation for this approach is shaky. Prof. Menachem Kellner[13] argues that the only Talmudic text that seeks to exclude some Jews is to be found in Sanhedrin 10:1. From the interpretation of this text by the Rambam we have slowly evolved to a position where, predominantly on the contemporary authority of Rav Moshe Feinstein (or rather an *ex post facto* interpretation of Feinstein), a minimum commitment to a literal application of the 13 principles of faith is required if one wishes to escape the label of heretic.

Kellner makes the suggestion that 'we expend less effort on determining whether or not our fellow Jews are heretical, and more effort on working with our fellow Jews to make their behaviour accord more with traditional norms. I think we should let G-d worry about who the kosher Jews are, and who gets into heaven, while we worry about trying to get Jews to become more Jewish in this world.'[14]

Another example of this second approach (although it also fits within the first strain) was the manner in which Orthodoxy generated a climate of unbending hatred to Yitchak Rabin. Rabbis the world over, including some in Johannesburg and Cape Town, thundered from their pulpits about the perfidious conduct of the democratically elected Israeli Prime Minister.[15] In this case, the discrimination was focussed on a Jew who had 'placed himself' outside of the community as defined by this strain of Orthodoxy. To an extent Rav Aaron Lichtenstein captured this pathology when, following the assassination of Mr Rabin, he said, 'May we know how to purify our camp, and through a spiritual Torah effort, we shall aspire as best we can to purify and sanctify our city.'[16]

3. Open society for all

In my view the third position must include the second. One cannot be contemptuous of fellow Jews and simultaneously be committed to a principle of freedom and equality for all. My reason for this argument is that if a Jew is concerned with the 'Other' then a commitment to the second and third alternatives must follow simultaneously.

This conclusion can be illustrated thus: In dealing with the question of the interpretation of Talmudic texts, Emmanuel

Levinas contends that Judaism mandates an engagement of subjective interpretation with an obligatory recourse to the tradition of commentators. As he writes, the aim of interpretation is not to appeal to authority but rather 'to refer to a context which allows the level of discussion to be raised and to make one notice the true import of the data from which the discussion derives its meaning. The transfer of an idea to another climate – which is the original climate – wrests new possibilities from it. Ideas do not become fixed by a process of conceptualisation which would extinguish many of the sparks dancing beneath the gaze riveted upon the Real.'[17] For Levinas this means that the very process of textual interpretation on which a tradition relies is predicated upon the position that the self is only being true when its truth is established by a response to the 'Other'. It is the other person who disrupts our complacency, self-sufficiency. Thus there is a Jewish tradition which by definition must concern both self and 'Other'. The special vocation of Jews is to remind the world of the 'Other' which can only be achieved by reference to the Jews' individuality and that of the 'Other'.

Developing this theme, Levinas contrasts the Greek to that of the Jewish model of society. Within the covenant each person finds herself responsible for everyone else. Each act of the covenant expresses more than 600 000 personal acts of responsibility. Society is thus formed by the bonds that tie on to the 'Other'. In the Greek world, society binds an individual to another individual through the intermediary of the state. The first allegiance is to the civil order – the good of the state. For Jews the world is founded on the inter-personal. It begins with humans facing humans, and grows into a community of individuals each of whom is an integral part of the whole.

Expressed differently, if much of Western philosophy is regarded by Levinas as the philosophy of subjectivity, Judaism is based on the idea of *hineini* – an act of conscience making possible the act of consciousness. This is the basis of the beginning of community. As he observes, 'The heirs of Abraham – men to whom their ancestors bequeathed a different tradition of duties toward the other man, which one is never done with, an order in which one is never free. In this order, above all else, duty takes the form of obligations toward the body, the obligation of feeding and sheltering. So defined, the heirs of Abraham are of all nations: any man truly man is no doubt of the line of Abraham.'[18]

So in a sense we return to Popper. We cannot but be committed to respect for the 'Other' – we cannot but help engage with the 'Other'. It shapes our being. So to cut off the other Jew but not the other person is as hopeless a pursuit as the opposite, namely to try cut off the fellow person but not the fellow Jew. It is truly difficult to see how the closure to the outside can be reconciled not only with the approach adopted by Levinas but with a far more immediate text for Jews – the *Aleinu* prayer which is said every day. Without an engagement with the 'Other' world, it becomes impossible as the beneficiaries of Abraham's bequest to see how we are supposed to engage in *tikkun olam* – the purification of the world which lies at the very heart of the *Aleinu* prayer. Retreating into an eighteenth-century ghetto within the demands of the twenty-first century can hardly represent anything other than an acknowledgement of defeat for such foundational aspirations. But does that mean that Orthodox Jews must forsake their values for a pluralism? The answer must be in the negative; for what the spirit of this aspiration entails is that we cannot simply disengage from the 'Other' and hope to be truly human.

But do the texts not bind us to *the* interpretation? Unquestionably there has been a blurring between a framework as encapsulated in the *Halachah* and the end, howsoever defined. But the framework itself has been the subject of change and interpretation. David Hartman provides a neat example to illustrate this point. He refers to Exodus 3:13-16 in which G-d gives Moses an answer to the question as to what name he should use to describe G-d to the people. To this G-d says that Moses must tell the people that Ehyeh asher Ehyeh sent you. To this Hartman comments, 'He is the G-d of history and community, the G-d of the ancestors, but also G-d who says that radical novelty and surprise are possible in a spiritual life in which the covenantal ancestors follow you constantly. I take Ehyeh asher ehyeh to mean "I will be – I will come in new ways."'[19]

The tradition is a contested one precisely because the engagement between G-d and humanity is an evolving one – requiring differing responses from both sides. This unquestionably invites debate and openness – which does not mean to establish a liberal state for which liberal as opposed to Jewish principles would be sufficient. But there is a possibility of openness of a unique Jewish kind.

But if we so impose but one literal view of the text and any engagement, we then begin to act for and like G-d. We then decide who is a Jew, who is a person and who is an 'Other'. We then deny the very possibility of a contest within our traditions, and insist that some Eastern European model of an eighteenth-century ghetto becomes *the* only version of Judaism. If correct, Judaism then becomes an enemy of a deliberative process.

The tragedy is that as fundamentalism takes hold, engagement dies and deliberation takes place no more. That is neither inevitable nor is there an absence of contrary authority. Take Parshat Korach as an example. Moshe was faced with a rebellion led by Korach. His initial response was to ask for time, designed so that Korach could reconsider his position. Thereafter Moshe entered into dialogue with a group whose unashamed object was to mount a challenge to the leadership of Moshe Rabenu. That such proposal of dialogue failed is another issue; that it was the first option employed by Moshe is indicative of its centrality within Biblical Judaism and of the overarching importance of engagement and deliberation.[20] The modern Orthodox establishment bothers neither to explain nor to debate; exclusion of the 'Other' is the only tactic bolstered as it is with an assurance of literal textual support.

Conclusion

The dominant strain within Orthodoxy is a commitment to closure to all but those who commit to the same theological position. It is one in which the dignity demanded by Soloveitchik's Adam I[21] is paramount and in which the role of the Jew is to build from within and not to bother about the outside world.[22]

Admittedly, there is a group of scholars who are concerned with the broader community but maintain an unbending approach to any other form of Judaism.[23] For some within the ultra-Orthodox establishment, a marketing ploy appears to be to be adopted, namely to purport to accommodate for a brief period in order to capture a constituency, for which period the foundational belief claims are blurred. But the theology remains exclusionist in its objective.

Where does it leave Jews and their relationship to deliberation? In my view, the past decade has seen a closure of the Jewish mind. The Orthodox establishment in South Africa is proud of these developments which have seen a marked rise in adherence to ritual, particularly in Johannesburg. On its own, this commitment may be admired. Indeed a position committed to openness and dialogue could hardly be anything other than supportive, subject to a major qualification. The caveat is that this swing to greater intensity of ritual has come at a serious price – the closure of the Jewish mind, the creation of a massive 'Other' within Jewish ranks, a hatred of difference and a consequent rejection of any possible reconciliation between Muslim and Jew, Palestinian and Israeli. Of equal importance, this form of Judaism promotes the group at all costs. The individual is then subsumed under the weight of obligations to the group, Judaism then becomes a custom-made product, and the possibility for individual development implodes. On this basis one wonder why the custodians of this uniformity do not change the introduction to the Amidah to read 'the G-d of Abraham, Isaac and Jacob' rather than its existing formulation of 'the 'G-d of Abraham, the G-d of Isaac and the G-d of Jacob', which is indicative of the very personal engagement required between G-d and the human being.

The purpose of this article is not claim that there is one superior position within the tradition. It is however to assert the cost of denial of that contest. For me, there is a strain within Jewish tradition that can fall within the third of the options. It is exquisitely defined by Abraham Joshua Herschel as follows: 'Who is a Jew? A witness to transcendence and the presence of G-d; a person in whose life Abraham would feel at home, a person for whom Rabbi Akiba would feel deep affinity, a person of whom Jewish martyrs of all ages would not be ashamed.'

Who is a Jew? A person whose integrity decays when unmoved by the knowledge of wrong done to other people.

Who is a Jew? A person in travail with G-d's dreams and designs; a person to whom G-d is a challenge and not an abstraction. He who is called upon to be involved in the sanctification of time and in building of the Holy Land; to cultivate passion for justice and the ability to experience the arrival of Friday night as an event.

Who is a Jew? A person who knows how to recall and to keep alive what is holy in our people's past and to cherish the promise and the vision of redemption in the days to come.'[24]

This is a definition which allows for engagement and dialogue. It opposes the present dominant strain in which G-d is seen as sitting in the sky with a bank of television screens deciding when to intervene in human affairs. After all, is that not what the predominant view of *bashert* actually means? For those who wish to pass on a tradition to our children where *tikkun olam* means adherence to justice tempered by compassion, the closure of the Jewish mind has come at too great a cost to the next generation. This anxiety is compounded when account is taken of the implications of our recent history. If South African Jews failed to promote an open society in the dark days of apartheid, when the moral issues were so starkly set out and when the cloud of Kundahar had not spread throughout the Jewish firmament, the question must arise as to the possibility of such a contribution in more nuanced moral times and within a faith community which has increasingly shown its affection for the darkness of such theological clouds.

Endnotes

Introduction

1. The colloquium was organised by the Isaac and Jessie Kaplan Centre for Jewish Studies and Research at the University of Cape Town in association with the new South African Jewish Museum. The themes chosen for the colloquium followed those that informed the design of the museum, which was formally opened by former president Nelson Mandela on 13 December 2000. All the contributions other than that of James Campbell arose out of the colloquium.

2. A special issue of *Jewish Affairs* was devoted to this question. See *Jewish Affairs*, 52:1, 1997. More recently the topic has been explored in Braude, Claudia Bathsheba, *Contemporary South African Jewish Writing*, University of Nebraska Press, Lincoln and London, 2002.

3. See Dubb, Allie A, *The Jewish Population of South Africa: the 1991 Sociodemographic Survey*, Jewish Publications – South Africa, Kaplan Centre for Jewish Studies and Research, University of Cape Town, 1994, p.7. For the early history of South African Jewry see Saron, Gustav and Hotz, Louis (eds), *The Jews in South Africa: A History*, Oxford University Press, Cape Town, 1955, and Shain, Milton, *Jewry and Cape Society: The Origins and Activities of the Jewish Board of Deputies for the Cape Colony*, Historical Publications Society, Cape Town, 1983.

4. See Shain, Milton and Frankental, Sally, '"Community with a Conscience": Myth or Reality?' in Abramson, Glenda (ed.), *Modern Jewish Mythologies*, Hebrew Union College Press, Cincinnati, 1999.

Between ideology and indifference: the destruction of Yiddish in South Africa (Joseph Sherman)

1. These are: Poliva, JA, *A short history of the Jewish press and literature of South Africa from its earliest days until the present time*, Johannesburg, 1961; Sherman, J (trans. and ed.), *From A Land Far Off: Yiddish Stories in English Translation*, Cape Town, 1987, p.198; Belling, V, *Bibliography of South African Jewry*, Cape Town, 1997.

2. These are the Landau Collection in the library of the University of the Witwatersrand, Johannesburg; the Gitlin Library, Cape Town; and the Jewish Studies Collection in the Library of the University of Cape Town.

3. The South African sections of this book have been published in English translation. See Hoffmann, ND, *Book of Memoirs*, translated by Lilian Dubb and Sheila Barkusky, Cape Town, 1996.

4. Wolpe, DE, *Ikh un mayn velt*, 2 Vols, Johannesburg-Jerusalem, 1997/1999.

5. Only the last of these has been translated and published in English. See Feldman, L, *Oudtshoorn: Jerusalem of Africa*. Edited, with an introductory essay, by Joseph Sherman; translated by Lilian Dubb and Sheila Barkusky; historical notes and commentary by John Simon, Johannesburg, 1989.

6. For a detailed study of these particular stories see Sherman, J, 'Serving the Natives: Whiteness as the Price of Hospitality in South African Yiddish Literature', *Journal of Southern African Studies*, 26:3, September 2000, pp.505-521.

7. See Feldman, R, *Shvarts un vays*, Warsaw, 1935; enl. and repub. New York, 1957; Levinsky, N, *Der regn hot farshpetikt*, Bloemfontein, 1959.

8. Goss, I, 'What are we to teach our children?' *Adventure of Jewish Education: Essays in Survival and Salvation*, Johannesburg, 1961, pp.33-4.

9. For a penetrating evaluation of the significance of Peretz's work, see Wisse, RR, *I.L. Peretz and the Making of Modern Jewish Culture*, Seattle, 1991.

10. For a brief but telling analysis of the extent to which Peretz ironically deployed the Hasidic material he used, see Wisse, Ruth R, 'Introduction' in Wisse, Ruth R (ed.), *The I.L. Peretz Reader*, New York, 1990, pp.xxii-xxiii. In those cases where Peretz chose to give both a Hebrew and a Yiddish version of individual stories (and the stories I mention here were not among them), Peretz did not simply translate them – he always rewrote them. For this reason, there are significant differences between Peretz's Hebrew and Yiddish texts. None of this was ever mentioned, of course.

11. Goss, I, 'Yitzchok Leibush Peretz – some reflections on his work', *Gleanings: Reflections on Judaism and Jewish Education*, Johannesburg, 1975, pp.52-3.

12. The quoted phrase is Goss's own, cited in the biographical sketch given by Katzew, H, 'Isaac Goss – Religious Intellectual who Guides Education', in Goss, I, *Adventure of Jewish Education*, South African Board of Jewish Education, Johannesburg, 1961, pp.xi-xv.

13. The kind of censorship exercised on my overview of the Yiddish-Zionist conflict in South Africa in the 1930s can easily be established by comparing its two published versions. Contrast the account in Arkin, M, *South African Jewry: A Contemporary Survey*, Cape Town, 1984, pp.152-8 with the account in Sherman, J, (trans. and ed.), *From A Land Far Off*, pp.7-9.

14. This uproar has been the subject of exhaustive and well-documented research. For the most detailed account, see Shain, M, *Jewry and Cape Society*, Cape Town, 1983.

15. Goss, I, 'Can We Produce Jewish Intellectuals?' *Adventure in Jewish Education*, p.227.

16. Goss, I, 'some Reflections on Zionism and Judaism', *Adventure of Jewish Education*, p.264.

17. I have elsewhere more fully discussed this polemic and the central role taken in it by Dovid Bergelson and Shmuel Niger. See Sherman, J, 'From Isolation to Entrapment: Bergelson and the Party Line, 1919-1927', *Slavic Almanach*, 6:9, 2000, pp.195-222.

18. For a fuller discussion of how the theories of Dubnov and Zhitlovsky were understood in South Africa, particularly by Leibl Feldman, see Sherman, J, 'With Perfect Faith: The Life and Work of Leibl Feldman', in Feldman, L, *Oudtshoorn: Jerusalem of Africa*, pp.27-38.

19. Levick, W, 'Yiddish in Limbo: A Personal View', Afterword in Sherman, J, *From A Land Far Off*, pp.193-4.

20. For an outline of the early history of the Johannesburg Yiddish *Folkshul* from 1929 to 1931 see Sherman, J, *From A Land Far Off*, pp.9, 160; for an overview of Feldman's despotic control over it from 1948 to 1967 see Sherman, J, 'With Perfect Faith: The Life and Work of Leibl Feldman' in Feldman, L, *Oudtshoorn: Jerusalem of Africa*, pp.20-3.

21. For details of both the official and the unofficial proscription of Hebrew and its use in the Soviet Union, see Gilboa, Yehoshua A, 'Hebrew Literature in the USSR' in Kochan, L (ed.), *The Jews in Soviet Russia Since 1917*, Oxford University Press, London and New York, 1972, pp.226-9. For details about the 'language revolution' and its impact on Yiddish orthography, see Pinkus, Benjamin, *The Jews of The Soviet Union*, Cambridge University Press, Cambridge, 1988, pp.116-8.

22. Khrushchev's speech, of course, was neither spontaneous nor secret, but the result of three years of agonised planning by the Soviet Central Committee and by Khrushchev himself. See Khrushchev, NS, *Khrushchev Remembers*, with an introduction, commentary and notes by Edward Crankshaw. Translated by Strobe Talbott, Boston, 1970, pp.346-53.

23. Wolpe, D, *Ikh un mayn velt*, Vol. 2, pp.211-3; my translation.

24. Dobrushin, Y, *Dovid Bergelson* [in Yiddish], Moscow, 1947.

25. Although the SABJE eventually succeeded in its aim of establishing Day Schools throughout South Africa, it did so in the face of antagonism, obviously for different reasons, from both religious and secular quarters in the community. See the brief and evasive outline of this negative

reaction to organised Jewish education in South Africa given by Mink, R, 'Education', in Arkin, M, *South African Jewry: A Contemporary Survey*, p.119.

26. Goss, I, 'Jewish Day and Afternoon School', *Gleanings*, pp.39-40.

The Boer War, the Great War, and the shaping of South African Jewish loyalties (Richard Mendelsohn)

1. For refugee life at the coast, see Bradlow, Edna, 'Jewish Refugees at the Cape in the Anglo-Boer War', *Jewish Affairs*, 54:3, Spring 1999, pp.37-42, and Van Heyningen, Elizabeth, 'Refugees and Relief in Cape Town 1899-1902', in *Studies in the History of Cape Town*, University of Cape Town, Cape Town. 1980.

2. The wartime minute books of the Bloemfontein Hebrew Congregation, for example, which are preserved in the well-managed archives of the present congregation, reveal a community of some 70 stay-behinds, determined on preserving communal life despite the disruptions of war. The principal wartime issue, it seems, was the shaky performance of its *mohel* (ritual circumciser). In the midst of a war zone, Bloemfontein was forced to do without a fully certificated minister for the duration of the war. Instead it relied on the services of Mr Zitron, a questionably qualified jack-of-all-trades who tripled up as *mohel*, *schochet* (ritual slaughterer) and prayer leader. Zitron's performance became a matter of serious wartime dispute. After a congregant complained about the circumcision of his son, medical and rabbinical opinion were solicited about Zitron's fitness for duty. The committee approached a respected gentile family doctor, Dr Kellner, who reported that 'the Mohel's fingers were not too clean and under the circumstances he would not allow any of his children to be circumcised by him'. The *shul* committee also

posted off Zitron's certificates to Chief Rabbi Adler in London for scrutiny. To their dismay Adler replied that while these proved that Zitron was competent to act as a *schochet*, there was 'not a word however ... in these Certificates touching his ability as a Mohel'. Challenged to explain, Zitron promptly resigned, on the eve of the Treaty of Vereeniging. (With the arrival of peace, and the community's greatly improved prospects, the congregation then advertised for a 'competent man' – at twice Zitron's salary.) Bloemfontein Hebrew Congregation archives: 1/1/1 minute book, 1901-1923; 1/1/26 letter book, 1898-1918.

3. This hitherto-hidden history of the uprooting of rural Jewry in the Transvaal and Orange Free State will be extensively documented in my forthcoming study of Jews and the South African War.

4. For this legal sleight-of-hand, again see my forthcoming book on Jews and the South African War.

5. For a case study of the Jewish 'bittereinder', see Mendelsohn, Richard, 'A Jewish Family at War: the Segalls of Vlakfontein', *Jewish Affairs*, 55:3, Spring, 2000, pp.22-5. The 16-year-old Joseph 'Jakkals' Segall (for example) had only arrived in the Orange Free State from Russia a year before the war, yet chose to serve on commando, alongside his friend Wolf Jacobson, till the 'bitter-end'.

6. See Mendelsohn, Richard, 'The Jewish Soldier: Anglo-Jewry at War', *Jewish Affairs*, 54:3, Spring 1999, pp.11-19, and Mendelsohn, '"Supporting the Fallen and Healing the Sick": Jewish Doctors of the Anglo-Boer War', *Jewish Affairs*, 56:2, Winter 2001, pp.10-15, for the fervid and large-scale participation of Anglo-Jewry in the empire's war in South Africa.

7. For Jewish civil disabilities in the South African Republic, see Mendelsohn, Richard, 'Between Boer and Brit: Jewish Immigrants in the Transvaal in the Late Nineteenth Century', in Newman, A and Massil, SW (eds) *Patterns of Migration, 1850–1914*, Jewish Historical Society of England and the Institute of Jewish Studies, University College London, 1996, pp.201-2.

8. Sammy Marks's fluid loyalties are themselves a demonstration of the ease with which the great majority of Jews – very few of them with anything approaching his level of personal and financial investment in the old order made the transition to their new allegiances. For Sammy's rapid and easy transfer of allegiances in mid-1900, with the British occupation of Pretoria, see Mendelsohn, R, *Sammy Marks. 'The Uncrowned King of the Transvaal'*, David Philip and Ohio University Press, Cape Town and Athens, Ohio, 1991, chapter 7.

By contrast, the Baumann-Leviseur clan of Bloemfontein, Free State-born anglicised German Jews, clung on to their republican loyalties long after the republican cause had apparently collapsed, and did so at some (moderate) personal risk. See Mendelsohn, Richard, 'Friends of the Free State: the Baumanns of Bloemfontein in the Anglo-Boer War', *Jewish Affairs*, 56:3, Spring 2001, pp.6-18, for the war service and intense republican loyalties of this Jewish family in a war in which most Jewish families in South Africa were more circumspect.

9. The participation of young Jewish maidens in street-collecting raised

Memories, Realities and Dreams

some moral anxiety. The *South African Jewish Chronicle* (9 March 1917) railed at those young girls who it alleged used 'the opportunities afforded them to invite the attentions of a more or less desirable section of the male population'.

10. *South African Jewish Chronicle* 21.9.17

11. *South African Jewish Chronicle* 13.8.15; 27.8.15; 24.12.15

12. The ugly *Lusitania* Riots of May 1915, directed at German property in South Africa in the wake of the sinking of the eponymous passenger ship, were a frightening reminder to Jews of these passions. German Jews and Jews with German names were particularly vulnerable.

13. In England, where conscription was introduced in mid-war, Jewish recruitment nevertheless remained a public issue. The conspicuous reluctance of young Russian Jews, not yet naturalised and therefore not liable for conscription, to volunteer for service, attracted public hostility, much to the embarrassment of the Anglo-Jewish establishment. See Cesarani, David, 'An Embattled Minority: the Jews in Britain During the First World War', in *Immigrants and Minorities*, 8:1 & 2, March 1989, pp.61-81.

14. *South African Jewish Chronicle* 27.7.17

15. *South African Jewish Chronicle* 23.3.17

16. *South African Jewish Chronicle* 23.3.17

17. See Cesarani for the strong parallels between the experience of South African and British Jewry with regard to Russian Jewish responses to the war.

18. *South African Jewish Chronicle* 29.7.17

19. *South African Jewish Chronicle* 9.2.17 The *South African Jewish Chronicle* (16.2.17) dismissed much of this as classic 'Jew Baiting' ...
While on the question of recruiting it is interesting to note that the *Cape Times* has recently been full of letters on this subject. Apparently the number of Jews of suitable appearance and age now sunning themselves on the sands at Muizenberg has led to certain individuals writing to the Cape Town dailies saying that our co-religionists are not doing their fair share. This recrudescence, from time to time, of attacks upon the Jews for slacking, some couched in very strong terms and some in milder form, is getting monotonous, more particularly to those of us who know that – as one of the *Cape Times* correspondents points out – were every Jew but one in the country to get killed in action and that one Jew be seen, he would be pounced upon by antisemites and designated as a slacker, his female relations – for there would be no Jewish males left – being equally condemned, possibly because they had no further human sacrifices to make.

20. *South African Jewish Chronicle* 16.3.17

21. *South African Jewish Chronicle* 5.4.17
A further instance of Jewish defensiveness in the face of wartime public criticism: in response to antisemitic aspersions by the resident magistrate of Kroonstad 'about the Jews not necessarily going to fight but for the purpose of making money', a Mr A

Michels wrote a letter to the local paper defending the patriotism of the anglicised Jew while explaining the reluctance of the Russian Jew to embrace the allied cause:

> He (Mr Leary) attacks the Jew for not going. I say emphatically that all the English-born Jews of Kroonstad that were fit to go, went. The remainder are the oppressed Russian Jews who were treated in their homeland worse than kafirs, whose parents were allowed to be slaughtered at the whim of the Russian and who, I regret to say, would rather see German (even Chinese) government over them. These facts should be borne in mind before insulting the Jews as a race and attacking them for lack of patriotism.

(*South African Jewish Chronicle* 23.3.17)

22. *South African Jewish Chronicle* 23.11.17; 18.1.18; 22.2.18; 27.3.18

Insiders on outsiders: some South African Jewish writers (Marcia Leveson)

1. *Sarah Gertrude Millin: A South African Life*, Ad Donker, Johannesburg, pp.1-21.

2. 'Blood, Taint, Flaw, Degeneration: The Novels of Sarah Gertrude Millin' in *English Studies in Africa*, 23:1, 1980, pp.41-58, rpt in *White Writing: On the Culture of Letters in South Africa*, Century Hutchinson, Sandton, 1988, pp.136-162.

3. 'Not Gobineau but Heine – Not Racial Theory but Biblical Theme: The Case of Sarah Gertrude Millin' in *English Studies in Africa,* 34 (1), 1991, pp.27-38, cited in Leveson, M, *People of the Book: Images of the Jew in South African Fiction 1880-1992*, Witwatersrand University Press, Johannesburg, 1996, p.78.

4. Unpaginated notes. SG Millin Papers, A539/9. Manuscript Collection, University of the Witwatersrand Library. Quoted in Braun, L, op. cit., p.29.

5. Millin, Sarah Gertrude, *The Night is Long*, London, Faber, 1941, p.148.

6. Interview, London, 3 Feb 1987, quoted in Lazerson, JN, *Against the Tide: Whites in the Struggle against Apartheid*, Mayibuye Books, Belville, 1994, p.82.

7. *Cutting through the Mountain: Interviews with South African Jewish Activists,* Viking (Penguin), Sandton, 1997.

8. Interview with Ian Hamilton, *New Review*, 4 October 1977, p.26.

9. Remark made by a member of the Commission of Enquiry into Labour

in the Cape Colony 1893. Cited in Shain, M *The Roots of Antisemitism in South Africa*, Witwatersrand University Press, Johannesburg, 1994, p.23.

10. Interview with Alan Ross, 1965, in Bazin, NT and Seymour, MD (eds), *Conversations with Nadine Gordimer*, University Press, Jackson and London.

'If it was so good, why is it so bad?' The memories and realities of antisemitism in South Africa, past and present (Milton Shain)

1. *Zakhor, Jewish History and Jewish Memory*, Schocken Books Inc., 1989, p.94.

2. Shain, Milton, *The Roots of Antisemitism in South Africa*, University Press of Virginia, Charlottesville and Witwatersrand University Press, Johannesburg, 1994.

3. See Shain, *The Roots of Antisemitism in South Africa*, p.109.

4. Shain, *The Roots of Antisemitism in South Africa*, p.144.

5. See Furlong, Patrick J, *Between Crown and Swastika*, Wesleyan University Press, Middleton, 1991, chapter 2, *passim*.

6. See LaCapra, Dominick, *History and Memory after Auschwitz*, Cornell University Press, 1998.

7. See, e.g., Millin, SG, *The South Africans*, London, 1926, pp.175-81; Herrman, L, *History of the Jews in South Africa*, London, 1930; Abrahams, I, *The Birth of a Community*, Cape Town, 1955; Saron, G and Hotz, L (eds), *The Jews in South Africa: A History*, Cape Town, 1955. Similar ideas have been appropriated by non-Jewish historians: see, e.g., Stultz, N, *Afrikaner Politics in South Africa 1934-1948*, Berkeley and Los Angeles, 1974, pp.44-45.

8. The origin of the word *smous* (pl *smouse*) is not certain. The word may be a corruption of the name Moses brought over from Holland in the Dutch East India Company's days.

The corruption arose from the manner in which the Dutch Jews themselves pronounced the name. It has been suggested that the word derives from *Mauschel*, the equivalent of Jewish trader. Another explanation claims that the word is derived from the German *schmuss* (talk, patter) and from the Hebrew *Sh'mu* (tales, news), the reference being to the persuasive eloquence of Jewish traders. While the former explanation seems plausible in a folk etymological sense, *Sh'mu* is problematic. The author may have meant *Sh'mu'a* which means rumour, report, news, tidings, gossip, tradition. Certainly *smous* usually referred to a Jewish trader or merchant.

9. Aschman, G, 'Oudtshoorn in the Early Days', in Saron and Hotz, *The Jews in South Africa*, p.136.

10. Anti-Jewish outbursts and movements have belonged exclusively to the realm of European or white parliamentary and extra-parliamentary politics. The majority black population – including coloureds and Indians – has never focussed specifically on the Jew when articulating grievances and aspirations. For them the issue was always one of 'white' oppression and domination.

11. Cohen, M, 'Anti-Jewish Manifestations in the Union of South Africa'; unp. BA (Hons) dissertation, UCT, 1968; Bradlow, E, 'Immigration into the Union, 1910-1948'; unp. PhD thesis, UCT, 1978; Shimoni, G, *Jews and Zionism. The South African Experience 1910-1967*, Cape Town, 1980; Furlong, *Between Crown and Swastika*.

12. Shain, Milton, *Jewry and Cape Society*, Historical Publication Society, Cape Town, 1983. Charles van Onselen, Riva Krut and Greg Cuthbertson have also indirectly touched upon conflict between Jew and non-Jews: see Van Onselen, Charles, 'Randlords and Rotgut, 1886-1903', in Van Onselen, Charles (ed.), *Studies in the Social and Economic History of the Witwatersrand 1886-1914, Vol I, New Babylon*, Johannesburg, 1982; Krut, Riva, 'The Making of a South African Jewish Community in Johannesburg, 1886-1914', in Bozzoli, Belinda (ed.), *Class, Community and Conflict: South African Perspectives*, Johannesburg, 1987; Cuthbertson, Greg, 'Jewish Immigration as an Issue in South African Politics, 1937-1939', in *Historia*, 26, 1981.

13. Quoted in Addleson, A, 'In the Eastern Province', in Saron and Hotz, *The Jews in South Africa*, p.307.

14. See for example, Boon, MJ, *Jotting's by the way or Boon's madness on the Road*, London, 1884.

15. Standard Bank Archives, Diamond Volume, Michell to General Manaher 13 April 1882 (Henry Files). Quoted in Turrel, RV, *Capital Class and Monopoly, the Kimberley Diamond Fields 1871-1889*, unp. PhD thesis, University of London, 1982.

16. 4.7.1883.

17. Grundlingh, MAS, 'The Parliament of the Cape of Good Hope, with special reference to Party Politics, 1872-1910', in *Archives Year Book for South African History*, II, 1969, p.182.

18. *Land en Volk*, 5.5.1891. See also Gordon, CT, *The Growth of Boer Opposition to Kruger 1890-1895*, Cape Town, 1970.

19. Report of the working of the Immigration Act 1902-1904, G 63-04,

Vol IX. *Annexures to the Votes and Proceedings of the House of Assembly*, Cape Colony, Cape Archives.

20. 6.5.1904.

21. 23.1.1897.

22. The term *Peruvian* is probably an acronym for Polish and Russian Union – a Jewish club established in Kimberley in the early days. It has also been suggested that the term refers to those immigrants who had sojourned in Argentina under Baron de Hirsch's settlement scheme before coming to South Africa. If that is the origin of the term, the lack of a geographical distinction between Argentina and Peru needs to be explained. It is interesting to note, however, that in a short story in *The Owl* (8.2.1901) by JE Corbett, the author refers to the English Jews struggling to compete against 'Hebrews from Peru and Argentina.' Similarly the *Johannesburg Times* (1.4.1896) description of the Peruvian mentions the 'generosity of Baron Hirsch'. Another theory is that the term is derived from 'Peruvia', a mistaken reference to the ancient Latin term for Poland.

23. Van Onselen, 'Randlords and Rotgut', *op.cit.*

24. Hirshfield, Claire, 'The British Left and the Jewish Conspiracy. A Case Study of Modern Antisemitism', in *Jewish Social Studies*, 43, Spring 1981, p.104.

25. See Davey, Arthur M, *The British Pro-Boers, 1877-1902,* Cape Town, 1978 and Galbraith, John S, 'The Pamphlet Campaign on the Boer War', in *The Journal of Modern History*, Vol. 24 (2), June 1952.

26. See, for example, *The Owl*, 20.12.1901.

27. Hobson, John Atkinson, *The War in South Africa: Its Causes and Effects*, London, 1900. For a very recent critique of British Jews and the Boer War see Mendelsohn, Richard, '"The Jewish War", – Anglo-Jewry and the South African War', paper presented at the 'Rethinking the South African War' Unisa Library Conference, 3-5 August, 1998, Unisa Library, Pretoria.

28. Shain, *The Roots of Antisemitism in South Africa,* pp.58-64.

29. See Shain, *The Roots of Antisemitism in South Africa,* pp.62-63.

30. 3.2.1917.

31. See Shain, *The Roots of Antisemitism in South Africa,* pp.92-99.

32. See Dubow, Saul, 'Race, Civilization and Culture: The Elaboration of Segregationist Discourse in the Interwar years', in Marks, Shula and Trapido, Stanley (eds), *The Politics of Race, Class and Nationalism in Twentieth Century South Africa,* London and New York, 1987.

33. 29.10.1927.

34. 3.2.1930.

35. 2.2.1930.

36. It is significant that even philo-semites supported the Quota Act. Jewish industriousness was equated with Jewish power, a source of concern.

37. Endelman, Todd, 'Comparative Perspectives on Modern Anti-Semitism in the West', in Berger, David (ed.), *History and Hate. The Dimensions of Anti-Semitism,* Philadelphia, 1986.

38. Furlong, p.13.

39. *Ibid*, pp.41-45.

40. Bradlow, 'Immigration into the Union 1910-1948', p.266.

41. 1.10.1937.

42. Shimoni, *Jews and Zionism*, p.130.

43. O'Meara, Dan, *Volkskapitalisme*, Ravan Press, Johannesburg, 1983, p.128.

44. Moodie, TD, *The Rise of Afrikanerdom. Power, Apartheid, and the Afrikaner Civil Religion*, Berkeley, 1975, p.21.

45. Vatcher, WH, *White Laager. The Rise of Afrikaner Nationalism*, London, 1965, pp.68-75.

46. Friedman, Sharon, 'Jews, Germans and Afrikaners: Nationalist Press reactions to the Final Solution', unp. dissertation, BA (Hons) UCT, 1982.

47. The National Party was organised along federal lines with each province maintaining an autonomous structure.

48. Shain, *The Roots of Antisemitism in South Africa*, pp.152-53.

49. See Saron, Gustav, 'A University's "Private Affair" or State Policy?', in *Jewish Affairs*, January 1962, p.6.

50. See Hoffman, Tzippi and Fischer, Alan, *The Jews in South Africa, What Future?* Johannesburg, 1988, p.392.

51. Richard Goldstone was a judge appointed by President FW de Klerk to investigate the security apparatus. *Antisemitism World Report, 1994*, London, p.192.

52. See Shain, Milton, 'South Africa' in David Wyman (ed.) *The World reacts to the Holocaust*, Baltimore, 1996.

53. Hellig, Jocelyn, *Anti-Semitism in South Africa Today*, Tel Aviv University, The Project for the Study of Anti-Semitism, 1996, p.12.

54. *Antisemitism World Report, 1998*.

55. See Pretorius, PJ, *Volksverraad. Die Geskiedenis agter die Geskiedenis*, Mossel Baai, 1996.

56. This was evident in a survey conducted under the auspices of the Kaplan Centre for Jewish Studies and Research at the University of Cape Town.

57. *Antisemitism World Report, 1995*, London, pp.280-81.

58. Edelstein, M, *What Do Young Africans Think?*, Johannesburg, 1972.

59. Hoffman and Fischer, p.42.

60. Edelstein, M, 'The Urban African Image of the Jew', *Jewish Affairs*, 27:2, 1972.

61. See Leveson, Marcia, *The People of the Book: Images of the Jew in South African English Fiction, 1890-1992*, Johannesburg, 1996.

62. Dubb, Allie A and Shain, Milton, 'South Africa' in *American Jewish Year Book 1992*, p.419.

63. In the 1930s in the United States, for example, the average American held the most appalling stereotypes of the Jew.

64. See e.g. Deedat, Achmed, *Arabs and Israel: Conflict or Conciliation?*, Durban, 1989.

65. *Antisemitism World Report, 1998*, London.

66. *Ibid*.

67. Interview, 'Prime Talk', 8.5.1998.

68. Lewis, Bernard, *Semites and Anti-*

Semites, New York, London, 1986, p.237.

69. See for example http//www.islam.co.za

70. See Moosa, Ebrahim, 'Islam in South Africa', in Prozesky, Martin and De Gruchy, John (eds), *Living Faiths in South Africa*, Cape Town, 1995.

71. Tayob, Abdulkader I, 'Islamism & Pagad: Finding the Connection', in Galant, Raashied and Gamieldien, Fahmi (eds), *Drugs, Gangs, People's Power. Exploring the Pagad Phenomenon*, Cape Town, 1996.

72. See Ebrahim Rasool interview in Hoffman and Fischer.

73. See Shain, Milton, 'South Africa', *American Jewish Year Book, 1997 and 1998*, Philadelphia.

Beyond the pale: Jewish immigration and the South African left (James T Campbell)

1. *Jewish Affairs*, 52:1, Autumn 1997. See in particular Auerbach, Franz, 'Do We Apologise? South African Jewish Community Responses to Apartheid'; Goldberg, Aleck, 'Apartheid and the Board of Deputies'; Shain, Milton and Frankental, Sally, 'Accommodation, Activism and Apathy: Reflections on Jewish Political Behaviour During the Apartheid Era'; Sherman, David, 'My Encounter with Apartheid: A Reform Rabbi's Perspective'; and Slier, Paula, 'What Does It Mean to be a Young Jew in South Africa Today?'

2. See *Mail and Guardian*, 27 March 1997, pp.2, 22. Yutar's conduct has also recently been examined in Frankel, Glenn, *Rivonia's Children: Three Families and the Cost of Conscience in White South Africa*, Farrar Strauss and Giroux, New York, 1999.

3. Saenger, Hanns and Sherman, Joseph, 'Shouting from the Grandstand: By Way of an Afterword', in *Jewish Affairs*, 52:1, Autumn 1997, pp.80-83. For samples of the ensuing debate, see *Mail and Guardian*, April, 11 April and 18 April

4. Suttner, Immanuel (ed.), *Cutting Through the Mountain: Interviews with South African Jewish Activists*, Johannesburg, Viking Penguin, 1997, pp.3, 601-2, 616, 620. On the phenomenon of 'non-Jewish Jews' – a category upon which Suttner relies – see Deutscher, Tamara (ed.), *The Non-Jewish Jew*, Hill and Wang, New York, 1968.

5. See Braude, Claudia, 'A Cure for

Fear?' in *Mail and Guardian*, 6 June, p.22. For a recent analysis of Jewish participation in the CPSA, and of the anxieties that such participation ignited in the wider Jewish community, see Israel, Mark and Adams, Simon, '"That Spells Trouble": Jews and the Communist Party of South Africa', *Journal of Southern African Studies*, 26, 1, March 2000.

6. Founded in 1921, the Communist Party of South Africa (CPSA) disbanded in 1950 to forestall prosecution under the Unlawful Organisations (Suppression of Communism) Act. The Party was relaunched in secret in 1953 as the South African Communist Party (SACP).

7. Basner, Miriam, *Am I An African? The Political Memoirs of HM Basner*, Witwatersrand University Press, Johannesburg, 1993; Hirson, Baruch, *Revolutions in My Life*, Witwatersrand University Press, Johannesburg, 1995; Podbrey, Pauline, *White Girl in Search of the Party*, Hadeda Press, Pietermaritzburg, 1993; Slovo, Joe, *Slovo: The Unfinished Autobiography*, Ravan Press, Johannesburg, 1995.

8. Hermann, Louis, *A History of the Jews in South Africa From the Earliest Times to 1895*, Westport, Greenwood Press, 1975, orig. pub. 1935, pp.38-89, 114-146; Rosenthal, Eric, 'On the Diamond Fields', in Saron, Gustav and Hotz, Louis (eds), *The Jews in South Africa: A History*, Oxford University Press, Cape Town, 1955, pp.105-120; Shain, Milton, *The Roots of Antisemitism in South Africa*, Witwatersrand University Press, Johannesburg, 1994, pp.9-18; Bradlow, Edna, 'Tikvath Israel,' in *Vuka SA*, 1:1, November 1995, pp.20-3. On Marks, see Mendelsohn, Richard, *Sammy Marks: The Uncrowned King of the Transvaal*, David Philip, Cape Town, 1991.

9. Gershater, C, 'From Lithuania to South Africa' and Saron, Gustav, 'Jewish Immigration, 1880-1913', both in Saron and Hotz, *The Jews in South Africa*, pp.59-84, 85-104. See also Shimoni, Gideon, *Jews and Zionism: The South African Experience, 1910-1967*, Oxford University Press, Cape Town, 1980, pp.1-26, 97-108, 116-8, 144.

10. Shimoni, *Jews and Zionism*, pp.5-12.

11. Shimoni, *Jews and Zionism*, p.18; Rabinowitsch, Wolf Zeev, *Lithuanian Hasidism*, Schoken Books, New York, 1971. On cultural ferment within the Pale, see, *inter alia*, Baron, Salo W, *The Russian Jews Under Tsars and Soviets*, Macmillan, New York, 1964, pp.135-186; Dubnow, SM, *History of the Jews in Russia and Poland From the Earliest Times Until the Present Day*, Volume 2, Katz Publishing House, New York, 1975, orig. pub. 1918, pp.206-242. On Yiddish literature, see Howe, Irving, *World of Our Fathers: The Journey of the East European Jews to America and the Life They Found and Made*, 2nd edition, Schocken Books, New York, 1989, pp.7-20; and Graftein, Melech, *Sholom Aleichem Panorama*, London, nd. On the 'affirmation of ordinary life' as a predicate of modern identity in the West, see Taylor, Charles, *Sources of the Self: The Making of the Modern Identity*, Harvard University Press, Cambridge, 1989.

12. For overviews of Tsarist persecution, see Dubnow, *History of the Jews in Russia and Poland*, and Baron, *The Russian Jews Under Tsars and Soviets*. See also Mendelsohn, Ezra, *Class Struggle in the Pale: The*

Formative Years of the Jewish Workers' Movement in Tsarist Russia, Cambridge University Press, Cambridge, 1970, pp.1-26; and Liebman, Arthur, *Jews and the Left*, John Wiley and Sons, New York, pp.70-87. (The quoted passage is on pp.76-7.)

13. Vital, David, *The Origins of Zionism*, Clarendon Press, Oxford, 1975, pp.65-186, ff; Mendelsohn, *Class Struggle in the Pale*, pp.63-125; Liebman, *Jews and the Left*, pp.70-134. See also Frankel, *Prophecy and Politics: Socialism, Nationalism, and the Russian Jews, 1862-1917*, Cambridge University Press, Cambridge, 1981; and Levin, Nora, *Jewish Socialist Movements, 1871-1917*, Routledge & Kegan Paul, London, 1978. (For Lenin's attack on the Bund, see Levin, pp.280-300.)

14. Mendelsohn, *Sammy Marks*, p.3. This portrait of family life draws primarily on Zborowski, Mark and Herzog, Elizabeth, *Life is With People: The Culture of the Shtetl*, 2nd edition, Schoken Books, New York, 1962, pp.291-360. See also Howe, Irving, *World of Our Fathers: The Journey of the East European Jews to America and the Life They Found and Made*, 2nd edition, Schocken Books, New York, 1989, pp.1-25, 171-3.

15. Howe, *World of Our Fathers*, pp.20, 73-6, 169-183, 249-263. (The quotation is on p.255.)

16. Shimoni, *Jews and Zionism*, pp.4, 10-1, 61-8, 105; Shain, *The Roots of Antisemitism*, pp.52, 136-7. On Johannesburg, see Krut, Riva, 'The Making of a South African Jewish Community in Johannesburg, 1886-1914', in Bozzoli, Belinda (ed.), *Class, Community and Conflict: South African Perspectives*, Ravan Press, Johannesburg, 1987. For an evocative rendering of Jewish immigrant Johannesburg, see Sachs, Bernard, *Multitude of Dreams: A Semi-Autobiographical Study*, Kayor Publishing House, Johannesburg, 1949.

17. See Van Onselen, Charles, 'Randlords and Rotgut, 1886-1903', and 'Prostitutes and Proletarians, 1886-1914', *Studies in the Social and Economic History of the Witwatersrand, 1886-1914. Volume 1: New Babylon*, Ravan Press, Johannesburg, 1982. (The quotation is on p.74.) The 'Jewhannesburg' comment is quoted in Krut, 'The Making of a South African Jewish Community', p.136. For the broader history of the 'white slave' trade, see Bristow, Edward J, *Prostitution and Prejudice: The Jewish Fight Against White Slavery*, Clarendon Press, Oxford, 1982. The origins of the term 'Peruvian' remain uncertain, with scholars variously tracing it to a short-lived Polish-Russian Union in Kimberley, to the arrival of Jewish immigrants from Argentina, or to a bastardisation of the Latin name for Poland; see Shain, *The Roots of Antisemitism*, pp.163-4, n.32

18. Sonnabend, H, 'Statistical Survey of Johannesburg's Jewish Population' (np, 1935), p.22. See also Shimoni, *Jews and Zionism*, pp.10, 104, 124, 162; Krut, 'The Making of a South African Jewish Community', pp.135-144; Adler, Taffy, 'Lithuania's Diaspora: The Johannesburg Jewish Workers' Club, 1928-1948', *Journal of Southern African Studies*, 6:1, October 1979, pp. 71-4; and Israel and Adams, 'That Spells Trouble', pp.148-9. On kaffireetniks, see Sherman, Joseph, 'Constructing Jewish Immigrant Identity: The "Kaffireatnik" in South African

Yiddish Literature', paper delivered to the Institute for Advanced Social Research Seminar, University of the Witwatersrand, 29 September 1997; and Sherman (trans. and ed.), *From a Land Far Off: South African Yiddish Stories in English Translation*, Jewish Publications, Cape Town, 1987, especially the stories by Feldman, Leibowitz and Tabatznik. On Jewish cabbies, see Van Onselen, 'Johannesburg's Jehus, 1890-1914', in *New Babylon*.

19. For relations of Jewish employers and employees, see 'Sweating in Native Stores Along the Reef', in *Forward*, 8 January 1926; and Sherman, 'Constructing Jewish Immigrant Identity'. cf. Saron and Hotz, *The Jews in South Africa*, p.xii, ff.

20. Shimoni, *Jews and Zionism*, pp.19-27. (The quotation is on p.27.) See also Alexander, Jack, 'South African Zionism', in Saron and Hotz, *The Jews in South Africa*, pp.270-282; and Gitlin, Marcia, *The Vision Amazing: The Story of South African Zionism*, Menorah Book Club, Johannesburg, 1950.

21. Shimoni, *Jews and Zionism*, pp.27-51, 90-2. (The quotation is on p.91.)

22. Shimoni, *Jews and Zionism*, pp.23, 29, 31-7. (The quotation is on p.32.). See also Kentridge, Morris, *I Recall: Memoirs of Morris Kentridge*, The Free Press, Johannesburg, 1959, pp.105, 146, 155, 161; and Adler, Taffy, 'Lithuania's Diaspora: The Johannesburg Jewish Workers' Club, 1928-1948', *Journal of Southern African Studies*, 6:1, October 1979, p.79, n.30.

23. Shimoni, *Jews and Zionism*, pp.13-8, 76-9, 90; Shain, *The Roots of Antisemitism*, pp.104-112; Krut, 'The Making of a South African Jewish Community', pp.144-153; Saron, Gustav, 'The Long Road to Unity', in Saron and Hotz, *The Jews in South Africa*, pp.226-269. Despite the clear intention of the legislation (and the public denials of Minister Patrick Duncan), it is clear that by the early 1920s section 4(1)(a) was being used 'to keep the Peruvians out'.

24. Krut, 'The Making of a South African Jewish Community', p.148; Shimoni, *Jews and Zionism*, pp.13-5, 146-151.

25. Saron and Hotz, *The Jews in South Africa*, pp.xvi, 374-5; Shimoni, *Jews and Zionism*, pp.76-84. (The comment from the Transvaal Board President is on p.76.)

26. Kentridge, *I Recall*, pp.164-5; Shimoni, *Jews and Zionism*, pp.137-168. (The Executive's request is quoted on p.149.) See also Cuthbertson, Greg C, 'Jewish Immigration in South African Politics, 1937-1939', *Historia*, 26:1, 1981.

27. All of these themes are pursued below.

28. Adler, Taffy, 'History of the Jewish Workers' Club', paper delivered to the African Studies Institute Seminar, University of the Witwatersrand, March 1973, pp.3-4; Shimoni, *Jews and Zionism*, pp.52-53.

29. On the white labour movement in South Africa, see, *inter alia*, Ticktin, D, 'The Origins of the South African Labour Party', unp. PhD thesis, University of Cape Town, 1973; Katz, Elaine N, *A Trade Union Aristocracy: A History of White Workers in the Transvaal and the General Strike of 1913*, African Studies Institute, Johannesburg, 1976; and Davies,

Robert H, *Capital, State and White Labour in South Africa, 1900-1960: An Historical Materialist Analysis*, Harvester Press, Brighton, 1979.

30. See Mantzaris, Evangelos A, 'Jewish Trade Unions in Cape Town 1903-1907: A Socio-Historical Study' and 'The Cigarette Makers and the First Workers Cooperative Society in South Africa, Cape Town, 1906-1907', both in Mantzaris, *Labour Struggles in South Africa: The Forgotten Pages 1903-1921*, Collective Resources Publications, Windhoek, 1995.

31. See Johns, Sheridan, *Raising the Red Flag: The International Socialist League and the Communist Party of South Africa*, Mayibuye Books, Bellville, 1995; Roux, Edward, *SP Bunting: A Political Biography*, 2nd edition, Mayibuye Books, Bellville, 1993; and Campbell, James T, 'Romantic Revolutionaries: David Ivon Jones, SP Bunting and the Origins of Non-Racial Politics in South Africa', *Journal of African History*, 39:4, 1998.

32. Sachs, Bernard, *Multitude of Dreams: A Semi-Autobiographical Study*, Kayor Publishing, Johannesburg, 1949, p.132; Adler, 'History of the Jewish Workers' Club', p.6. On the Yiddish-Speaking Branch, see Mantzaris, Evangelos A, 'Radical Community: The Yiddish-Speaking Branch of the International Socialist League, 1918-1920', in Bozzoli, *Class, Community and Conflict*.

33. Adler, 'History of the Jewish Workers' Club', p.5; Slovo, *Unfinished Autobiography*, p.41.

34. On anti-Jewish stereotypes, see Shain, *The Roots of Antisemitism in South Africa*. See also Shimoni, *Jews and Zionism*, pp.90, 107.

35. The quotation is from a 1919 speech by the President of the SAJBD; see Shain, *The Roots of Antisemitism*, p.88.

36. Basner's story is told in Basner, Miriam, *Am I An African? The Political Memoirs of HM Basner*, Witwatersrand University Press, Johannesburg, 1993, a book based on Basner's own unfinished autobiography. All parenthetical page references are to this work.

37. In his memoirs, Basner attributed his victory to the common law principle of *lex non cogit ad impossibilia* – 'the law does not contemplate the impossible' – but in fact the alternative accommodation requirement was embedded in the 1923 statute. The requirement stymied municipal urban removal efforts for a generation. See Davenport, Rodney, 'African Townsmen? South African Natives (Urban Areas) Legislation Through the Years', *African Affairs*, 68, 1969, pp.95-109.

38. Adler, 'Lithuania's Diaspora', p.84. On the Friends of the Soviet Union (not to be confused with the Society of Friends of Russia a generation before). On Sidney Bunting, see Roux, Edward, *SP Bunting: A Political Biography*, new edition, Mayibuye Books, Bellville, 1993.

39. Podbrey, *White Girl in Search of the Party*, p.48. Joe Slovo tells a story with an almost identical punchline – 'If you knew her you'd realise that no self-respecting kaffir would ever marry my sister' – but attributes the remark to Issy Wolfson, General Secretary of the Tailoring Workers' Union; see Slovo, *Unfinished Autobiography*, pp.22-3.

40. Adler, 'Lithuania's Diaspora', p.81.

41. See Bradford, Helen, *A Taste of Freedom: The ICU in Rural South Africa*, Yale University Press, New Haven, 1987. On the AME Church, see Campbell, James T, *Songs of Zion: The African Methodist Episcopal Church in the United States and South Africa*, Oxford University Press, New York, 1995.

42. On both the Communist Party's role in the countryside and the rural revolts of the 1950s, see Delius, Peter, *A Lion Amongst the Cattle: Reconstruction and Resistance in the Northern Transvaal*, Heinemann Press, Portsmouth, 1996.

43. On First, see below.

44. Hirson's works include *Year of Fire, Year of Ash: The Soweto Revolt, Roots of a Revolution*, Zed Books, London, 1979; *Yours for the Union: Class and Community Struggles in South Africa, 1930-1947*, Witwatersrand University Press, Johannesburg, 1989; and *The Delegate for Africa: David Ivon Jones, 1883-1924*, co-authored with Williams, Gwyn A, Core Publications, London, 1995.

45. Hirson, Baruch, *Revolutions in My Life*, Witwatersrand University Press, Johannesburg, 1995. All parenthetical page references are to this work.

46. On *Amalaita* gangs, see La Hausse, Paul, '"The Cows of Nongoloza": Youth, Crime and Amalaita Gangs in Durban, 1900-1936', *Journal of Southern African Studies*, 16:1, 1990, pp.79-111.

47. Ever ready to grind a theoretical axe, Hirson insisted that these migrants were not peasants (as some socialist writers suggested) but proletarians, the neglected key to socialist revolution; see *Revolutions in My Life*, p.45.

48. On the intellectual roots of *Hashomer Hatzair*, see Borochov, Ber, *Nationalism and Class Struggle: Essays in Zionism and Socialism* (np, nd). (My thanks to Mitchell Hart for a copy of this rare pamphlet.) See also Frankel, *Prophecy and Politics*, pp.329-363; and Biale, David, *Eros and the Jews: From Biblical Israel to Contemporary America*, Basic Books, New York, 1992, especially chapter eight. (The quotation is from Biale, p.178.)

49. Biale, *Eros and the Jews*, p.176.

50. See also Hirson, 'The Trotskyist Groups in South Africa' and 'The Trotskyists and the Trade Unions', both in Liebenberg, Ian *et al* (eds), *The Long March: The Story of the Struggle for Liberation in South Africa*, HAUM, Pretoria, 1994.

51. Hirson's critique of the role of the CPSA in the Second World War, which he develops in greater detail in *Yours for the Union*, has itself been criticised by Jeremy Krikler; see Krikler, 'Activists and Historians', *Southern African Review of Books*, February/May 1990, pp.30-1.

52. Nelson Mandela, who played a central role in the ANC's move to armed struggle, has offered an identical assessment: 'Violence would begin whether we initiated it or not. If we did not take the lead now, we would soon be latecomers and followers in a movement we did not control.' See Sampson, Anthony, *Mandela: The Authorized Biography*, Alfred A Knopf, New York, 1999.

53. See Hirson, Denis, *The House Next Door to Africa*, David Philip, Cape Town, 1986.

54. Hirson begins each chapter of

Memories, Realities and Dreams

Revolutions in My Life with a short anecdote from his years in prison. For a fuller account of these years, written by one of Hirson's co-accused, see Lewin, Hugh, *Bandiet*, Penguin, Harmondsworth, 1974.

55. Podbrey, Pauline, *White Girl in Search of the Party*, Hadeda Press, Pietermaritzburg, 1993. All parenthetical page references are to this work.

56. Roux is best known to historians as the author of the classic *Time Longer Than Rope: A History of the Black Man's Struggle for Freedom in South Africa*, 2nd edition, University of Wisconsin Press, Madison, 1964. See also *Rebel Pity: The Life of Eddie Roux*, London, 1970. Bach's fate after his arrest in the Soviet Union in 1937 was for decades a mystery. Recently uncovered documents suggest that he died (of 'natural causes') in a Soviet labour camp in 1941; see Roux, *SP Bunting*, pp.191-2, n.49.

57. See Suttner, *Cutting Through the Mountain*, pp.49-70.

58. On the significance of renouncing food, see Zborowski and Herzog, *Life is With People*, p.303.

59. Suttner, *Cutting Through the Mountain*, p.70.

60. *Ibid.* pp.56, 58.

61. See Zborowski and Herzog, *Life is With People*, pp.270-3, 300.

62. Podbrey's SACP comrade, Lionel Forman, had a similar response to life in Eastern Europe after working as a Party journalist and student organiser in Prague, though he kept silent about his feelings until after Kruschev's 'Secret Speech' to the Twentieth Party Congress. Even then, he remained a committed Party member. See 'Stalin and Democracy' and 'Lessons from Hungary, 1956', in Forman, Sadie and Odendaal, Andre (eds), *A Trumpet from the Housetops: Selected Writings of Lionel Forman*, David Philip, Cape Town, 1992, pp.163-170.

63. Slovo, Gillian, *Every Secret Thing: My Family, My Country*, Little, Brown and Co., London, 1997. The intersection of personal and political is also explored with great sensitivity in Clingman, Stephen, *Bram Fischer, Afrikaner Revolutionary*, David Philip, Cape Town, 1998; and Frankel, Glenn, *Rivonia's Children: Three Families and the Cost of Conscience in White South Africa*, Farrar, Strauss and Giroux, New York, 1999.

64. Slovo, Joe, *Slovo: The Unfinished Autobiography*, Ravan Press, Johannesburg, 1995, p.xii. All parenthetical page references are to this work.

65. See Bristow, *Prostitution and Prejudice*, pp.114-145, 246-7, 309-323.

66. Slovo, G, *Every Secret Thing*, pp.34, 150. Shawn Slovo describes Wolfus as 'in and out of debtor's prison', though she may be referring to Eastern Europe; see her interview in Suttner, *Cutting Through the Mountain*, p.448.

67. Immanuel Suttner has used the story of Jonas as the basis of a short story, which is included in the *Jewish Affairs* special apartheid issue. See Suttner, 'Kaddish for Kefilwe', *Jewish Affairs*, 52:1, 1997, pp.84-7.

68. On student politics at Wits in this period, see Murray, Bruce K, *Wits: The Open Years*, Witwatersrand University Press, Johannesburg, 1997.

69. Slovo, G, *Every Secret Thing*, p.193.

Footnotes

70. Frankel, *Rivonia's Children*, p.178.

71. First described her experience of detention in a harrowing memoir, *117 Days*, Penguin, Harmondsworth, 1982.

72. Slovo, G, *Every Secret Thing*, p.35.

73. See Zborowski and Herzog, *Life is With People*, pp.304-7.

74. Podbrey, *White Girl in Search of the Party*, p.118.

75. See the interviews with Robyn, Gillian and Shawn Slovo in Bernstein, Hilda (ed.), *The Rift: The Exile Experience of South Africans*, Jonathan Cape, London, 1994, pp.442-458.

76. *Ibid.* pp.447-451, 456.

77. When Gillian informed him, shortly before his death, of her intention to publish a family memoir, Slovo erupted in anger. 'I'm not going to tell you anything,' he snapped. 'It's my life, my life. Not yours.' See Slovo, G, *Every Secret Thing*, p.183.

78. Slovo, G, *Every Secret Thing*, pp.97-8.

79. See Sampson, *Nelson Mandela*, pp.149-153, ff.

80. The visit was sponsored by the Party-sponsored World Peace Council; see Frankel, *Rivonia's Children*, pp.51, 62.

81. Slovo, Joe, 'Beyond the Stereotype: The SACP in the Past, Present and Future', in Liebenburg, Ian *et al*, *The Long March*, pp.35-41.

82. Slovo, Joe, 'Has Socialism Failed?' *The African Communist*, 121, 1990, pp.25-51.

83. Frankel, *Rivonia's Children*, p.320.

84. Slovo, 'Beyond the Stereotype', pp.38-9.

85. See interview with Shawn Slovo in Suttner, *Cutting Through the Mountain*, p.452.

86. Hirson, *Revolutions in My Life*, p.329; Suttner, *Cutting Through the Mountain*, pp.190, 475, 598.

87. Kasrils, Ronnie, *Armed and Dangerous: My Underground Struggle Against Apartheid*, Heinemann, Oxford, 1993, p.9.

88. Sachs, Bernard, *Multitude of Dreams: A Semi-Autobiographical Study*, Kayor Publishing, Johannesburg, 1949, pp.72-3, 132-4, 235.

Accounting for Jewish radicals in apartheid South Africa (Gideon Shimoni)

1. A trend-setting exposition of this view is Fuchs, Lawrence, *The Political Behavior of American Jews*, Free Press, Glencoe, Illinois, 1956.

2. See Suttner, Immanuel (ed.), *Cutting Through the Mountain: Interviews with South African Jewish Activists*, Viking, London, 1997, pp.620, 602, 605. Together with all interested in the present subject, I am much indebted to this invaluable collection of interviews.

3. See e.g. the objections to Fuchs's theory in Liebman, Charles S, *The Ambivalent American Jew: Politics, Religion and Family in American Jewish Life*, Jewish Publication Society, Philadelphia, 1973, pp.139-144. c.f. Cohen, Percy, *Jewish Radicals and Radical Jews*, Academic Press, London, 1980. Percy Cohen was a British sociologist who was South African-born and Jewish. Cohen's analysis deals mostly with phenomena in the 1960s and emphasises the marginality condition of Jews, but retains the assumption that there is a sense in which social values inherent to Judaism play a role.

4. Suttner, *Cutting Through the Mountain*, p.351.

5. Sachs, Albie, 'Being the Same and Being Different', in *The Jewish Quarterly*, Spring 1993, p.13.

6. Interview in Suttner, *Cutting Through the Mountain*, pp.60, 59, 70.

7. Slovo, Joe, *Slovo: The Unfinished Autobiography,* introduction by Helena Dolny, Ravan Press & Hodder & Stoughton, Johannesburg, 1995, p.3.

8. The author of this paper can attest to this, as he was himself a pupil at this school, although belonging to a later generation.

9. *Slovo: The Unfinished Autobiography*, p.22.

10. Quoted in Suttner, *Cutting Through the Mountain*, p.602. As it happened, it might be said that Barney Simon had been exposed to 'Jewish values' but in the form manifest in the Zionist youth movements. He told an interviewer: 'A clear influence on me was being a member of *Habonim*, which I was from about ten to about 17.' Interview in Suttner, *Cutting through the Mountain*, p.122.

11. Rabbi Harris's eulogy is reproduced in *Slovo: The Unfinished Autobiography*, pp.201-5.

12. Interview in Suttner, *Cutting through the Mountain*, pp.361, 362.

13. c.f. Levey, Geoffrey Brahm, 'Toward a Theory of Disproportionate American Jewish Liberalism', in Medding, Peter Y (ed.), *Studies in Contemporary Jewry*, Volume X1, 1995, pp.64-85.

14. Autobiographical records and interviews provide plentiful illustrations of Jewish radicals' estrangement, alienation and resentment in relation to the Jewish community. Particularly bitter experiences are related concerning contact with rabbis while in prison, and also concerning the unsympathetic attitude of community bodies to the problems faced by the wives of detainees and prisoners. See e.g. Hirson, Baruch, *Revolutions in My* Life, Witwatersrand University Press, Johannesburg, 1995, pp.55-6;

Podbrey, Pauline, *White Girl in Search of the Party*, Hadeda Books, Pietermaritzburg, 1993, pp.130-31; and Wolpe, AnnMarie, *The Long Way Home*, David Philip Publishers, Cape Town, 1994, p.227.

15. See Shimoni, Gideon, *Jews and Zionism: The South African Experience*, Oxford University Press, Cape Town, 1980, pp.201-2, 261-7, 297-9.

16. Interview in Suttner, *Cutting Through the* Mountain, pp.23-47.

17. See Podbrey, *White Girl in Search of the Party.*

18. Also most of the earlier generation of Jewish radicals was rooted in this ambience; Hyman Basner, for example, of whom Tom Lodge perceptively notes that 'marginality of existence was an essential ingredient of Basner's upbringing ... Being an outsider may have helped to cultivate his capacity for social observation.' See Basner, Miriam, *Am I an African: The Political Memoirs of HM Basner*, Witwatersrand University Press, Johannesburg, 1993, p.xvi.

19. Lazerson, Joshua N, *Against the Tide: Whites in the Struggle Against Apartheid*, Westview Press & Mayibuye Books, Boulder, Colorado, 1994, p.87 based on interview London, 27 January 1987. The resourceful research of Lazerson, which includes many oral interviews, makes an invaluable contribution, *inter alia*, to the subject of the present paper.

20. On the Barsels see the article based on an interview: Suttner, Immanuel, '48 Regent Street', in the Israeli newspaper (English edition) *Ha'aretz*, 19 September 1999. On Turok and also Barsel see Lazerson, *Against the Tide,* pp.87, 92.

21. Lazerson, *Against the Tide,* pp.37-9.

22. See Shimoni, *Jews and Zionism,* pp.53-4, 173-4; Feldman, *Yidden in Johannesburg*, South African Yiddish Cultural Federation, Johannesburg, 1956 [in Yiddish]. Also, Mantzaris, Evangelos, 'Bund in dorem afrika', in *Unser Zeit*, no. 6, 1981, pp.44-6, and *idem.*, 'Sergei Riger (Baron) in dorem afrika', in *Unser Zeit*, no. 9, September 1983, pp.42-43. See also *idem.*, *Labour Troubles in South Africa: The Forgotten Pages 1903-1921*, Collective Resources Publication, Durban, 1995.

23. See Mantzaris, Evangelos, 'Radical Community: The Yiddish-speaking Branch of the International Socialist League', in Bozzoli, Belinda (ed.), *Class, Community and Conflict: South African Perspectives*, Johannesburg, 1987, pp.160-176.

24. Feldman, Leibl, *Yidden in dorem afrika,* Johannesburg & Wilno, 1937 [in Yiddish], pp.102-16.

25. See Adler, Taffy, 'Lithuania's Diaspora: The Jewish Workers Club, 1928-1948', *Journal of Southern African Studies*, 6:1, October 1979, pp.71-92.

26. See e.g. *Proletarishe Shtimme*, September 1932.

27. See Shimoni, *Jews and Zionism,* pp.56-60.

28. The quotations are from *Geserdword*, Feb. 1932; May 1935. See Shimoni, *Jews and* Zionism, pp.56-8.

29. *Jewish Opinion. A Newsletter*, July 1954. This newsletter of the Jewish Democratic Association appeared monthly from April 1954 until June 1962.

Memories, Realities and Dreams

30. Interview in Suttner, *Cutting Through the Mountain*, p.467.

31. *New Outlook*, April 1985, p.32.

32. Interview in Suttner, *Cutting Through the Mountain*, p.466.

33. Interview in Suttner, *Cutting Through the Mountain*, p.374.

34. 'Speaking to Jews in the Next Two Years: An Interview with Ronnie Kasrils', in *Jewish Affairs*, Autumn 1994, p.17.

35. Interview in Suttner, *Cutting through the Mountain*, p.507.

36. *Ibid.*, p.514. See also 'A Question of Identity: An interview with Raymond Suttner', in *Jewish Affairs*, Autumn, 1994, p.25-7.

37. Interview in Suttner, *Cutting through the Mountain*, p.500.

38. See Saks, David, 'Sam Kahn and the Communist Party', in *Jewish Affairs*, Autumn 1999, pp.25-9.

39. Hirson, Baruch, *Revolutions in My Life*, p.125.

40. Author's interview with Arthur Goldreich, 15 February 1972.

41. Interview with Harold Wolpe, conducted on the author's behalf by Steven Ascheim, London, 1 June 1971.

42. Bernstein, Rusty, *Memory Against Forgetting*, Viking, London, 1999, pp.2,10.

43. Bernstein, *Memory Against Forgetting*, pp.14,15.

The road to Rivonia: Jewish radicals and the cost of conscience in white South Africa (Glenn Frankel)

1. Bernstein, Hilda, *The World That Was Ours*, SA Writers, London, 1989, pp.80-1.

2. Rusty Bernstein's role as principle author of the charter was obscured until recently; but he has revealed his role in interviews with me and in his own published memoir. See Frankel, Glenn, *Rivonia's Children*, Farrar, Strauss and Giroux, New York, 1999, pp.64-5; and Bernstein, Rusty, *Between Memory and Forgetting*, Viking, London, 1999, pp.143-56.

3. Howe, Irving, *World of Our Fathers*, Harcourt Brace Jovanovich, New York, 1976, pp.101-2.

4. Dawidowicz, Lucy S, *From That Place and Time*, WW Norton, New York, 1989, pp.28-51.

5. *Rivonia's Children*, p.21.

6. Biographical details of Joe Slovo are from *Slovo: The Unfinished Autobiography*, Ravan Press, Johannesburg, 1995; and Slovo, Gillian, *Every Secret Thing*, Little, Brown, London, 1996, pp.27-8.

7. Suttner, Immanuel (ed.), *Cutting Through the Mountain*, Viking, London, 1997, p.52.

8. Mandela, Nelson, *Long Walk to Freedom*, Little, Brown, Boston, 1994, p.62.

9. Nkosi, Lewis, *Home and Exile*, Longmans, London, 1965, p.19.

10. Segal, Ronald, *Into Exile*, McGraw-Hill, New York, 1963, pp.16-9.

11. *Rivonia's Children*, p.191.

12. *Dagbreek en Sondagnuus*, 1 Sept. 1963.

13. South African Jewish Board of Deputies Press Digest, No. 54, 5 Sept. 1963, p.343.

14. 'The Yutar Legend', *Sunday Chronicle*, 29 Aug. 1965.

15. For Yutar's biography, see *South African Jewish Times*, 14 Feb. 1975; and *Rivonia's Children*, pp.187-191.

16. *South African Jewish Times*, 23 July 1963.

17. *Ibid.*, 24 April 1964.

18. *Ibid.*, 24 April 1964.

Jews and the open society (Dennis Davis)

1. *The Lonely Man of Faith*, Tradition, Spring 1965, p.5.

2. Popper, KR, *The Open Society and its Enemies*, Routledge, London, 1945.

3. Popper is hardly my philosopher of choice. Not only did he misconstrue Hegel and Marx, but his own approach to freedom is too much an apology for a free-market system to amount to a meaningful conception of a free society. For a presentation of Hegel and Marx that represents a careful reading of their texts and which sets out a nuanced analysis of totalitarianism, see Fine, Robert, *Political Investigations*, London, Routledge, 2001. However, as I was given the title by the conference organisers, I have chosen to employ Popper who did make the phrase 'open society' famous.

4. See for example the interviews conducted with Jewish activists in which Jewish tradition appeared to play but a miniscule role, in Suttner, I, *Cutting through the Mountain*, Viking, Sandton, 1997.

5. *Jewish Affairs*, May 1972, pp. 9-10.

6. *Jewish Affairs*, June 1974, p.29.

7. See *Jewish Affairs*, May 1976, p.12.

8. There is now the wonderful irony of activists such as Ronnie Kasrils, once claimed by the community as an example of a Jewish activist, now campaigning in favour of legitimate rights for the Palestinians, claiming to be a South African of Jewish descent, thereby drawing a barrier between himself as a Jew and as a South African. After all, save for the few converts, Jews are Jews by descent!

9. This is a controversial question which requires a separate analysis. Briefly stated, the claim to openness to all but Jews is one that has been made by many groups throughout the vicissitudes of Jewish history. In 2001 the UN Conference against racism illustrated this tendency better than the most eloquent treatise on the subject. Antisemitism of the most egregious kind saturated proceedings yet received little in the way of universal condemnation. Recently a self-styled group of Jewish dissidents have mounted a campaign in favour of asserting rights of Palestinians as well as condemning Israeli breaches of human rights. Anyone committed to an open society must be sympathetic to the sentiments expressed in the petition. The problem (which should not be employed as a defence against the assertion of the legitimate case of Palestinian statehood) is the absence of any condemnation of Muslim sexism and xenophobia or breaches of human rights, including virulent antisemitism; the case then becomes that of Jews for selective justice. See *Sunday Independent*, 9 December 2001.

10. See Shimoni, Gideon, *Jews and Zionism: The South African experience 1910-1967*, Oxford University Press, Cape Town, 1980.

11. Recollection of author attending Wolmarans Street Synagogue, December 1983.

12. Interview with Rabbi Ginsburg, *Jewish Week*, 26 April 1996.

13. Kellner, Menachem, *Must a Jew believe anything?* Litman Library, London, 1999.

14. Kellner p.112.

15. I had two distressing personal experiences of this ferocity from the pulpit. Rabbi Yossi Goldmann of the Sydenham Synogogue and Rabbi Ivan Lerner of the Claremont Synagogue gave sermons which I heard during 1995, both of which effectively classified Rabin as an 'Other'.

16. Cited in Peri, Y (ed.), *The assassination of Yitzchak Rabin*, Stanford University Press, California, 2000, p.152.

17. Levinas, Emmanuel, *Nine Talmudic Readings*, Indiana University Press, Bloomington, 1994, p.21.

18. Levinas p.xxx.

19. Hartman, David, *Conflicting Visions*, Shocken Books, New York, 1990, p.258.

20. There is other textual support for this view. Take the example of Jacob, whose preparation for his meeting with brother Esau after such a long lapse of time was first to be able to provide Esau with presents, then to pray, and only if the first two failed to fight. In short, dialogue and prayer precede any attempt at exclusion, of which military victory is but an extreme example.

21. This is a reference to the two typologies employed by Soloveitchik in *The Lonely Man of Faith*, being Adam I who seeks to control the world and thus assert his dignity, and Adam II whose concern is a relationship with G-d and a faith community, and whose intellectual universe is not about 'how' but about 'why'.

22. See for example Bleich, David in Sacks, J (ed.), *Orthodoxy confronts Modernity*, New Jersey, Ktav, 1991, pp.97-108.

23. Heschel, AJ, *More Grandeur and Spiritual Audacity*